THE NORTH AMERICAN WOOD HEAT HANDBOOK

THE NORTH AMERICAN WOOD HEAT HANDBOOK

GORDON FLAGLER

Charles Scribner's Sons
New York

38212001297362
Main Adult
697.04 F574
Flagler, Gordon, 1951-
The North American wood heat

Revised edition copyright © 1982 Deneau Publishers & Company Ltd.
Copyright © 1979 Deneau and Greenberg Publishers Ltd.

Library of Congress Cataloging in Publication Data

Flagler, Gordon, 1951-
    The North American wood heat handbook.

    Rev. ed. of: The Canadian wood heat book. 1979.
    Bibliography: p.
    Includes index.
    1. Stoves, Wood—North America. 2. Fireplaces—North America. 3. Furnaces—North America. 4. Fuelwood—North America. I. Title.
TH7438.F52   1981   697'.04   82-5489
ISBN 0-684-17491-X   AACR2

This book published simultaneously in the
United States of America and in Canada—
Copyright under the Berne Convention.

All rights reserved. No part of this book
may be reproduced in any form without the
permission of Charles Scribner's Sons.

1 3 5 7 9 11 13 15 17 19   F/C   20 18 16 14 12 10 8 6 4 2

Printed in the United States of America.

Grateful acknowledgment is made to the following
organizations and individuals for permission
to quote from their publications:

Garden Way Publishing Co., Charlotte, Vermont
Jay Shelton and Shelton Energy Research,
   Santa Fe, New Mexico
Harrowsmith Magazine, Camden East, Ontario
The Institute of Man and Resources,
   Charlottestown, Prince Edward Island
Tekton Corporation, Conway, Massachusetts
Wood 'n Energy Magazine, Concord, New Hampshire
Richard Jagels
WoodenBoat Magazine, Brooklin, Maine

Acknowledgments

Had I not been assisted by a sizable number of friends and wood heating professionals, the task of preparing this book would have been much more difficult.

I would like to thank my previous employers, the *Canadian Renewable Energy News* and *Harrowsmith* magazine, and their respective editors, Doug Nixon and James Lawrence, for providing me with positions that broadened my knowledge of wood heating.

I want to give special appreciation to Ken Daggett, Susan Salls, and Richard Wright, of *Wood 'n Energy* magazine, who allowed me access to the huge quantity of valuable information found within their periodical. A number of other publishers and authors also cooperated. While there is not room to mention them, I am grateful for being able to draw on important, earlier works.

I wish to thank the four men who acted as advisors: C. H. Anthony, Charlie Page, Paul Stegmeir, and Clarence Coons. All gave freely of their time and considerable expertise. There were others who answered my questions, including Brian Park, Michael Sciacca of the Wood Heating Alliance, Michael Jorgenson of the Underwriters' Laboratories, Inc., James Polzine, Bea Bryant, John Creelman, Cal Wallis, Robin Tully, and Trygve Husebye.

I must express my gratitude to friends and family who, as always, stood close by. Christina Kloepfer assisted me cheerfully from beginning to end and my mother Clare lent her considerable typing skills, while Elinor Campbell Lawrence, Kathleen Milne, Beth Symes, my brother Greg, and my sister Nancy all helped in a major way.

I also wish to thank Ian Grainge, who created the excellent illustrations, Michael Pietsch, my editor, who was exceptionally patient and supportive, Jacek Galazka, also of Scribners, who conceived this project, and Denis Deneau, my Canadian publisher, who along with his editor, Thelma Cartwright, was among the first to believe in my writing on wood heat.

Contents

Introduction
ix

PART ONE
Background
1

1. *History*	3
2. *Terms and Theory*	7
3. *Basic Design Features*	14

PART TWO
Types of Appliances
19

4. *The Cookstove or Woodrange*	21
5. *Fireplaces, Fireplace Inserts, and Fireviewers*	26
6. *Central Systems: Furnaces and Boilers*	39
7. *Heaters*	56
8. *Used Appliances*	70

PART THREE
Choosing the Right Appliance
81

9. *Size, Quality, and Safety*	83
10. *The Dealer*	101

PART FOUR
Installation
105

11. The Chimney and Smokepipe	107
12. Installing the Appliance	139

PART FIVE
Operation
153

13. Starting a Fire and Keeping It Going	155
14. Maintenance and Fire Safety	164

PART SIX
Fuel
181

15. Bringing in the Wood	183
16. The Harvest	194
17. Bucking up Wood	208
18. Chain Saws and Axes	217

Bibliography
231

Index
235

Introduction

A century ago, most Americans who inhabited towns, villages, and farms were well acquainted with the accoutrements of wood heating: saws, axes, stoves, chimneys, and ash pails. In 1870, wood supplied 75 percent of the country's energy needs.

The peak period of wood heat did not last long, however. In 1900 wood's contribution had declined to 25 percent. By 1972, when heating oil was selling for less than 15 cents a gallon, wood use stood at less than 2 percent, and that was mostly in the commercial and industrial sectors; residential use was nearly nonexistent. The woodpile and the stove it fed had become endangered examples of American folk culture. Pioneer museums, cantankerous bachelors, and scattered pockets of back-to-the-landers were the only ones still attracted to this nearly forgotten form of home heating.

Of course this all changed dramatically with the scare presented by the OPEC oil embargo of 1973. Stoves were resurrected from back sheds and community dumps; the few firms that had continued to manufacture wood appliances found themselves overwhelmed with orders. Hundreds of new companies began operation and, by 1979, annual sales of wood stoves reached 1.5 million (some estimates put the figure at 3 million). It is believed that between 7 and 16 percent of all homes in the United States now use some type of wood heater or furnace at least part-time. The woodpile, once an object of scorn, has become a hot status symbol.

When you have a shed full of dry split wood and access

to further supplies, oil shortages and price hikes seem much less threatening. Independence from the world's political imbroglios gives the wood stove owner great satisfaction. And although all other popular residential heating units are crippled or paralyzed by a power blackout, wood systems are not hindered except for furnaces or heaters equipped with electric blowers, and boilers or water heaters employing electric water circulators. This knowledge can be especially comforting in rural areas where severe blizzards and ice storms knock down power lines with regularity.

While independence is pleasant, it is not the prime reason that wood heating is again so popular. The wish to avoid the family checking account's midwinter malaise, brought on by repeated payments to a fuel oil or gas dealer, is the true cause.

These bills can be reduced by several hundred dollars annually if the consumer has access to a free or inexpensive source of wood. However, serious problems can occur if an attempt is made to scrimp unrealistically when assembling a stove system. Before a single fire is lit, expect to spend at least six hundred dollars if you need only an appliance, and over a thousand dollars if a chimney is also required. Chances are that the total expenditure may be substantially higher. This may shock those who believe articles with titles like "How I Got Started in Wood Heating on $79.21." But if my suggestions in the forthcoming chapters are heeded, the equipment acquired will heat a home easily without being a source of worry, will pay for itself in one to five years, and will last ten to twenty years or even longer.

There is no doubt that wood heat can assist in mitigating both personal and societal energy-related difficulties. In most parts of North America the wood appliance is the most economical to install of all renewable energy equipment. In New England alone approximately 230 million gallons of home heating oil are displaced yearly by wood. Presently it is not as convenient to use as oil, natural gas, propane, or electricity, but sophisticated new central heating systems will change this. In most locales the price of fuel wood remains below that of the conventional fuels (except when wood is bought from a dealer). As long as we manage and replenish our forests, an infinite supply of wood is guaranteed. This cannot be said of most fuels now utilized for residential heating.

However, heating with wood is not for everyone. Until the

above-mentioned automated appliances become commonplace, fuel wood will have to be procured, split, transported, and stacked; the appliance will have to be tended a minimum of two or three times daily; ashes will have to be removed from the firebox, and soot and creosote cleaned from the smokepipe and chimney regularly. What is novel in October can become drudgery by February.

Wood heat can restrict one's life-style significantly—if it is the sole provider of warmth. Without an auxiliary oil, gas, propane, or electrical system, you can be absent from the house for only twelve to twenty-four hours before the interior temperature will plummet, causing plants to die and liquids to freeze. Returning to a home heated solely with wood after a midwinter absence of even one night is discomforting. I therefore recommend that conventional heating equipment not be torn out the moment a wood appliance is purchased.

Each unit has its own characteristics. The type of unit, length and condition of the smokepipe and chimney, species of wood being burned, size of the dwelling, geographic location, severity of the winter, and several other factors all influence performance. Figuring out how to operate a heater or furnace for greatest efficiency can be frustrating, especially in frigid weather; it is also a challenge that, once mastered, is extremely rewarding.

Approach wood heat carefully. Due to the proliferation of equipment and the accompanying "hype," plus the breadth of the subject, it is natural for the newcomer to feel completely overwhelmed. Anyone thinking of buying his first wood appliance should read this book through and examine a variety of equipment before spending a penny.

A perusal of the now-ubiquitous energy shelf in any bookstore will attest to the fact that I am not the first author to tackle wood heating. However, this book has several unique traits. While a good number of other wood heat books do impart important information, many are highly specialized. You would have to purchase three or four titles to learn everything that is needed to heat with wood safely and efficiently. I have taken a different approach. You will find here at least basic information on nearly every facet of this expansive subject.

Many of the more widely circulated books are several years

old and out of date in key sections. I have included state-of-the-art material wherever possible. My aim has been to explain new developments as well as to point out products, still widely sold, that have become obsolete.

In recent years, the wood heat industry has been paying increasing attention to aesthetics. When one installs a wood appliance it is no longer necessary to adopt a rustic decor. I have made a special effort to include material pertaining to urban wood heating and contemporary interior design.

Air pollution from wood heating has become a major concern in a number of mountain-surrounded towns and cities. I have detailed tips on how to use a stove to keep efficiency up and smoke output down and have described new approaches to reducing such harmful emissions.

Wood stoves can be dangerous; an appliance improperly installed, operated, or maintained is akin to a loaded gun—it has the potential of wreaking havoc at any time. I have done everything I can to prevent triggers from being squeezed; safety has been a prime concern.

I have devoted many pages to addressing the needs of wood heating neophytes, but I have not forgotten those who have already burned many cords of wood during several winters. If they have not done their homework over the last few years, chances are they have missed important safety and technological advances. If this description fits you, I hope you heed my recommendations and make any needed changes in your system. A stubborn burner of wood is often the one who ends up singed.

Wood heating is not all warmth and enjoyment. You will sweat hard while collecting your fuel supply, probably fill the room with smoke during your first attempts to use the appliance, and may experience a harrowing chimney fire. But chances are good that you will immensely enjoy your new appliance—even before you realize that the oil truck hasn't been around nearly as often, or that the gas meter isn't spinning around like the hands on a stopwatch.

PART ONE

Background

1
History

Long before the first waves of European immigrants neared the shores of America, scores of native tribes depended on wood for warmth and the cooking and preserving of food. The fuel was burned in outdoor firepits and within the portable tepees and more elaborate lodges and longhouses.

The European settlers soon realized that, in most regions, the forest would have great significance in their new lives. Wood was hewn into square logs and beams, primitively cut into lumber, shaped into wagon wheels and furniture, and, as it was with the native Americans, employed both for cooking and heating.

Soon after their arrival, the immigrants moved the campfire inside, but instead of allowing the smoke to meander on its own up to a hole cut in the roof, as was the practice in tepees and lodges, they adopted a device whose design was brought from Europe—the massive fireplace. In the original colonies along the eastern seaboard, one was usually located in every room.

As time passed and tons of wood were consumed, these settlers came to realize what we have relearned in the last decade: that the open fireplace, though romantic, is very inefficient. It allows the operator little control over the rate of burning, since the huge opening causes the fire to burn quickly and much of the heat is sucked up the chimney. To combat this, inventors began to construct cast-iron boxes of varying sizes and shapes.

Testimony to the variety of wood stoves invented can be found at the Bryant Stove Museum of Thorndike, Maine.

Opened by Bea Bryant in 1980, after thirty years of stove collecting, the museum contains about two hundred appliances and is growing constantly. The most popular varieties of stoves from America's past are all represented, among them massive cooking ranges, the still-common rectangular box stoves, tall column models, hexagonal laundry stoves designed to warm flatirons, and elaborate parlor heaters. The oldest appliance in the collection dates from 1780, but according to Mrs. Bryant, there were stove manufacturers in operation in this country even before that.

The peak of the first wood stove boom was between 1840 and 1850, with 350 foundries in Albany and Troy, New York, the main production centers. Another hotbed was New England, where large firms included the Weir Stove Foundry of Taunton, Massachusetts (Glenwood stoves), the Wood and Bishop Foun-

Early American stove.

dry of Bangor, Maine (Clarion models), and the Portland Stove Foundry of Portland, Maine, which manufactured the Atlantic line of appliances.

Nearly all stoves were of cast iron. Some of the loveliest were made of the lighter, imported Russian iron, which had a gray, smooth surface when highly polished. By the time the peak occurred, shapes and designs had become quite refined. Castings were elaborate. Most units had grates for burning both wood and coal, and a popular feature was a door that opened so that the fire could be seen.

The wood stove's demise as a primary heat source began when the Reverend Eliphalet Nott, head of Union College in Schenectady, New York, developed the Base-Burner coal appliance. A tall unit shaped like a cemetery monument, its unique feature was a hopper on top of the stove through which coal was fed down into the fire. When properly loaded with a sizable amount of good-quality anthracite coal, the Base-Burner would virtually take care of itself for many hours. By the 1880s the Base-Burner and coal furnaces had taken over in the more populated centers. Eventually, even most farm families tired of wood heat's inconvenience. Most chose to retire their venerable box stove or furnace, even when they had their own woodlot providing fuel that was less expensive to prepare and use than coal or cheap heating oil.

Although the 1973 oil embargo instantly made wood heat more cost effective, it would never have become so popular again had airtight stoves not been available. While "airtight" stoves are not truly airtight, since air must be allowed in for combustion to occur (they are more accurately known as "controlled-combustion appliances"), they are built so that all joints are tight and doors fit snugly. As a result, a fire can be better managed; instead of initially heating the house to a point of near suffocation and then consuming the wood supply within two or three hours, a fire in an airtight stove burns steadily and slowly. These stoves need to be fed less often than appliances that do not have tight joints, so a home can be comfortably heated from bedtime nearly until breakfast without someone having to rise before sunup to tend the fire. The improved performance also results in a significant decrease in wood consumption.

During wood heat's first golden era, only a handful of controlled-combustion models, such as the Revere and Stanley, were available. Now, a high percentage of all types of appliances have the controlled-combustion feature incorporated into their design. And as consumers, businessmen, and even many governments recognize the importance of wood as a fuel, other types of improvements are being introduced and tested at a faster rate than ever. Not all "improvements" are necessarily safe or ultimately cost effective, but the attention now being paid to wood heat is bound to result in wood-burning appliances that are more convenient and efficient. In the meantime, be sure to read Part Three, "Choosing the Right Appliance," so that you don't end up the victim of some inexperienced manufacturer's experiment.

2
Terms and Theory

Before further territory is covered, a number of readers will need a grounding in the terms used frequently and in the scientific processes central to the burning of wood. Mountains of complicated data are not required; only facts essential to understanding how, why, and where wood burns within a residential appliance will be discussed. Those who wish to gain more than a rudimentary grasp of this subject should read the *Woodburners Encyclopedia* by Jay Shelton.* First published in 1976, it remains the most approachable technical explanation of heating with wood.

Unit, appliance, and *stove* refer to any type of woodburning device. A *cookstove* or *woodrange* is primarily used for preparing food, while a *furnace, boiler,* or *central heating system* is usually found in the basement and uses water pipes or metal ducts to transfer heat to the rest of the home. A *heater*, nearly always situated within the living area, simply releases heat into the surrounding space, either by direct radiation or by convection, which is the circulation of heat using an electric blower or gravity-assisted pipes or channels built into the appliance.

Fireplace refers to the traditional open model. A *fireplace liner* or *Heatilator* is a metal box used within many brick or stone fireplaces that facilitates circulation of air and the installation of glass doors. A *zero-clearance* or *factory-built fireplace* has primarily the same functions, but it can be installed on its own,

---

* *Publishing data on all books and periodicals mentioned in the text can be found in the bibliography on page 231.*

using a metal chimney instead of the masonry model employed with stone or brick fireplaces. A *fireplace insert* is a heater designed to fit into an open fireplace, while a *fireviewer* or *fireplace-stove* is a heater (generally airtight in design) that sits out in the room but has doors that open, or a window that allows observation of the blaze within. A *freestanding fireplace*, which is also installed in the room, usually has a large hood but rarely the controlled-combustion feature.

The *firebox* is the chamber in the stove—square, round, triangular, oval, or rectangular in shape—that contains the blaze. The *heat exchanger* is a chamber found above the firebox of some heaters and furnaces that provides additional surface area for the transfer of heat. The *plenum* is a sheet-metal box found on top of most furnaces. It collects heat for distribution through ducts. While the heat exchanger is incorporated into the appliance proper, the plenum usually is separate.

The *chimney*, also referred to as the *stack*, is the vertical metal or masonry chamber that carries smoke and unburned gases out of the home. A *flue* is the inner channel of the chimney. A steel *chimney connector, fluepipe, smokepipe,* or *stovepipe* connects the chimney and appliance. The fitting on the stove that accepts the smokepipe is known as the *flue* or *smokepipe collar*.

The fuel itself is traditionally measured in *cords*. A full cord contains 128 cubic feet and must be stacked neatly so that it measures 4 feet high, 8 feet long, and 4 feet wide. Though it is not legal for trade, the *face* or *short cord* is also common; while its height and length are generally the same as the full cord, the width varies from 12 to 16 to 24 inches.

The heat output available from a cord of wood is traditionally defined in *British thermal units* (*BTUs*), the amount of energy needed to increase the temperature of one pound of water by one degree Fahrenheit. A dry cord of sugar maple, a deciduous hardwood, will turn out 28.7 million BTUs, while the same quantity of balsam fir, a coniferous softwood, will supply about 16.4 million BTUs. Chapter 15 has an extensive chart of BTU ratings that further demonstrate why hardwoods such as the sugar maple, red oak, beech, and hickory are of more value for heating than softwoods like balsam, spruce, and cedar.

Draft is technically defined as the movement of air caused by differences in pressure, which are related to temperature. Draft is best in midwinter, when interior and exterior temperatures vary significantly. It can be poor in spring and autumn, when the air outside is not much cooler than that inside. Other factors, including height of the chimney and its inner dimensions, can also influence the draft. The air flow should also be channeled and regulated. On closed appliances, the *primary draft intake, inlet,* or *opening* routes the oxygen from the room or directly from outdoors into the firebox. The *draft control,* or *cap,* allows the operator to dictate the quantity of oxygen flow. Some units also have a *secondary air intake* and others require a *damper,* usually found on the smokepipe, a few feet above the stove, which keeps a check on the flow of smoke and gases out of the appliance.

Of extreme importance is *combustion,* the process by which the chemical energy inherent in wood is converted into heat and other energy forms. For combustion to take place, fuel, oxygen, and high temperatures must be present simultaneously. The *Woodburners Encyclopedia* states (page 26) that "combustion is different from many other chemical reactions because it is self-propagating—if one corner of a piece of paper is ignited, it in turn will ignite adjacent portions and ultimately the whole piece is burned." Thus, once the initial reaction occurs, combustion will be repeated—if the three essential elements remain—until the entire chunk of wood turns to ash.

Combustion has several stages. The first is vaporization of the moisture in the wood into steam, which occurs at 212 degrees.* Then at 350 to 400 degrees, the cellulose and lignin fibers that make up most of wood begin forming new chemical compounds such as carbon monoxide, methane, hydrogen, and paraffin, which are emitted as gases and liquid droplets. These "volatiles" feed the fire, increasing the temperature. Once a temperature of 1,100 degrees is reached, the gases turn into flames, causing the temperature to rise to 2,000 degrees.

The solid mass of the wood ignites at the much lower

---

* *All temperatures are given in Fahrenheit.*

temperature of 600 to 700 degrees. However, because the gases hold up to 50 percent of the wood's inherent energy, it is best if temperatures are reached that allow their consumption. Combustion starts on the outer surface of the wood and gradually spreads throughout the entire chunk. The inner core can still be driving off water while the next layer is emitting gases and the outer skin has turned to charcoal.

Neophytes commonly make two mistakes that affect the rate and even the occurrence of combustion. The first is the use of freshly cut wood having a high moisture content. Besides cellulose and lignin, with their primary components hydrogen and carbon, water can account for more than half the total composition of certain species of trees. Most hardwoods, which are highly suitable as fuel due to their dense makeup and lack of pitch and gum, are one-quarter water when newly cut. It is far easier and much more efficient to burn wood that has been allowed to dry or season for eight to twelve months. With wet wood, as much as half of the heat can go to simply drying the wood in preparation for combustion.

The second and more serious error is keeping the draft control too far closed. This severely restricts the inflow of oxygen and leads to incomplete combustion, and allows gases to rise in the flue at a relatively low temperature. This improper process often generates a potentially dangerous substance called *creosote*. Found within the chimney and smokepipe, this is not a new substance; it has been generated for as long as wood has been burned within enclosed appliances. However, due to the proliferation of airtights operated by neophytes, creosote deposits are now thicker, harder to remove, and much more common.

These buildups originate as condensed organic vapors or condensed tar fog. As the cellulose and lignin are heated, acetylene, ethylene, hydrogen, and other gases are released, as are liquid tars such as benzol, naphthalene, paraffin, phenol, and resins. If the three elements necessary for combustion are present and the chimney is insulated or located where it is not greatly influenced by frigid winter temperatures, these gases will either be consumed or escape upward. But if the chimney is cold, the intake of air is restricted, or green wood is employed, these substances will condense and adhere to the smokepipe and chimney walls. These liquid and solid creosotes are highly combustible and will ignite if the smokepipe and chimney are heated to a relatively high temperature.

Keeping the draft control at too low a setting can also increase the emissions released by the system. These include particulates such as soot and ash, and hydrocarbons given off as the cellulose and lignin are heated. The hydrocarbons that are of special concern are the polycyclic organic materials (POMs) such as pyrene, anthracene, phenol, aldehyde, and naphthalene. Tests have shown these to be carcinogenic in certain conditions, so their presence in wood smoke is alarming. While some particulates and organic compounds are always present in emissions from a wood-burning appliance, it has been proven that incomplete combustion increases the problem.

Wood stove emissions become a menace in populated zones where there are many appliances used in a small area, and the situation is especially severe in mountainous regions. Here temperature inversions can cause the smoke to hang over the town or city, similar to the infamous hydrocarbon smog from automobile engines that envelops Los Angeles.

Some critics lay the blame for creosote formation and increased emissions squarely on the airtight feature itself, but this explanation misses the mark. When correctly used, controlled-combustion stoves are a major improvement on past models. But, encouraged by irresponsible manufacturers who advertise possible burning times of well over ten hours on one charge of wood, many people operate their controlled-combustion stove so that smoldering fires result. This causes the aforementioned difficulties.

One solution to these problems is education of the operator, a task central to the purpose of this book. A second solution is the development of equipment that takes increased control of the burning process. Appliances from the new generation, which are just starting to be widely sold, do address this need. Some decrease the creosote and emission problems by burning the wood quickly and storing the heat. Others make the use of wood far more convenient than even the controlled-combustion unit can manage, by using small wood pellets and auger feeding systems to automate the loading of fuel into the appliance.

Those who read wood stove advertisements as a method of narrowing the field of suitable appliances will encounter phrases such as "most efficient stove marketed today" and "has an efficiency of nearly 100 percent." With scores of models to choose from, and the legendary American penchant for performance, this battle to prove which appliance is the most efficient is an expected development. However, what most consumers do not realize is that three different efficiency measurements are commonly calculated, and the methods used to determine and rate efficiency often vary with each testing facility.

The highest efficiency figure gained by any product is always *combustion efficiency*, which simply measures how well the stove converts the energy inherent in the wood into heat. Scores of between 80 and 95 percent are normal. Be forewarned, though, that this measurement does not give a true idea of the stove's overall performance.

A reading that reveals more is the *appliance efficiency*, which measures the amount of excess air required for satisfactory combustion and the ability of the unit to take heat out of the combustion process for possible use in the house. Appliance efficiency runs from 50 to 80 percent, with 60 to 70 percent being commonplace.

The most useful statistic of the three is the *overall efficiency*, which is a combination of the combustion and appliance efficiency figures. While different test methods arrive at different ratings, 50 to 60 percent is commonplace, 65 to 75 percent is very good, and a few advanced units perform even better.

It must be remembered that these figures are arrived at under laboratory conditions. Although there are experts who feel that some laboratories reach marks that are below those achieved in the field, this is not always the case. The efficiency gained by a consumer will first of all depend on the species of wood burned and how seasoned it is. Furthermore, how well the potential of the appliance and the fuel is utilized can vary with the skill of the operator, the size of the house and how well insulated it is, the climatic zone, and the severity of the winter.

Once testing agencies and manufacturers have standardized

their efficiency testing and advertising procedures, the consumer will be able to compare performance figures, but until then the situation is confusing.

3
Basic Design Features

Since burning a significant percentage of the gases created during the second phase of combustion is essential to efficient functioning of a wood stove, most controlled-combustion apliances now being manufactured have design features whose aim is to achieve this. In addition to the essential features of all wood stoves—a metal box with a door through which wood is loaded, a grate or solid floor on which the wood is placed, and a pipe through which smoke exits—a number of additional features for improving the stove's performance are now common.

BAFFLES

Skip Hayden of the Canadian Combustion Research Laboratory in Ottawa, Ontario, states that "any of the airtight units that do not allow the passage of flame into the chimney, that is, units that are not just an empty box but do have significant baffles, perform significantly better."

While there is controversy as to whether some new features actually work, most wood heat professionals agree with Mr. Hayden about baffles, which have become a feature on a large number of units. The baffle's basic effect is to act almost as a hanging mirror to reflect heat back into the fire, thus raising the combustion temperature. To be effective a baffle must be

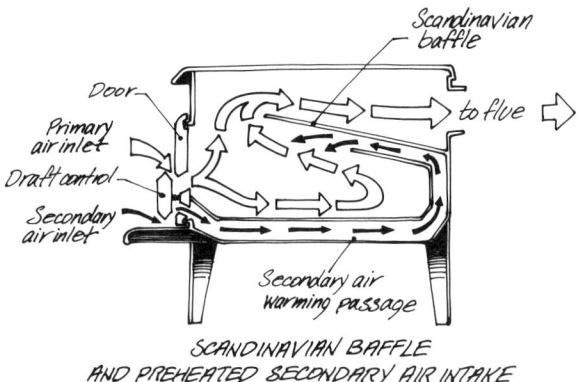

SCANDINAVIAN BAFFLE
AND PREHEATED SECONDARY AIR INTAKE

at the proper angle and not too far from the fire area; most are located above and just back of the primary combustion zone.

There is widespread agreement that the Scandinavian-type baffle is especially effective. Found within many of the popular stoves imported from Denmark and Norway, as well as in some of the more progressive North American units, this substantial baffle extends from side to side and from the back nearly to the front of the firebox. It directs all gases to the front; thus they must always pass through the primary combustion zone before exiting. Baffles are susceptible to deterioration because of their proximity to hot flames and high temperatures, so they should be rugged and replaceable.

PREHEATING THE INCOMING OXYGEN

The manufacturers of several appliances on the market stress that the air coming into their firebox is preheated before it is released, by passing through a tube adjacent to the firebox. Most experts believe that this can theoretically facilitate reaching the needed combustion temperature, but they point out that the devices used in some appliances are not satisfactory.

For optimal preheating, the tube must be several feet long. Only a few massive industrial furnaces have such a device. This is not to say that the much shorter tube employed by some heaters does not have some influence. It simply appears that the potential of this feature is not being fully realized.

SECONDARY DRAFT INTAKES

In an airtight stove, the secret of attaining conveniently long burns is in the limiting and regulating of the oxygen flow into the stove. However, many experts believe that oxygen is either all used up in passing through the primary combustion zone, or it is not hot enough when it reaches the secondary combustion region to inspire the burning of gases. This is thought to be particularly the case in stoves that do not significantly preheat the incoming air.

Several designers have therefore added a secondary air intake to their stoves. Jay Shelton believes that some of these arrangements are more practical than others. Proper situation of the intake is critical, he says: "A rough rule of thumb is that secondary air will help only if admitted into a region where flames already exist." This is particularly important with low or medium rates of firing. The effect on the secondary burning rate must be dramatic; an escalation of several hundred degrees is necessary for there to be any impact.

SPECIAL FLOW PATTERNS

The traditional flow pattern of air through a firebox has been from the bottom front diagonally to the top and back of the unit. To encourage secondary combustion, designers have come up with new routes.

While the gases in all stoves rise from the primary combustion area, in a design called the downdrafter they must travel back down into that zone to exit through the grate that contains the fire.

The sidedrafter is a variation of this approach that Skip Hayden has found, in a series of tests, to be more efficient than the downdrafter. Instead of leaving through the grate, gases exit at the side of the firebox. Some feel that the sidedrafter has the advantages of the downdrafter—exposure to flames and quite high temperatures—without its problems, since the plugging of holes in the grate with coals and ashes does not inhibit the draft.

THE CATALYTIC COMBUSTOR

A great stir was caused by the introduction, in late 1980 and early 1981, of the first wood appliances equipped with catalytic combustors. Manufacturers claimed that overall efficiency was increased dramatically, and tests at Ryerson Polytechnical Institute in Toronto showed an increase in overall efficiency over similar noncatalytic stoves of between 12 and 17 percent. Manufacturers also stated that the combustor reduced the potential for creosote production and virtually eliminated the possibility of pollutants emerging from the stove.

A catalyst is a substance that promotes and effects a chemical reaction but is not destroyed or chemically altered in the process. Catalytic converters have been used extensively in automobiles to reduce emissions. The first wood appliance combustors used the noble metal palladium, which was coated onto a round ceramic substrate with an interior resembling a honeycomb. Once the fire reached a temperature between 500 and 700 degrees, the smoke and gases rising up through the "cells" of the combustor were stimulated and instantly boosted to 1,200 degrees, with nearly complete combustion occurring. The stove operator would be made aware of this reaction taking place because the combustor would "light off," emitting a red glow.

The combustor is now being used by a number of stove companies. However, as time passes, more research is carried out, and field findings come in, the excitement that greeted its appearance is waning somewhat.

It is now believed by many experts that the combustor will not remove all or even most pollutants, and it has been outperformed by other equipment in laboratory tests. The combustor increases the price of a stove substantially, and the stove must have a sizable heat exchanger to distribute the increased heat generated by the combustor. It will not work if the stove is improperly operated and does not function optimally unless it is situated directly above the hottest part of the fire. Current models of the catalytic combustor have a maximum life expectancy of only two or three years, can be plugged by excessive paper or cardboard, and can be ruined if aluminum foil, paint, or a few other substances are present in the fuel.

When the stove is correctly designed to accept a combustor and the appliance is operated by a knowledgeable person, the combustor will have a positive influence on performance. It is also likely that second-generation models will cost less and be more durable. However, the combustor is clearly not a panacea for all problems connected with the burning of wood that it was initially thought to be.

ANOTHER APPROACH TO SECONDARY COMBUSTION

Tests have now shown that many appliances designed to encourage secondary combustion in fact rarely provide the conditions needed for its occurrence in normal use. The failure of these models, together with the aforementioned drawbacks to catalytic combustors, has led some manufacturers to look in another direction.

One appliance, released during the spring of 1982, tries to achieve the same results aimed at by the designers of catalytic combustors, without using the combustor device. The firebox is insulated to keep the gases emitted during the primary combustion phase warm. These gases then pass into a completely separate secondary combustion chamber that is also insulated. Air that has been warmed by an effective preheating system is then introduced through a primitive carburetor. Designers claim that this provides the correct ratio of oxygen and gases and causes complete mixing of the two.

While full data on these units is not yet available, it appears that their overall efficiency is in the same range as combustor models, and that they allow fewer emissions. The increase in price is similar, but there are no components that need cleaning or replacing, and this appliance is said to function equally well at almost all temperatures. The first of these appliances was developed in Norway, but domestic manufacturers will probably introduce their own versions soon.

PART TWO

Types of Appliances

There are four basic kinds of wood heat appliances: cookstoves, fireplaces, central systems, and heaters. Each type has essentially different features and purposes, and within each type there are a number of models. These chapters will help you decide which type of appliance will best suit your particular needs and desires.

4
The Cookstove or Woodrange

In years past, nearly every country kitchen held one of these iron and chrome monsters. Now, however, the numbers have declined and there are opposing views on their value. While all but the most dogmatic proponents will readily admit that only a few cookers are capable of supplying all of the heat a house requires, many feel the woodrange can play a worthy role. It can supply supplementary heat during the daytime, save energy costs by handling cooking, baking, heating of water (at least in the winter and perhaps other seasons as well), and take the chill off damp late spring and early fall mornings.

Critics point out that having both a wood-fired heater or furnace and a cookstove in operation means that two appliances must be bought and looked after. As the firebox in nearly all ranges will hold a blaze for only two or three hours, it requires a substantial amount of tending even if it is being used simply for preparing three meals a day. There is also the woodrange's complexity. For the uninitiated, it resembles something from the Dark Ages, with its massive size, numerous cavities, mysterious draft intakes and dampers, and a phalanx of heavy, round lids.

There are several distinct genres of new cookstoves. These include traditional, no-frills models manufactured by older American foundries; more lavish copies of elegant "classics"

Contemporary small Scandinavian woodrange

made by some of the same firms, often in collaboration with dynamic entrepreneurs; small, sophisticated units produced by a number of Scandinavian companies; and large, state-of-the-art ranges from Austria, West Germany, Belgium, and the United Kingdom, which, when hooked to a network of radiators located throughout the home, can provide heat and hot water as well as handle cooking and baking.

The traditional foundries are situated primarily in New England, Georgia, Alabama, and the Pacific Northwest. Many of these firms have been in business since the turn of the century, and the cookstoves they produce—the most economical type available in the United States—reflect their belief that what worked then will still work now. There is little that is fancy here. These products are simple, quite sturdy, and rustic. The flashy, chromed versions that are more expensive are aimed squarely at antique collectors and affluent segments of the back-to-the-land movement.

John Creelman, a Toronto wood stove dealer, warns that U.S. woodranges may be too large for modern, well-insulated kitchens. He points out that in this case oversizing can cause creosote buildup (since small fires that tend to smolder will be built to prevent overheating the room) and prohibit the use of hot fires required for some types of cooking and baking.

While these American woodranges appear Gibraltar-durable beside contemporary electric ranges, a comparison of cookstoves made recently and those produced several decades ago will usually reveal that the castings are not quite as good and parts are a little lighter. Be careful of traditional models advertised as "modern airtights." Some companies raise the price by several hundred dollars but then make only a perfunctory effort to seal the unit. The fastest way of spotting such a misrepresented stove is to check between the plates that compose the cooking surface. If there are gaps through which the firebox can be observed, the stove is not a controlled-combustion model.

The small Scandinavian woodranges are suited to highly insulated kitchens. These are beautifully made and often contemporary in design. However, there are drawbacks: the cost, generally higher than the heavier American models, and the almost Lilliputian size of the oven.

The bigger European cookstoves resemble American models in weight and dimensions only. These units tend to be sleek, airtight, and extremely sophisticated. They have not caught on here, mainly because they can cost several thousand dollars if an entire radiator installation is necessary. Also, the principle of using one appliance for both cooking and heating is somewhat alien to Americans accustomed to having the furnace in the basement.

From a strictly financial perspective, careful consideration of the investment represented by a cookstove is warranted. In most cases, cookstoves are capable of playing only a supple-

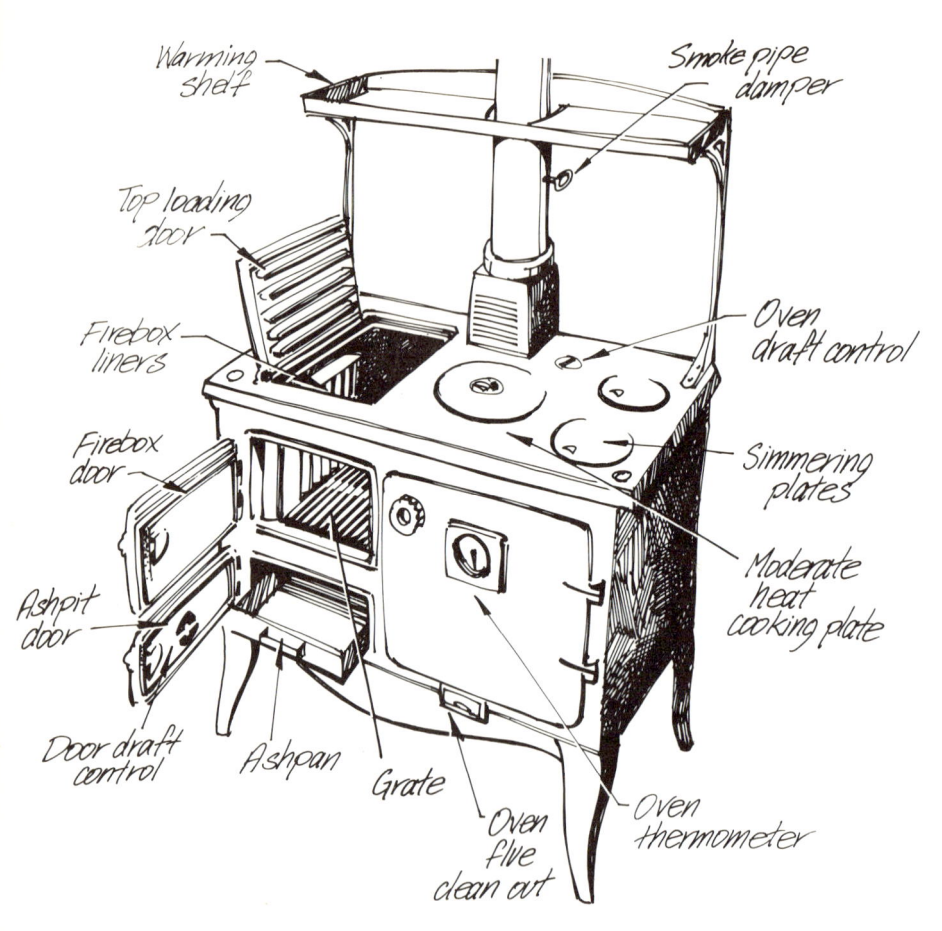

EUROPEAN STATE-OF-THE-ART COOKSTOVE

mentary heating role, but they often cost more than an appliance that can warm the entire dwelling. However, the cookstove can provide a wonderful focal point for the kitchen and in fact the entire home, it presents baking conditions that remain unrivaled, and it is not difficult to master.

To get an idea of the quality of workmanship possible in cookstoves, examine some of the European models. The firebox and oven doors should fit tightly and shut with a "thud" rather than a "ping." There should be no rough edges, and the cooking surface should be free of pockmarks and ripples.

Handy features in a cookstove are a reservoir that warms water; a spigot that provides easy access to the water; a top-warming oven; an accessible opening that allows quick cleaning of the stove's nether regions, and a chrome-plated rail, close to the firebox, which is excellent for warming one's feet after a frigid outdoor trek.

5
Fireplaces, Fireplace Inserts, and Fireviewers

According to *Wood 'n Energy*, a professional wood heat magazine based in Concord, New Hampshire, a survey carried out by the National Association of Home Builders revealed that 84.4 percent of the people looking at new homes want a fireplace. According to the study, this is now the most desired option, edging out carpeting, which had held the number-one position for thirty years.

A fireplace is something of a status symbol, and watching a roaring, crackling blaze is a wonderful experience. But what many people do not realize, until they have used one, is that the effectiveness of a fireplace in heating a house is startlingly poor: The overall efficiency of most traditional open fireplaces ranges from an astonishingly low −10 percent to a still-disappointing +10 percent. The minus rating is a result of the fireplace's actually sucking up the chimney all of the heat it creates, as well as some of the heat generated by other heating devices. When a fireplace's results are compared with results attained by more efficient airtight heaters, it is understandable that many homeowners who already have a fireplace are desperate to find ways of improving its performance.

There are a number of options open for someone who wants the visual effects of a fire without completely sacrificing efficiency. These include both retrofit devices and new appliances. Jay Shelton, one of America's leading wood heat researchers, prepared in 1979 a still-respected paper entitled "Measured Performances of Fireplaces and Fireplace Accessories," which sheds light on the various approaches to fireplace efficiency.

To begin, the person who does not have the money to buy any of the efficiency improvers can increase the performance of an open fireplace with several operating procedures. These include building full-sized, long-lasting fires; setting the fireplace damper—if it is adjustable—at the most closed position that does not lead to smoke flowing into the house; not using the unit on extremely frigid days; covering the fireplace opening with sheet metal or tight glass doors when the fire begins to wane; and shutting the damper and fireplace opening when they are not in use.

It should be pointed out that the amount of heat released into a room through the stone or brick walls of the fireplace can be significant—half again as much as given off through the front of an open fireplace, if the proper factors are present. These include regular firings, which enable the walls to remain warm, plus the design and location of the fireplace. If it is situated in the middle of the room, it will conduct and radiate a considerable amount of energy. However, a fireplace located on an outside wall will suffer sizable heat loss and be far less useful in the circulation of heat.

GLASS DOORS AND TUBULAR GRATES

A good deal of attention has been given to glass doors and tubular grates, which are hailed by some for increasing the efficiency of traditional fireplaces. If glass doors are attached, it is felt they should be left open—with a fireplace screen in place for safety reasons—while the fireplace is in use. Shelton discovered that having glass doors shut when the appliance was in operation caused a 40 to 50 percent reduction in overall heat output.

Manufacturers of glass doors usually claim that these doors

will greatly reduce the flow of air into the unit, making the fireplace virtually airtight and thus increasing efficiency. However, test results show otherwise: Having the doors shut inhibited the flow of heat up the chimney by only 20 to 25 percent. This lack of effectiveness is attributed to the fact that there is almost always space between each outside edge of the door unit and the fireplace, and that the surface of these outside edges can amount to ten or more linear feet. (The poor fit is usually due to the anything-but-smooth surface generally found with stone or brick.) To see for yourself this lack of airtightness in most glass door installations, examine such a setup owned by a friend or neighbor. Even with the doors shut, a blaze will generally burn brightly, a sign that a sizable amount of air is reaching the fire.

Glass doors have two positive but hardly earth shattering uses: They prevent sparks from jumping out into the room, and they limit somewhat the movement of air up the chimney overnight, when there is a smoldering fire.

Tubular grates, which can help prevent heat loss in certain installations, are hollow. In principle, relatively cool air enters these grates at the bottom, is carried around the back of the fire where it is warmed, and then exits at the top. However, in certain instances the air can be sucked back into the fireplace, instead of flowing out into the room. There are solutions. With a passive system (not using an electric blower), the grate unit should be set up so that the tube ends are flush with the fireplace opening; if this is not possible due to the design of the fireplace, extension tubes need to be added to carry the heat beyond the edge of the hearth. It is important that the upper tubes not be more than two inches below the top of the fireplace opening. Another method of preventing the hot air from being drawn back up the chimney is to purchase a model that has a blower.

CIRCULATING FIREPLACES

Two kinds of circulating or convective fireplaces appear to function reasonably well. The first is the factory-built, also known as a zero-clearance unit. This appliance is used in thousands of new homes and by consumers who desire a quickly installed, economical fireplace in their existing dwelling. A rectangular box that rests on one of its sides, this unit can be set directly on a wooden floor and against a combustible wall. It is then connected to a metal, factory-made chimney and given a cosmetic covering of ceramic tiles, brick, or stone. The unit can be so installed because of its four-wall-thick composition. Two of the three spaces between walls are open, to allow air to circulate through; the outer cavity is filled with insulation that prevents the temperature of the outer skin from exceeding 194 degrees.

The second type of circulating fireplace is the fireplace liner, often called a Heatilator, after the brand name of one of the better-known liners. Containing all the main elements of a fireplace, including the fire chamber and damper, it is built into a new masonry model. Similar spaces carry air around the firebox.

Many of these models are equipped with a blower designed to push more heated air into the room. It has been found that only a huge fan, six times larger than the one normally included, noticeably improves energy efficiency. Such a mammoth fan is believed to be beneficial from a heat transfer standpoint, but its operating noise level would probably be irritating. With standard-sized blowers, the improvement noted by Shelton was no more than 5 percent (the models employed were rated at 118 and 134 cubic feet per minute). The purchase and operating costs of these blowers would cancel out the slight positive effect on performance.

An increasing number of factory-built fireplaces are fed by air ducted in from the outdoors. While there is some debate over the worth of this feature, there is no doubt that the use of outside air will lessen floor drafts, which result when air inside the dwelling is pulled into a fireplace. Such a pipe can be one way of providing combustion air for an appliance located within an extremely well insulated and sealed home; without an outside duct or other devices to bring in fresh air the occupants of such houses can have health problems, from a scarcity of oxygen. Skip Hayden feels that cool air is beneficial, since it is denser and thus contains more oxygen than warm air.

Jay Shelton does point out that cool air may decrease

combustion efficiency and that the use of outside air will almost surely result in some cold air's leaking into the living areas of the home, as the system carrying the air is rarely well sealed. Such a device should always have a shut-off switch for when the fireplace is not in use.

Some mortgage-lending bodies require that any appliance burning wood or coal have an outside air source supplied by such a duct running directly into the unit, or by a window situated on the same wall as the stove. If you are buying or building a new home, investigate whether your mortgage holder stipulates this.

The best factory-built fireplaces are, according to Shelton, close in energy efficiency to Franklin-style wood stoves, the least efficient heaters on the market. While this may not seem much of an achievement, consider that the net heat efficiency of these appliances was found to range from 36 to 46 percent (with closed glass doors). This compares with the -10 to $+10$ figures for open fireplaces.

Since 1979, factory-built-fireplace manufacturers have been active in refining their products. It is highly likely that some current models have higher ratings than indicated by the figures just noted. Also, sophisticated fireplace-boiler units from Sweden, Great Britain, and South Africa are beginning to arrive on the North American market. As do cookstove boilers, these heat water that is then distributed to radiators. These appliances are well built, efficient, and still allow observation of the fire.

FREESTANDING FIREPLACES

Tests conducted by the Canadian Combustion Research Laboratory show that freestanding fireplaces, which somewhat resemble heaters and use a metal chimney, have even better efficiency levels than the finest factory-built models, in spite of the fact that those examined were nonairtights, with little care given to the sealing of seams. According to the laboratory, this efficiency is due to the sizable smoke hood these appliances possess, which acts as a large heat transfer surface.

Many homeowners like these units because they are contemporary in design and often available in a variety of colors. Models introduced in the last two years are using efficiency features found on most heaters, as manufacturers are realizing that demand for their units would increase if performance could match their aesthetic appeal.

FIREPLACE INSERTS

Three years ago, less than a handful of fireplace inserts were available, and consumer demand was minimal. Models were generally ugly, and the concept of placing an airtight box in the heat chamber of a masonry fireplace was a new one.

> WARNING: Only a limited number of inserts are designed for use within factory-built fireplaces. Be sure that you purchase one certified by Underwriters' Laboratories or another agency for use in this situation.

Now, several hundred brands of fireplace inserts are marketed, and it has become one of the best-selling types of wood-burning appliance. The reasons for this newfound popularity are several: The insert can be quickly installed and operated with an existing chimney; it is by far the most efficient of the retrofit devices that can be placed within a fireplace, and most models still allow observation of the fire; and its overall efficiency can range from approximately 40 to 60 percent, far above that of the open fireplace. These factors have led some to hail the insert as the most important advance, along with the catalytic combustor, since the widespread adoption of the airtight firebox. But others have serious reservations about the safety of inserts. There are two main areas of concern: difficulties caused by the fireplace the unit is set into, and those caused by the insert itself.

Many fireplaces, constructed simultaneously with the home, contain wooden structural components. When used as an open model, the heat generated within the fireplace either rises quickly up the chimney or moves out into the room, directly or through the walls. But with an airtight insert, temperatures within the fire chamber are localized and can reach very high levels, causing wooden structural members to eventually catch fire. To prevent this occurrence, a careful inspection of the

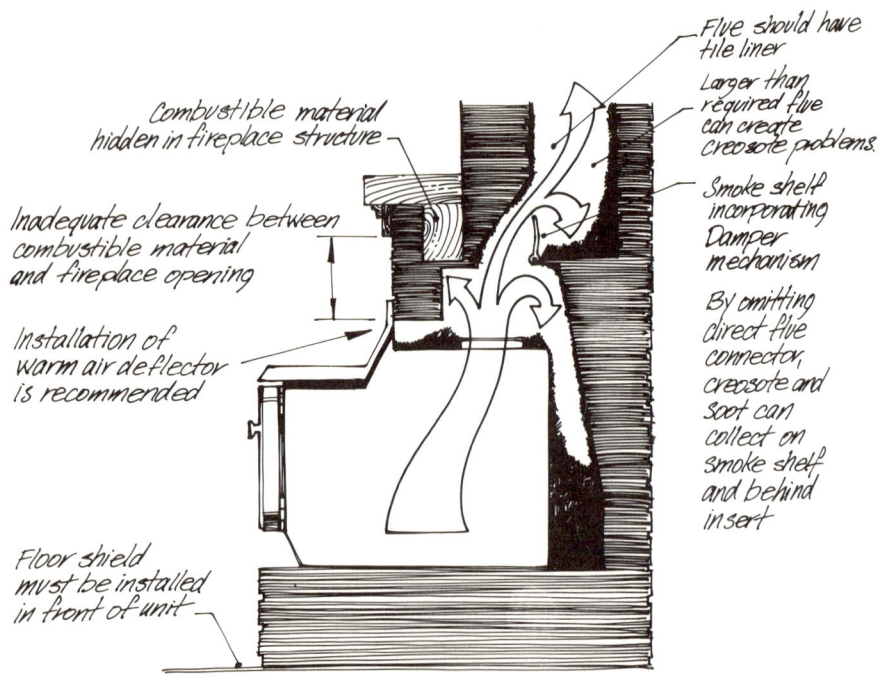

POTENTIALLY HAZARDOUS INSTALLATION OF FIREPLACE INSERT

Labels (clockwise from top right):
- Flue should have tile liner
- Larger than required flue can create creosote problems.
- Smoke shelf incorporating Damper mechanism
- By omitting direct flue connector, creosote and soot can collect on smoke shelf and behind insert
- Floor shield must be installed in front of unit
- Installation of warm air deflector is recommended
- Inadequate clearance between combustible material and fireplace opening
- Combustible material hidden in fireplace structure

fireplace and surrounding area, or blueprints, should be made before an insert is bought. There must be two inches of clearance between all portions of a masonry fireplace or chimney and wooden structural components.

Another inherent problem is the size of the chimney flue. Since an open fireplace handles a great deal of oxygen, smoke, and gases, the flue must be quite large in diameter to prevent back-puffing of smoke into the home. However, such stacks are greatly oversized for nearly all airtight appliances, and the connection of an efficient insert can lead to severe creosote deposits. Since chimney fires are rarely a problem with open fireplaces, it is very possible that the masons who built such units did not leave clearances between the fireplace and combustibles adequate for all the heat of an insert. A substantial chimney fire, which is a possibility with any airtight appliance, can cause the wood around the fireplace to catch fire.

A further complication has to do with the dimensions of the fireplace's front opening. Since people generally want to see the fire from every part of the room, the mouth of a fireplace tends to be massive—perhaps two feet high and three feet wide. Some dealers will try to sell the customer an insert that fits this space, without taking the size of the room into consideration. Be sure to buy one that suits your heating needs. (See Chapter 9 for a formula for calculating the correct size of heater for a given room size.)

Furthermore, much of the heat generated by an insert is simply absorbed by the stone or brick and mortar of the fireplace. While Jay Shelton has found that some of this heat does make its way into the room, the units that extend out into the room deliver more heat more quickly. It should be noted, however, that some insert manufacturers claim that a model that sits flush with the edge of the mouth is safer (as there are few hot surfaces that can be touched), and better looking.

Many inserts have a surrounding system of ducts for improved air circulation. Cool air flows along the bottom and hot air is then pushed (often with the aid of an electric blower) into the room. This does distribute some heat and helps to keep temperatures within the fireplace at safe levels, but the mass still prohibits much of the generated heat from reaching the room.

The primary problem that can exist with an insert concerns the passage of smoke from it to the chimney. The first inserts, and some models still sold today, simply shove into the fireplace cavity. This easy type of installation has been appreciated by the consumer but, soon after these units began to make their way into many homes, alert consumers and wood heat professionals realized that a major crisis could occur. When there is no direct or positive smokepipe connection between the appliance and the flue, the smoke and gases simply meander out of the unit—especially if the fire is smoldering—swirl around behind it, and eventually rise if the chimney has a strong draft. If it doesn't, and a kitchen exhaust fan or a furnace is in operation, the smoke can be drawn into the home.

If the chimney is built against an outside wall, the smoke and gases can be cooled rapidly, increasing the possibility of creosote being formed. If creosote does appear, it will adhere to the walls of the fire chamber, behind and above the insert. Furthermore, if soot and creosote fall down from the chimney, they too will land behind the insert. To remove this buildup, or to fight a fire should the creosote ignite, the insert must be pulled out. But when early models were designed, it appears this was not considered. Inserts can weigh up to 500 pounds and often lack the most basic handles or track for extricating the unit. Thus, the absence of a few feet of smokepipe can cause several problems.

These faulty design features have sent many manufacturers back to the drawing board. Most inserts now have a direct or positive connection and removal of the unit has been facilitated.

The best positive connections have smokepipes running past the damper directly into the flue. These are capable of fitting around the smoke shelf, a component of many fireplaces, which juts into the fire chamber. This arrangement does not completely eliminate the possibility of creosote buildup, because most inserts are airtight and because of the preponderance of mammoth fireplace flues, but it certainly helps. It also eases cleaning of the chimney, since the soot and creosote will collect within the stove, not behind it. If the smokepipe makes an especially tight turn around the smoke shelf, the person cleaning the chimney may have to reach up from below with a flexible rod and brush. Many chimney sweeps charge higher than normal rates for servicing an insert system. It is recommended that a professional install every insert, as some direct connections are quite difficult to make.

Underwriters' Laboratories, Inc. (UL), has developed the UL 907 standard for inserts. Selecting a certified insert should guarantee that it can be safely installed and easily cleaned. As with all other appliances, examine the stove for workmanship and ease of use. The unit should be quite rugged, have a firebox liner, efficiency increasers such as a baffle, and shields to protect combustible wooden mantels.

If, as most people do, you still want to observe the fire, ascertain that the unit you are considering allows this; some

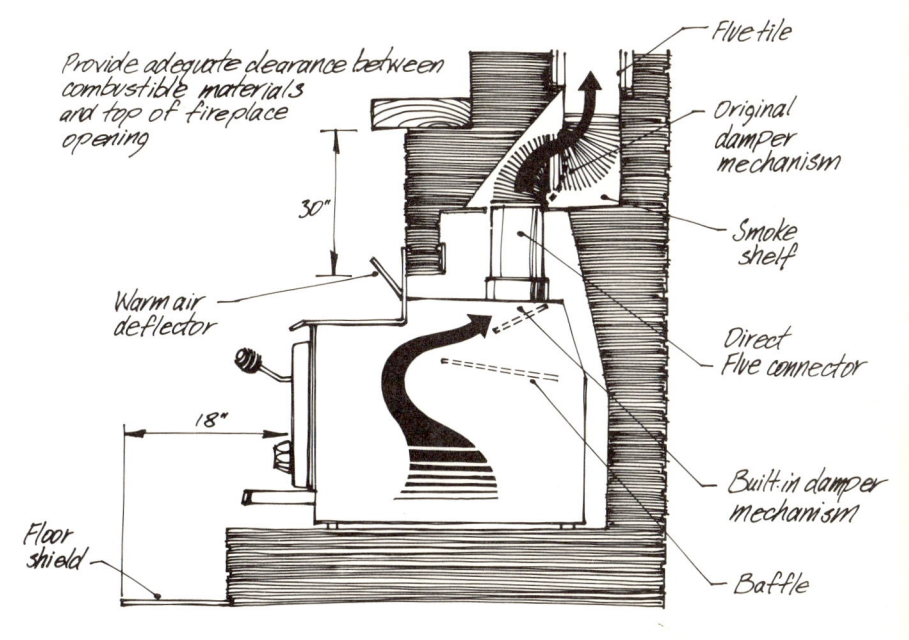

PROPERLY INSTALLED AIRTIGHT FIREPLACE INSERT

don't. Some units have solid cast-iron doors that swing back to allow placement of a protective screen, while others use glass windows. The glass is rarely covered under warranty. Most of the glass doors available as accessories for open fireplaces, or that come with factory-built models, are tempered. This glass should never be jarred when hot, as it will shatter into small pieces. Also, quite hot blazes should be built as far back in the fire chamber as possible. Many manufacturers are switching to glass with a high silica content. Used in most heaters that have windows, this is stronger than the tempered type, except when being moved. All glass used can be scratched fairly easily, and unless the stove has built-in channels that run air past the inside of the glass, it will quickly be covered in soot. The use of glass doors does allow easy monitoring of the fire, but some may wish to opt for the simpler solid cast-iron doors.

Have a careful look at your chimney *before* buying an insert. If its dimensions are nine inches square, nine by twelve inches, or twelve inches square, it should remain relatively free of creosote as long as reasonably hot fires are frequently used. If the flue is too large as is, a special tepee- or cone-shaped chimney cap, which will improve the flue's draft, is a simple and safe solution.

While there certainly can be problems with the insert, there is no doubt that it is one of the better methods of improving an existing fireplace. However, caution is needed in both the purchase and operation of the unit.

THE FIREVIEWER

The insert is one attempt to provide the consumer with a combination fireplace-heater. However, there is another hybrid that is inherently safer and more efficient than most inserts.

These units are known as fireviewers, fireplace-stoves, and combi-fire units. They are high-quality (for the most part) cast-iron or steel heaters equipped with a glass window or doors that swing back. Since the unit sits in the room, not the fireplace cavity, it generally has a high heat transfer efficiency.

The original fireviewer was the now-scorned, inefficient Franklin-style heater. The fit of the wall panels and doors in this type of stove is usually so poor that having the doors closed makes little difference in how fast the fire burns.

However, many companies realized some years ago that the principle of combining the two functions of fireplace and heater was a sound one. There are now several styles of fireviewers, some being American-made, cast-iron appliances with solid doors. The Scandinavians use the same approach with their cast units, except that some have a sophisticated mechanism that swings the door underneath the appliance. There are also some solid-door steel fireviewers and others with glass windows.

A fireviewer can be installed in a number of ways. The procedures detailed in Chapter 12 for installing any heater can be used, or the unit can be set on the hearth of the fireplace and use the fireplace flue. If you install the fireviewer in this way, employ the protective pad that must be placed in front of the firebox door. Unless you want to break a hole into the flue above the mantel, ensure that the smokepipe exits the ap-

American-made Fireviewer with double front doors, gasket sealed!

Snap-in screen for safe viewing of fire

pliance at a level low enough to allow it to enter the fireplace opening. Having the flue collar on the rear of the appliance works best. With this style of installation, always run smokepipes up past the damper and make sure that an airtight seal is made at the damper. Fiberglass insulation is not suitable for this, since air can pass through it and since fiberglass insulation breaks down when exposed to high temperatures. Using a metal adapter prepared by a sheet-metal shop is best. A professional stove installer should be called on in such a case.

Using an existing fireplace flue is generally not recommended with a coal-burning appliance, which needs the size of flue suggested by the manufacturer.

There will be some who will read this and remain determined to install a masonry fireplace regardless of the consequences. Simply remember that if you select an appliance for aesthetics initially, chances are that you will later wish you had spent more time and money on efficiency. To construct a mammoth stone fireplace and then install an insert is very expensive. Have a long, careful look at the fireviewers. Their aesthetics are pleasing, several styles are available, and an installation complete with a stone, brick, or ceramic-tile backdrop will be not only as visually pleasing as most fireplaces but also as efficient as almost anything on the market.

6
Central Systems: Furnaces and Boilers

During the first years of the current wood heating renaissance, the majority of consumers bypassed furnaces and boilers in favor of a cookstove, heater, or fireplace. They desired an uncomplicated, reasonably priced appliance that was visible, instead of being sequestered in a cellar, and that produced heat that could readily be felt.

However, increasing numbers of people—including many who already burn wood—are beginning to yearn for the comfort offered by a central system.

Regardless of how hard one tries to distribute the warmth generated by a space heater, the region directly around the appliance is nearly always warmer than the perimeter. Many people tire of needing a sweater in one room while wanting windows open in another. The uniform heat provided by a forced-air or hot-water central system then becomes appealing.

As well, a safely installed heater needs a sizable amount of space on all sides; no furniture can be within three feet. Smokepipe is generally black and, to most eyes, ugly. Carrying wood to the appliance from a shed, basement, or outdoor pile leaves a trail of bark, chips, dried mud, and, on occasion, insects and melting snow. Cinders can ruin rugs and floors, and it is impossible to avoid releasing smoke into the home occasionally. Having the unit situated in the basement also reduces the possibility of children, particularly, being burned by falling against the appliance.

Most furnaces and boilers are not visually satisfying. Some are painted bright colors and others have digital readouts but, in essence, these are bland boxes. However, due to their isolated location, aesthetics is rarely a concern.

There is little doubt that technological advances will develop the heater further, but it can be confidently predicted that if wood heating is to become as convenient as burning oil or gas, and therefore appeal to the majority of homeowners in areas where wood can be easily obtained, refined central systems will lead the way. It is clear that thousands of potential woodburners desire heating equipment that is not seen.

Central appliances are often appealing for a home that already has heating ducts or water pipes and radiation devices. Manufacturers are meeting the demand for retrofit equipment to replace an oil- or gas-fired unit with a multi-fuel appliance that safely allows the burning of wood while retaining for the operator the option of using other fuels. There are also boilers and add-on furnaces that can be connected to an existing system without removal of the original appliance.

It cannot be claimed that central systems are perfect; there are weak points. Since the cost of an entire installation can run to five figures—beyond the reach of many consumers—central wood-fired units are generally best suited to existing buildings where the heat distribution network is in place. Additionally, the wise person will take advantage of proven energy conservation and passive solar processes to build a new home that does not require the services of a heating unit as large as most central systems. Passive solar homes often need only a small heater.

In homes with poorly insulated basements, a significant percentage of the generated energy will be lost unless the duct or pipe network is well insulated. Canadian stove designer Brian Park once experimented by installing a furnace in the living area of his home before transferring it to his basement. In the latter location, it burned 50 percent more wood with the thermostat set at the same level. Thus, even-heat distribution and isolation of the heating device will generally escalate annual fuel requirements.

Some multi-fuel furnaces and boilers that depend on one heat exchanger or plenum for distribution of all created heat generally have a lower heat transfer efficiency when burning oil or gas than does a unit that operates solely on such fuels. It is harder for the heat to be emitted when soot and creosote, produced by the burning of wood, build up on the inner surface of the heat exchanger.

While newer units sometimes require tending as little as once every two or three days, traditional furnaces and boilers have to be charged three or four times a day. When the unit is in the basement instead of more frequented areas such as the den, living room, or kitchen, additional effort is required to carry out daily routines.

A power failure can knock out electric blowers or water pumps, rendering a central heating system virtually useless unless such a situation is carefully planned for prior to installation. (A reputable seller of this equipment can offer advice on how a boiler or furnace can be installed and operated in such a way that some heat can be produced without electricity.) Also, many furnaces and boilers are massive and heavy. Homeowners and installers may have difficulty moving the unit or heat storage tanks through cellar doors.

Finding a dealer who is knowledgeable about central systems in general, and who also knows about currently preferred equipment and safety practices, may require a lengthy search. The technical expertise tends to be possessed by established plumbing and heating contractors. The dealer must be aware of modern regulations relating to clearances between the ductwork of a solid-fuel system and combustibles. In a retrofit situation, unless the first few feet of the duct are lowered, the wood appliance, which produces much higher temperatures than an oil or gas unit, can cause dangerous overheating of combustible floor joists.

While the conscientious handyman can put a space heater in as long as recommendations of the manufacturer are strictly obeyed, very few furnace or boiler purchasers will have the option of performing this process themselves. Expertise is required in moving heavy objects and in working with electricity and water systems or sheet metal. Therefore, the cost of the installation must automatically be added to the overall price.

FURNACES

Since furnaces and boilers have intrinsic differences, it is important to discuss these appliances separately. There are three types of solid-fuel furnaces: wood furnaces, multi-fuel models, and add-ons.

The Wood Furnace

The wood furnace is the least popular of the trio because it costs substantially more to buy and install than most heaters, without offering one of the prime perquisites of most central units—convenient auxiliary heating provided by oil, gas, or electricity. But wood furnaces do tend to be uncomplicated and dependable, as the two technologies used, a simple firebox and a forced-air distribution system, are well proven.

The Multi-Fuel Furnace

The multi-fuel or combination furnace is quite popular in Canada, where add-ons are just gaining acceptance by safety officials. Multi-fuel units often have two fireboxes that feed into one plenum. As mentioned previously, this arrangement can harm the efficiency of the fossil-fuel-burning part, especially if cool air is allowed to infiltrate into the heat exchanger while a wood fire is burning, allowing creosote buildup. To prevent this, the fossil-fuel firebox must be completely sealed when the wood side is employed.

Not all wood and multi-fuel furnace manufacturers have yet adopted the combustion-improving devices found on many heaters. As with North American cookstove makers, some have turned out the same furnace for several decades and see no reason to modify it. Wood heat professionals familiar with all types of appliances are often appalled at how archaic some of these furnaces remain. For example, a good number do not have a well-sealed loading door. Since the blaze burns below this opening in the "firepit," cool air that seeps in flows straight into the secondary combustion zone. As with air that leaks from the oil-side firebox of a combination furnace, this can cause creosote in the heat exchanger and even in the combustion area itself. Furthermore, few of these older appliances have as simple a secondary combustion device as a baffle, let alone more complicated ones.

The catalytic combustor is being utilized by a few more progressive furnace makers, and an increasing number are going to controlled-combustion fireboxes and baffles. These can have an overall efficiency as much as twenty percentage points higher than the primitives.

Combination furnaces are often designed to burn oil and wood (and sometimes coal), but wood/gas and wood/electric versions are appearing. The wood/electric is essentially a wood furnace with heating elements placed between the firebox and plenum. This model is an excellent purchase when wood will be burned from 75 to 85 percent of the time, since the installation usually costs less than with oil or gas, and little ongoing maintenance is required by the electrical section of the appliance.

Multi-fuel furnaces generally have two thermostats that allow the homeowner to set the electric, gas, or oil thermostat a few degrees below the wood's, so that the auxiliary fuel will cut in whenever the fire dies down.

The firebox of a multi-fuel furnace should be lined with cast iron or refractory bricks. If the door is located far above the firebox, it can be made of steel. It should fit tightly into its frame. Compare models for thickness of materials and quality of workmanship. Since these models contain electric components, it is essential that a model listed to a UL standard be selected.

The Add-on Furnace

Similar to the fireplace insert, the add-on furnace is, in principle, a wonderful advance, allowing the homeowner to augment an existing furnace and duct system with a bare-bones, inexpensive wood unit. The person who has a capable oil appliance can have a multi-fuel arrangement without replacing the existing device or employing a more expensive, proper wood furnace.

When an oil or gas furnace is designed, built, and certified, the manufacturer and testing agency know the exact temperatures electrical components can withstand and what clearances are required between combustibles and the furnace's plenum and ducts. These limits will not be exceeded because the flow of oil and its rate of burn can be easily regulated. However, an unsafe add-on installation can raise temperatures far beyond what electrical components and clearances can handle. It is critical to buy a certified add-on and follow the manufacturer's installation directions.

There are two correct ways of setting up an add-on, known as the *series* and the *parallel* methods. Both use "downstream" locations whereby the hot air of the wood furnace never comes close to the firebox and electrical components of the oil appliance.

The series approach is the preferred of the two, but it is much harder to engineer. At those times when the oil furnace is in use (wood and oil should not be burned simultaneously), hot air leaving the oil furnace goes to the cold-air intake of the add-on, through its firebox, and out the plenum to the duct. The blower of the existing furnace pushes all the air along. This installation will deliver heat to room registers at between 105 and 120 degrees, comparable to the performance attained by an oil or gas furnace. There are two drawbacks to series models, though. The amount of ductwork that must be used is substantial; some basements simply don't have the space to accept it. Also, this ductwork can create what is known as excess static pressure. This can cause the existing blower to function improperly and burn out prematurely. A professional installer should calculate the static pressure; needed tables should be supplied by the manufacturer. It may be necessary to purchase a larger blower.

With the parallel process, warm air from the wood furnace feeds into the plenum of the existing furnace. To prevent this hot air from penetrating into the workings of the oil unit, both furnaces must have blowers that operate simultaneously when-

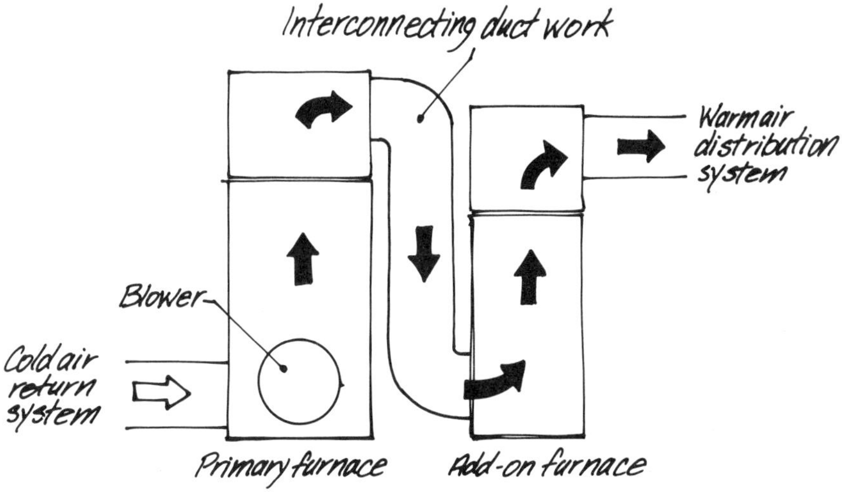

SERIES INSTALLATION

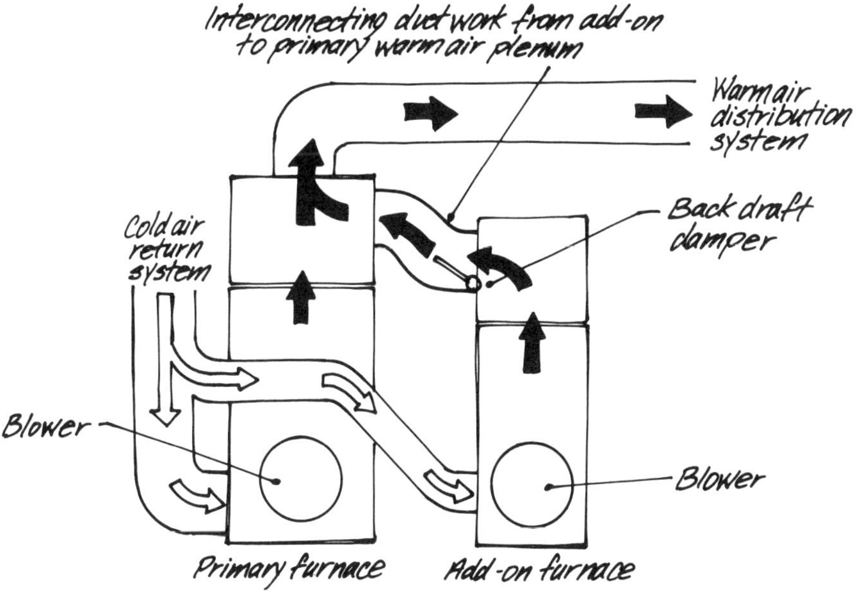

PARALLEL INSTALLATION

ever the wood furnace is pumping out heat. If blowers with an output of 500 cubic feet a minute or more are employed, there must be a back-draft damper located above the firebox of the wood furnace. If the blower on the wood furnace is considerably smaller than the other fan, it must have a high dynamic-pressure rating.

Since the warm air flowing out of a parallel add-on into the plenum of the existing model will be joined by cooler air coming up through the oil unit, the air that enters the duct is reduced to between 80 and 95 degrees when it reaches the room registers. The parallel method thus has a lower performance than the series, but it is generally cheaper to install, since it often requires less ductwork.

Three problems will arise if the wood furnace is hooked in upstream to the cold air return of the existing furnace. First, the oil appliance's blower motor can overheat and fail. Second, if the power goes off or the blower malfunctions, hot air will gravitate into the cold air return, which does not have sufficient clearance from combustible materials to safely handle such warmed air. Third, and most serious, if there is a leak in the firebox of the wood appliance, poisonous carbon monoxide gas can be drawn into the cold air return and infiltrate the living area of the home. (With parallel systems, each furnace should have a separate cold air return.)

To give the operator sufficient control over the rate of burning to prevent overheating in the ducts, a controlled-combustion add-on must be used. Furthermore, it is recommended that a professional heating contractor be hired to install it. See that he adjusts the ductwork to provide the proper clearances.

BOILERS

The boiler, and the network of pipes needed to distribute heated water to radiation devices located throughout the home, is the most complicated residential wood heating system. It should be considered only by those who already have a network of water pipes and radiators, unless the homeowner is wealthy or is a plumber with access to inexpensive pipe and pumps.

There are thousands of North American homes, especially

along the Atlantic coast, which are already heated with an oil- or gas-fired boiler. If the unit is aging, the wise homeowner with access to firewood will install a multi-fuel unit. It is also possible to hook a wood boiler into a system with a healthy existing boiler. Larger, older buildings use steam units, but almost all residential appliances now on the market are forced-hot-water models that heat the liquid to approximately 180 degrees.

The assortment of multi-fuel boilers can be confusing. Some burn wood and leave the consumer the option of adding coal grates. There are oil/gas boilers that can be converted to use solid fuel during an emergency. Some accept wood and either oil or gas, and others run on oil, propane, gas, wood, coal, or electricity; these last two styles generally allow the operator to switch fuels quickly. The consumer may find one firebox or two, and a single heat exchanger or a pair. All available models in the size range suitable should be examined before deciding which fits your needs and budget.

Some boilers, known as wet-base units, have water around the sides, top, and bottom of the firebox. Manufacturers of these warn that they will not function properly with green or wet wood. Other (dry-base) units have water only above the firebox. The smoke and gases within many boilers generally run through hollow tubes surrounded by water. A drawback of these air-to-water heat exchangers is that the tubes must be cleaned regularly, especially if they have a small inside diameter.

The water pipes that distribute the heat to the radiators are constructed of a number of different materials. The homeowner must ensure that the boiler is suitable for use with the type and diameter of pipe in place.

In many North American homes heated with hot water, there are a number of "zones." Each has a thermostat and circulating pump, so that residents can vary the temperatures in different parts of the house. These circulators do not run nonstop, but come on when so instructed by the thermostat. In Europe, most homes have only one zone, allowing the regulating of the water temperature in the distribution network to be handled by a mixing valve. This device adds a selected quantity of quite cool water to the hotter water flowing between the boiler and radiators. The valve can be controlled either manually or automatically. The circulator generally operates all the time.

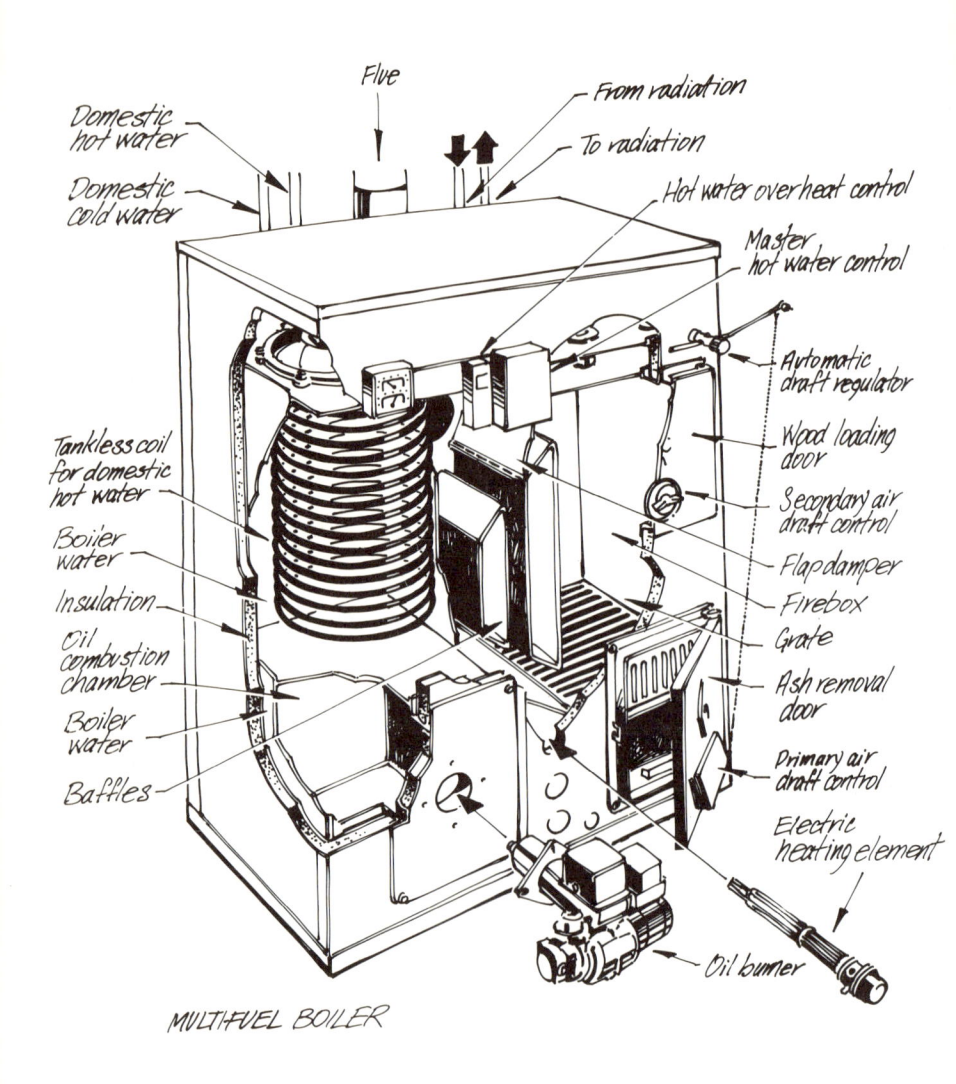

Figure labels:
- Flue
- From radiation
- To radiation
- Domestic hot water
- Domestic cold water
- Hot water overheat control
- Master hot water control
- Automatic draft regulator
- Wood loading door
- Secondary air draft control
- Flap damper
- Firebox
- Grate
- Ash removal door
- Primary air draft control
- Electric heating element
- Oil burner
- Tankless coil for domestic hot water
- Boiler water
- Insulation
- Oil combustion chamber
- Boiler water
- Baffles

MULTIFUEL BOILER

If an existing home has only one main zone, the mixing valve should be used. The owner's manual included with the Tarm line of boilers explains why:

> The valve leads to longer boiler life due to the elimination of thermal shock to the boiler caused by surges of cold return water at circulator start-up. There is longer circulator life as most wear in cir-

culators occurs during motor start-up. The home is quieter during the heating season, as the noises caused by sudden changes in water temperature in the radiation are eliminated. The house is more comfortable, because the heat is more even.

A great number of boiler water jackets (where the water is heated) contain a coil for producing domestic hot water. Taking advantage of the heating appliance to handle this energy-intensive chore makes a great deal of sense. (This topic will be dealt with in Chapter 7 as well.)

It is essential that any such system contain a pressure relief valve, either in the cold water line running into the coil or on the hot line exiting from it. There cannot be check or shutoff valves between the coil and relief valve. The absence of a relief valve will be questioned by safety authorities and can lead to the system's exploding if the water becomes too hot.

Some boilers that burn only wood do not have this coil, but if such an appliance is being added to a system with an existing boiler that does have a water coil, the wood unit can be used to heat the water. A parallel connection is needed to hook the boilers to one another. Water from the wood boiler flows into the water jacket of the existing unit, in which the hot water coil is immersed. This arrangement demands an extra circulator for the wood appliance.

As well as possessing a pressure relief valve on the domestic hot water pipe, quality boiler installations have a pressure relief valve and expansion tank on the main boiler water line. They also have a high limit or overheat control that, according to C. H. Anthony, writing in the January 1981 issue of *Wood 'n Energy*,

> will function when the water temperature rises above a predetermined point (usually 200 to 205 degrees F.). This overheat aquastat normally is set to activate one or more system circulators in order to "dump" excess heat into the radiation of the house. This type of control is necessary because, even when shut down, a solid-fuel boiler still is producing heat that in turn can lead to overheating of the boiler water.

SCHEMATICS FOR THREE BOILER INSTALLATIONS

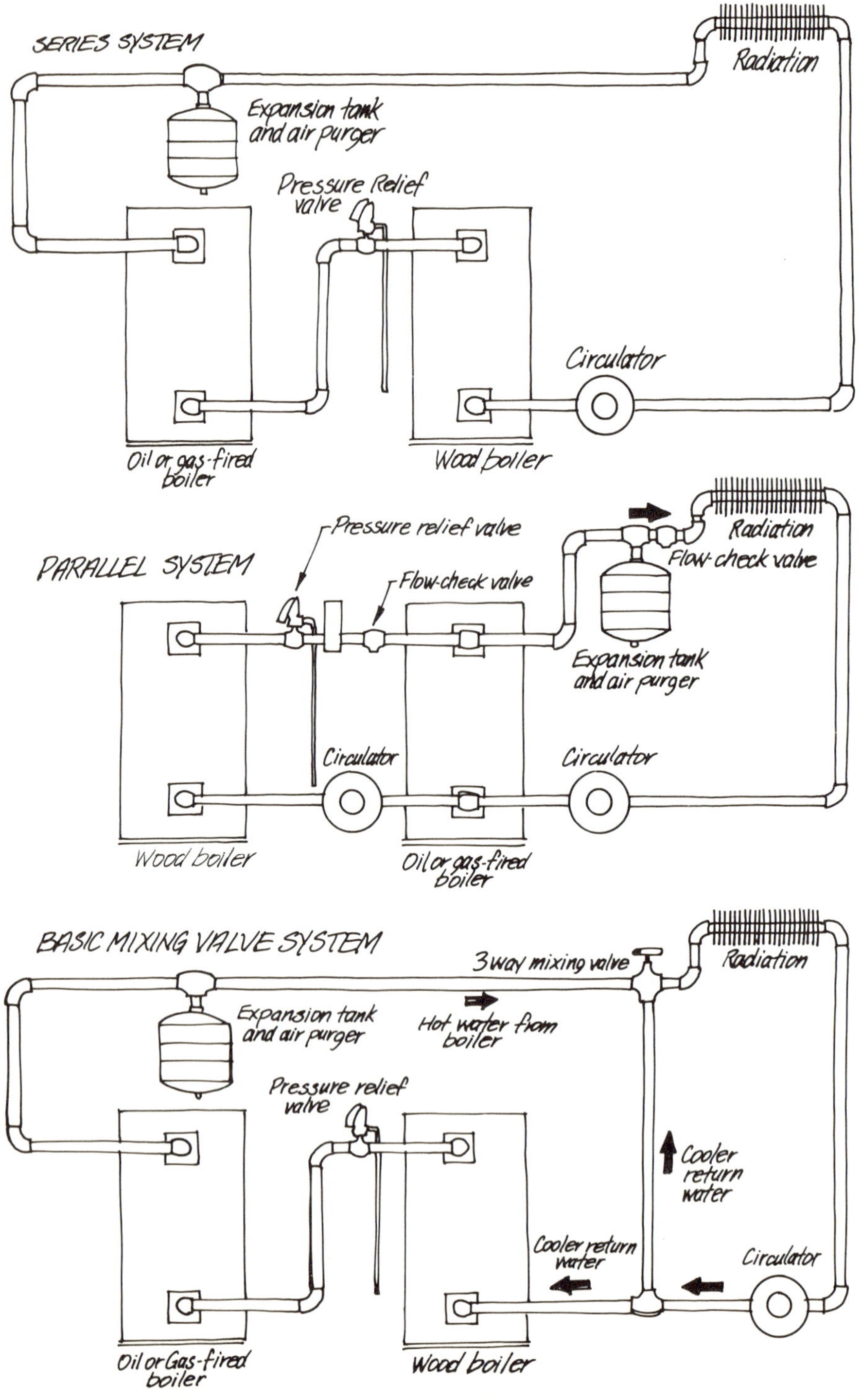

Central Systems: Furnaces and Boilers 51

The more sophisticated boilers have electrical or mechanical automatic draft controls, and secondary combustion features that can include the adding of preheated secondary air and flow routes that require gases and smoke to pass back through the primary combustion zone before exiting.

While an instrument panel is optional on some boilers, its presence is recommended to improve ease of operation. Since the tubes within the heat exchanger of the wood side's firebox will need regular cleaning, make certain they are accessible.

Every boiler should be certified by a recognized testing agency. While an approval by the American Society of Mechanical Engineers (ASME) is not essential, it does signify that the unit is especially rugged. The Tarm manual includes cautions that should be followed by any boiler purchaser:

> All boilers must be installed in accordance with national, state, and local plumbing, heating, and electrical codes and the regulations of the serving electrical, water, and gas utilities. All systems should be designed by competent contractors and only persons knowledgeable in the layout and installation of heating systems should attempt installation of any boiler. It is the responsibility of the installing contractor to see that all controls are correctly installed and are operating properly when the installation is complete.

It is thus important to approach the selection of a boiler with special care, because of the sizable investment and the safety concerns. Ensure that the dealer is experienced. Conscientious stove retailers who are entering the central heating market will often use installers employed by a heating contractor.

RECENT ADVANCES

Prince Edward Island is a compact province in eastern Canada, with a population of 120,000 and forests that cover more than half of its 1.2 million acres. Since the island has no oil or natural gas deposits and little hydroelectric development, it must rely on energy brought across the Northumberland Strait from other provinces. As Islanders pay more for heating oil than most Canadians, the province established the Institute of Man and Resources, a nonprofit corporation with a mandate to carry out imaginative renewable energy research. Much of the institute's funding is provided by the Canadian government through the Canada-P.E.I. Agreement on Renewable Energy Development.

Its innovative experiments with sophisticated wood-fired central systems are being closely watched by North American wood heat professionals. While the project has since been expanded, ten systems were originally installed in 1979. These fell into four categories: conventional boilers and furnaces; similar appliances equipped with heat storage (water) tanks; pellet burners; and wood-chip-fired appliances.

The three conventional "off-the-shelf" units were a wood furnace, a wood boiler, and a wood/oil boiler. The heat storage devices were attached to a Scandinavian multi-fuel boiler and a state-of-the-art boiler, built at that time in Prince Edward Island and based on a design developed by Dr. Richard Hill of the University of Maine. The pellet burner was a conventional furnace originally designed to burn coal fed into the firebox by an electric auger. This was modified to burn densified wood pellets less than an inch long. The wood-chip units consisted of two multi-fuel boilers and a pair of wood furnaces connected to Swedish-made, automatic feed systems specifically designed for use with wood chips.

Wood heat professionals have become extremely interested in these pellets and chips. Since the chips and pellets are made from poor quality logs, plus branches, twigs, and bark, they allow more complete utilization of the forest resource than does the round or split log traditionally used for fuel. Since these are much easier to load and transport than fuel wood, it has been predicted that there could be potential for using pellets and chips in urban and industrial settings. Finally, it has been hoped that by combining these with stokers that keep the fire fed, wood burning could be made far more convenient.

The Institute of Man and Resources has confirmed that these fuels do in fact "promise a high level of convenience. Although combustion equipment for these fuel forms does not yet offer the same level of convenience as oil-fired equipment, it does represent a significant improvement over conventional round log equipment." The chip and pellet systems required tending as often as twice a day and as little as once every second day. The pellet burner produced the lowest emissions of any of the ten units initially tested.

The institute believes these fuels are cost effective. However, it found that chips were difficult to transport and concluded that they were best suited to localized rural use. Farmers could prepare their winter's supply by renting a chipper that would attach to their tractor. The chips must be stored in a covered bin to prevent saturation by rain or snow that can cause the chips to freeze, creating problems with the feeding equipment. Since the chips themselves are quite wet when harvested, they raise humidity levels within the home. There is some cause for concern over reports from Sweden, where chips are widely used, that they can generate fungi that lead to respiratory problems.

The pellet is not as easily manufactured as the chip, requiring a costly and elaborate process. The first pellets used in Prince Edward Island were imported from the United States in barrels weighing three hundred pounds, which were taken directly to each home. Now they are delivered loose in a large truck that uses a blower to send the pellets into the home's storage area.

The predominant problem with the pellet has been dust, which tends to cover the area around the appliance. Says the institute's report on the project, "Although this concentration did not appear to approach the level at which a dust explosion was a danger, this factor must be considered when examining the longer term safety questions."

Further research and development should cure humidity and fungus problems with increased air circulation within the stored chips, and the institute feels that the amount of dust accompanying the pellets can be reduced by refining the manufacturing process.

The heat storage appliances functioned well and proved to be far more convenient than similar boiler systems without storage capability. For example, the Scandinavian boiler needed to be fired only twice a week. However, there were problems with the original storage tanks, which were essentially plywood boxes faced with fiberglass. After suffering massive leaks, these were replaced with steel or fiberglass tanks, narrow enough to fit through cellar doors. The institute believes that plastic film liners capable of withstanding near-boiling temperatures, and high-density polyethylene tanks, could also be employed.

While these units were outperformed in the emission tests by the pellet burner, later research carried out by Oregon's Department of Environmental Quality revealed that the boiler designed by Dr. Richard Hill had the lowest emission readings of any equipment tested. Since heat storage units usually have their charges of wood fired at very high temperatures that lead to near complete combustion, these should become very popular if communities and states begin to demand clean-burning appliances. While the conventional boiler hooked to water tanks had larger creosote deposits than were expected, the Hill boiler, the pellet furnace, and some of the chip units produced only small amounts of creosote and soot.

Although much of the equipment is quite sophisticated and unlike any ever seen by some of the local contractors who installed the systems, there were few initial problems—as long as installation manuals were present and comprehensive. Experts familiar with the new types of systems emphasize the importance of having the manual followed exactly and suggest that the work be closely observed as the installation progresses.

The overall efficiencies ranged from 21 to 52 percent and averaged about 40 percent. The test method used determined the amount of heat that actually reached the home. It was concluded that significant heat leakage was occurring through the walls of the various appliances. It was also seen that performance dropped considerably with nearly all appliances during late spring—unless the operator was careful to build only small, hot fires. Furthermore, the report concluded that season-long efficiency would be substantially improved if the operator kept a close eye on the unit, charged it often, and kept the air intake open.

The more sophisticated systems did not perform better than the conventional models. While some researchers may argue that this should not be the case, the institute believes that "the benefits offered by more advanced units are mainly in the area of convenience, that is, less frequent stoking and less maintenance. These are more expensive, and the extra cost purchases convenience rather than performance."

The results of the institute's studies are valuable. The potential offered by heat storage systems, new fuel forms, and automatic feeders has been confirmed—herein lies much of wood heat's future. However, the consumer who yearns to be on the cutting edge of the use of these new technologies may get more than he bargained for. Purchase costs will be high until North American sales increase. The systems do function well once the bugs are ironed out. A local heating contractor may well be able to handle the installation, but don't be surprised if he is a frequent visitor during the first winter of operation. Unless you live near one of the small number of pellet plants now in production, or are able to prepare your own chips, such fuels may be difficult to acquire as very few communities outside of Prince Edward Island have pellet or chip delivery services.

For the time being, heat storage equipment is the most perfected and the most easily obtained. Additionally, it functions well with conventional fuel wood. However, before this decade has ended, sophisticated stoker systems burning pellets and chips will be in widespread use.

7
Heaters

The majority of heaters are radiant models, in which the energy created simply moves out into the room through the walls of the heat exchanger or firebox. While central heating systems are becoming increasingly popular and fireplace inserts constitute a sizable portion of most stove dealers' inventory, space heaters remain the simplest and least expensive means of attaining energy independence.

A decade ago, before the wood stove regained widespread acceptance, only a few drab heaters were available. Now, there is a dizzying selection of shapes, sizes, and sound-alike brand names. It is little wonder that, upon crossing the threshold of a stove store to commence shopping for a heater, one is immediately confused.

BOX STOVES

While some manufacturers are trying hard to make their space heaters look as untraditional as possible, the majority of these units remain rectangular or square, close cousins to the box stove that warmed thousands of American homes a century ago. There are three primary styles of box stoves: Scandinavian- and American-made cast units; steel-plate stepstoves; and lighter, sheet-steel appliances. (For an example of the Scandinavian variety, see the illustration on page 123.)

Cast Stoves

Cast models are generally rectangular, with the firebox door at one end. A good number have wildlife or outdoor scenes sculptured into their side panels; some are available in bright enamel colors. While the new wave of cast stoves originated in Scandinavia, there are a few American manufacturers, primarily located in New England and Pennsylvania, who now produce quality units. These domestic cast models tend to be cheaper than the imports and cost competitive with American steel-plate heaters.

The majority of cast stoves are certified and equipped with baffles and other combustion-improving features. Cast units are available to suit all residential demands, with a particular emphasis on smaller models.

Stepstoves

For the past several years the most popular steel heater has been the stepstove, a box unit with a bi-level top. Developed in 1973 by Robert Fisher of Springfield, Oregon, the stepstove configuration has been adopted by scores of firms.

Since the stepstove is easy to manufacture and, in the opinion of many, more attractive than the unmodified box design, it became the favorite product of fly-by-night stove copiers. However, the situation has settled down and most stepstoves now sold are solid, certified products. Common features are a firebrick liner, cast-iron firebox door, and a steel lip in front of the door to catch ashes. Some designs preheat combustion air, introduce secondary oxygen, and employ a baffle. Electric blowers that connect to channels in the appliance are often optional. These will be discussed later in this chapter.

While some makers claim the bi-level top of the stepstove creates a pair of cooking surfaces that have varying temperatures, a heater cannot substitute as a cookstove. Food can be warmed or fried, and a pot of tea or coffee can be boiled, but extended use of a heater at the high temperatures needed for cooking some foods can permanently damage the walls of the appliance.

Most stepstoves are constructed of 5/16-inch and 1/4-inch

Typical, popular Stepstove type Radiant Heater. Flat top surfaces offer two-level, two temperature cooking areas

Plate steel construction with cast iron door.

steel plate. A good percentage of these units, designed with glass windows or doors that swing back, qualify as fireplace-heaters or fireviewers.

Sheet-steel Stoves

Square or rectangular sheet-steel appliances load from the front or top, and are generally modified downdrafters that sell for less than the heavier steel-plate units. Since the stove's walls are quite thin, it is essential that a complete refractory brick or cast-iron liner be present.

VERTICAL HEATERS

Most appliances burn wood horizontally, but there are a few heaters—often cylindrical, but sometimes rectangular or square—that fire the wood vertically. For simplification, I have deemed all of these *vertical* or *upright* appliances. Their prime advantage is their need of less floorspace. Most of the vertical heaters available in the United States are either combination wood/coal burners, or stoves designed only for coal, coke, and peat. (For an example of a wood/coal burner, see the illustration on page 123.)

C. H. Anthony, writing in the December 1980 issue of *Wood 'n Energy*, suggests that combination heaters have some drawbacks:

> There are no true combination stoves on the market today that will burn wood and both types of coal (anthracite and bituminous) equally well. The design characteristics of each type of stove are so different that any stove which claims to be a combination must sacrifice burnability and efficiency in one or more of the different fuels. Most wood stoves are NOT well suited to burning coal, and many coal stoves are too small to accept a healthy charge of wood.

Therefore, the person who requires a space-saving wood burner must either try to find an upright that is designed solely for that fuel or purchase a combination that favors wood.

While a wood appliance generally works best with a solid firebox floor and the primary combustion intake situated a few inches above it, most coal burners have the primary air enter beneath the fire to allow oxygen to reach all the small chunks of coal. This requires the use of cast-iron grates upon which the fire is constructed. The firebox must also be airtight, and a liner of refractory brick or cast iron is essential.

Stoves used to burn the hard anthracite coal employed primarily in the Northeast must have grates designed specifically for this coal. Stoves that use the softer bituminous coal have larger grate openings; the gaps cannot be very wide if wood will be burned, however, as the chunks of charcoal will fall through. Every coal appliance must have shaker grates that can be cleared from outside the firebox.

Coal appliances always load through a door found either on the top or high on the front or side of the stove. Some units that use the latter location may limit the length of wood that can be used. Since the preparation or purchasing of fuel wood is complicated if the pieces must be shorter than 12 or 14 inches, ensure that the stove will accept wood of at least this length. Also determine the depth of the firebox, as some coal stoves have a very shallow box.

Only a few wood heaters have a separate ash compartment, but a combination unit must have one. Since coal dust is so fine, the door to the ash compartment must fit snugly.

Anyone who desires a true combination unit should purchase one of the handful of wood stoves that has an optional coal grate kit. A drawback to this approach is that the conversion is a messy, complicated affair that most people will not want to perform more than a few times each season. It is important that the coal grate be bolted and cemented into place. Models that are simply dropped into the firebox perform poorly.

Those who wish to enter the world of coal burning in earnest should pick up one of the books published in recent years. Reliable titles include *Heating with Coal* by John W. Bartok, *Central Heating with Wood and Coal* by Larry Gay, *Coal Comfort: An Alternative Way to Heat Your House* by Peter Hotton, and *Home Heating with Coal* by Steve Sherman (see bibliography).

CIRCULATORS

While a radiant heater can distribute heat effectively if it is properly located, there are some situations, such as in a rambling house, where a circulator can be practical.

A true circulating heater does not use electricity, but design and gravity—the tendency of hot air to rise—to push heat farther than a radiant unit can manage. A second advantage is that passive circulators can be located closer to combustibles than radiant models.

All circulators function by running air around the firebox, but there are two exterior designs used. The older type has the air enter from the room through louvers built into a cosmetic outer cover. Inspect these carefully; some are neither as rugged nor as efficient as most radiant heaters. (For an example of a traditional circulator, see the illustration below.)

Some more recently developed circulators expose the tubes or ducts that surround the firebox. These probably work somewhat better than the older design, but many consumers find them ugly. Be sure that there are no leaks in the welds that join these tubes to the firebox.

Passive circulators do work, but the homeowner should not

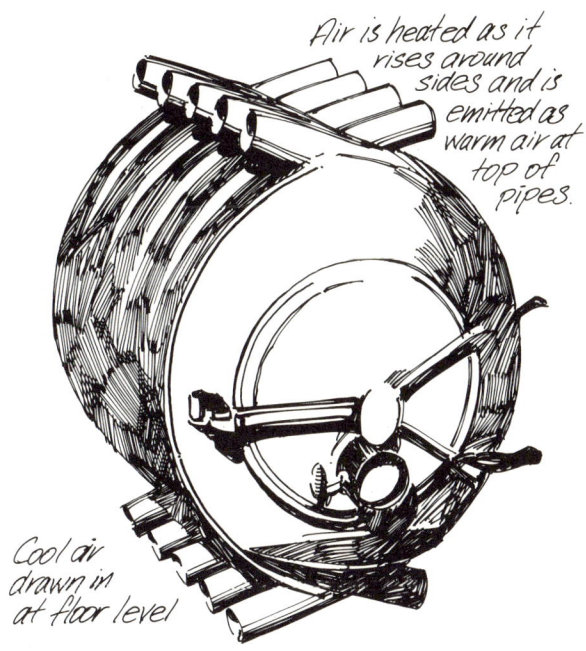

Passive Circulator Unit.

expect dramatic movement of heat. If warm air has to be sent to remote areas, it may be necessary to use an electric blower built into a radiant heater or a small but powerful electric fan installed in a doorway or staircase. Since these fans will not function during a power blackout, a radiant heater equipped with a blower must be installed with the clearances from combustible materials needed for a standard radiant unit.

KITS AND HOMEMADE APPLIANCES

Compared with other types of heating equipment, wood heaters are inexpensive. However, there are always people who want to do something for less.

There are kits available that allow a homeowner to make a stove using a steel barrel. These kits generally include legs, a flue collar, and a cast-iron firebox door. The barrel should be in good condition, without any holes or dents. Placing sand in the bottom will protect the barrel from the extreme heat, but expect to replace the barrel every few years. Before welding or sawing a steel drum, find out what it previously contained—even a few ounces of gasoline or a flammable chemical can cause a violent explosion.

Due to the utilitarian appearance of steel drums, and the massive volume of the firebox, most people find the barrel stove either aesthetically unappealing or oversized for use in the living area of a home. However, it can be used within a basement or in a large workshop or garage.

A much more sophisticated stove built from two sizes of drums was invented by Ken Kern, a Californian architect and builder. His barrel heater can also cook, bake, smoke food, and warm water. Complete instructions are found in Supplement 19/1 of Kern's *The Owner-Built Homestead*.

Anyone eager to take energy independence a step beyond the norm and build his own appliance should be aware of a few facts. A homemade stove will not be certifiable due to the cost involved for this procedure, and therefore its safety will be uncertain. Unless the builder has friends working in a stove factory, he will have difficulty finding cast-iron doors, handles, and other parts required for an efficient appliance. In general, one should not embark on such a project without expert-level metalworking and welding skills and access to an impressive array of tools. Always have a homemade stove inspected by a fire safety official or dealer before it is fired.

MASONRY HEATERS

The masonry heater—widely used in Europe and now gaining in popularity here—is the antithesis of a compact steel or cast-iron stove, as it is several feet square and can weigh a number of tons. Wood is burned at a high temperature within a controlled-combustion cast-iron firebox located deep in the appliance. Radiant heat moves into nearby firebrick. As the smoke and gases rise from the primary combustion zone, they travel through a series of channels. Between these channels are additional layers of firebrick that absorb more of the generated heat. Models include the kachelofen (pronounced ka-ka-LOW-fen) and the Russian Grubka.

The major drawback of these models is that it takes a long time for a masonry heater to begin radiating heat through its ceramic tile walls and into the home. It is also difficult to lessen the emission of warmth once the interior of the appliance has been heated. Kachelofens, Grubkas, and the other masonry heaters will dominate their surroundings and most of the year's home renovation budget. They require a concrete block base that begins below the basement floor, many bags of refractory cement, great numbers of firebricks, and scores of ceramic tiles or, in some cases, bricks or stone. A handful of American companies make custom masonry heaters, and plans are available for those who wish to construct their own.

For those who like this style of appliance but do not have the space and money required, there are smaller movable ceramic tile heaters that may be appropriate. There is debate over how successfully these imitate the performance of larger models. It is obvious that they cannot store as much heat since they do not possess much of the mass central to the masonry heater principle. However, the ceramic tile heaters and somewhat similar soapstone appliances do retain far more warmth than the average steel or cast-iron unit.

Traditional European Kachelofen tile stove

The tiles used on some models are garish, but the majority of tile and soapstone heaters are elegant. Check these for workmanship; better models are certified.

WATER HEATERS

Aside from using a boiler, there are three methods of preparing domestic hot water with a wood appliance: installing a water jacket or coil in a heater, purchasing a unit designed specifically for this purpose, and using a cookstove with a water reservoir. (The latter approach is discussed in Chapter 8, "Used Appliances.")

Families who own or plan to buy a heater should consider a device such as a jacket, coil, or plate that fits inside (or against

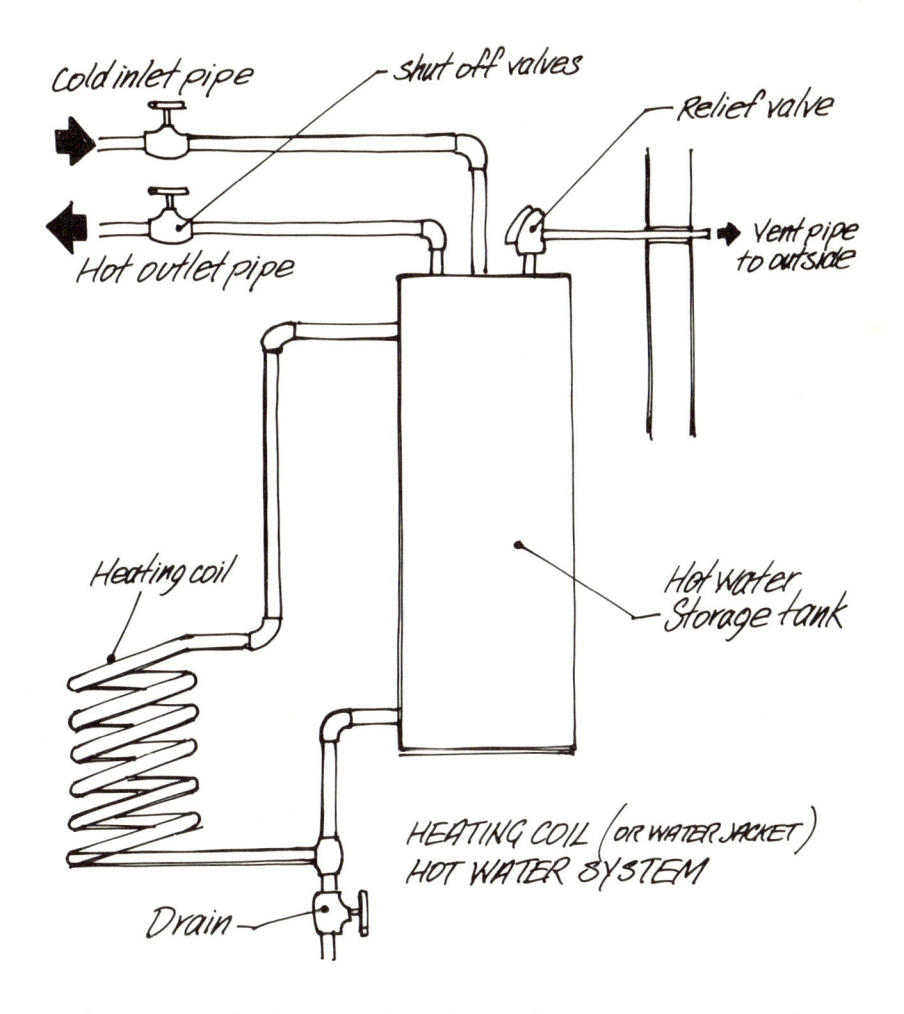

Cold inlet pipe
Shut off valves
Hot outlet pipe
Relief valve
Vent pipe to outside
Heating coil
Hot water Storage tank
HEATING COIL (OR WATER JACKET) HOT WATER SYSTEM
Drain

the exterior of) this type of appliance. It can supply many gallons of hot water daily, and if the main storage tank or an uninsulated preheat tank can be set above the device, gravity will move the water around, avoiding the need for an electric pump.

The water-jacket type of domestic water heating is appealing because only one appliance is needed; the consumer does not have the expense and labor associated with buying, installing, and using two heaters and chimneys. However, while such a system functions well during the chilly months when the appliance itself is operated daily, it is not nearly as convenient in the summer when hot water is still required but use of the appliance can overheat the building.

Some European manufacturers try to solve this problem by equipping the tops of their cookstoves with insulated covers. Three-component systems are also used. The wood unit serves as the primary domestic water heater during the winter; in summer this role is assumed by a solar collector that can feed into the same storage tank used by the wood stove's water jacket; and an electric water heater acts as the auxiliary unit. Such a system is often expensive and complicated to install, but it can supply sizable quantities of hot water year round, saving the homeowner hundreds of dollars in electricity or gas.

Most water jackets or coils inserted into appliances must always be full of water. Since this device cannot be easily removed from the firebox, the homeowner must be sure of his commitment to heating water with wood before installing the necessary components. Copper coils, lightweight steel water jackets, those lined with porcelain, and most made of stainless steel will be harmed by being heated when empty. Only those made of very heavy stainless steel or plain steel can withstand the temperatures. Cold water should never be allowed to enter hot, empty pipes, as steam will immediately be created that expands beyond what even the largest pressure relief valve, located on the top of the storage tank, can handle.

Only a few stoves come equipped with the tappings or openings needed to insert cold and hot water pipes, but any stove can be modified to accept them. Before modifying a stove that does not have them, check the unit's warranty to see what policy is put forward by the manufacturer. The easiest way of making the needed holes is to use a special electric drill attachment (available at plumbing and heating supply stores) that simplifies drilling through steel or cast iron. When sealing around the pipes, by welding a steel appliance or by using stove cement and nuts with a cast stove, be sure to leave room for the pipes to expand. The water jacket or coil must also be installed so that it can expand when warm.

Those who work with wood-fired domestic water-heating systems have no doubt that this is the most dangerous type of wood heat installation. People have been killed or maimed by improperly installed systems that exploded. *Extreme caution is necessary with any hot water system.* Always install pressure relief valves with the proper rating for the system, and expansion tanks. Hire a professional plumber who has had experience working with such setups. Be sure he follows instructions given within the manual supplied with most of these products. If your plumber is not experienced, obtain for him a book on the subject, such as *Handmade Hot Water Systems,* by Art Sussman and Richard Frazier, or *Heating the Home Water Supply,* by Larry Gay (see bibliography).

A smokepipe coil must never be used in conjunction with an airtight or controlled-combustion appliance. The smokepipe of an airtight unit is often too cool to begin with, without adding a coil that draws heat from it.

An approach that uses a separate water heater can be ideal for the household with minimal hot water needs. These appliances do not use a storage tank—the unit is designed to heat a few gallons of water very quickly, as it is required. These units come in various sizes and can be used year round without significantly increasing the temperature within the home. They are generally equipped with a short-term warranty and usually have a first-rate owner's manual that should be studied carefully before the unit is installed or operated. The use of small pieces of wood is recommended, allowing the opportunity to burn scraps that accumulate.

SHIP STOVES

While safety officials may cringe at the thought of having a wood appliance aboard a yacht, others believe that wood stoves and ships go well together. Writes Richard Jagels in *WoodenBoat* magazine:

> The radiant heat provided by a wood burning stove is ideal in poorly insulated and drafty surroundings—standard conditions on the boats of my acquaintance. For those who ship to exotic ports, the wood stove has another favorable feature: worldwide fuel availability. And if wood is difficult to obtain in a particular area, another solid fuel can often be sub-

stituted, such as coal, coke, charcoal, peat, sugarcane bagasse, and rice hulls.

To ensure a safe installation, Jagels instructs the consumer to ask,

> Can the stove be anchored to the floor or bulkhead; or, if no direct provision is incorporated in the stove, can it be easily modified so as to be securely held in place in a pitching boat? I know of no scarier thought than scurrying about capturing flying coals in a tossing boat.

The need for a door that cannot open accidentally is important in all cases, but it is even more essential that the door latch on a ship stove be rugged and fail-safe. While many boats may be drafty, as Jagels claims, there are some that are extremely tightly sealed. It is important that sufficient oxygen supplies always be present. It may be necessary to have a cabin door or hatch open when the stove is in operation, or, if you intend to use the stove when the boat is under way, an outside air duct.

To avoid problems with bulky fuel wood, Jagels suggests the use of wood pellets, which can be kept within a sack in a storage locker. Pellets should be fired in small quantities, since they burn at a very high temperature.

There are special ship stoves, the smallest space heaters on the market, built by companies primarily located along the Pacific and Atlantic coasts. The most compact Scandinavian and American residential cast appliances can also function admirably in this role.

Some wood stove dealers in coastal areas are catering to those desiring ship stoves. Marine outfitters may have a better selection of appliances and accessories, but it is likely that they will not have so much wood heating knowledge.

MOBILE HOME STOVES

Installing a solid-fuel appliance within a mobile home can make a great deal of sense, as these homes are often used in remote boomtowns where housing is at a minimum but trees are plentiful.

As with ships, mobile homes present special problems because they can be moved. Therefore, the stove should be secured to the floor of the home. Furthermore, if beams or studs are severed to permit the wood system's installation, new structural members must be fastened in place.

Mobile homes tend to be quite tight. As a result there is a UL standard that requires that every stove certified for mobile home usage have an outside air duct—usually found in the base of the appliance.

The federal government's Department of Housing and Urban Development (HUD), which regulates the safety of mobile homes in the United States, stipulates that a number of other features appear. The outside air duct must have a screen to keep out mice and other small animals, and it must be impossible for hot coals to fall through the duct and land beneath the home. This intake should also be tightly sealed to prevent cool air from seeping into the dwelling.

The installation must be carefully handled, since mobile homes contain many highly combustible substances, some of which release poisonous gases when heated. HUD requires that a metal factory-built chimney equipped with a spark arrester be employed and that it hook directly to the appliance.

The person who lives in a controlled mobile home community should check with the management before purchasing wood-burning equipment, as bylaws may prohibit its use.

A stove that does not conform to HUD regulations may be unsafe within a mobile home, and its use may invalidate mortgage and insurance policies and any warranty that exists on the dwelling. Make certain that the dealers you visit realize that you require a certified mobile home stove.

8
Used Appliances

Some consumers purchase used appliances simply to save money, while others desire an older, nonairtight stove in order to decrease the potential of creosote being created. There are also those who buy antique appliances because they prefer the charm and workmanship of objects crafted by past generations.

If you know where to search, what to look for, have patience, and are ready to apply elbow grease to your acquisition, a foray into the world of used stoves can be successful. If you enter this market armed only with enthusiasm and a checkbook, however, you may well purchase a lovely stove with permanent internal defects that is useful only as a plant holder.

Since a number of the factors involved in choosing a used appliance differ with each type, this section is divided into three categories: older cookstoves, older furnaces and heaters, and secondhand modern appliances. Nonetheless, many of the points laid out in the section on cookstoves will apply to the purchase of any "experienced" unit.

OLDER COOKSTOVES

Where to Look

The styles and number of appliances available will vary from region to region. Close to major cities, it is likely that diamonds-in-the-rough will be rare. If you want a classic woodrange without traveling out of such locales, expect to pay top dollar to an antique dealer or a full-time stove restorer. In isolated places where these professionals do not congregate at every farm auction, bargains are likely to be more plentiful.

Before you set out to snare the cookstove of your dreams, decide how much money you can spend and whether you would prefer to handle restoration work yourself. Buying a stove that has been refurbished by a pro saves sweat and time—as much as several months. As well, it virtually guarantees that the stove is in good condition.

Buying a stove that has not been restored is more of a gamble. But unless rebuilding is needed from top to bottom, the unit should be much less expensive, it should be possible to fix it yourself, and personal involvement in the project makes it a more satisfying purchase.

There are several places to look for such an appliance. Hardware stores and some stove dealers may have cookstoves that they have taken in on trade. Many rural retailers cannot be bothered restoring the unit and will sell it as is—without any guarantee.

Peruse the classified ads of small-town newspapers, especially during the spring—when an older couple may decide to retire from burning wood—or in late summer and early autumn. Attend farm auctions in regions that are not prowled by antique dealers. Check laundromat and general store bulletin boards for stove ads.

Steve Cawker, a Canadian stove restorer, points out that the physical appearance of a farm usually reflects the condition of any type of used appliance. Families who keep buildings painted and yards clean are likely to have treated their stoves with equal care.

What to Look For

After examining a few appliances—which you should always do before making a purchase—you will be able to tell if a stove has been abused, even if it has undergone a recent cleaning and painting. Avoid stoves that have been repaired by an amateur welder or with parts that do not quite fit. A cookstove that has been cherished by a family for decades will generally not be missing parts or tools such as pokers and lid handles. Some evidence of use can be expected with an appliance that is fifty or sixty years old.

Be careful about buying a stove that is missing parts. The following removable parts and tools should be present:

- All cooking lids or plates
- One or two lid lifters
- All grates for the firebox
- Removable ashpan
- All doors, for the firebox, ashpit, oven, and warming closet
- Copper liner, if stove has a water reservoir
- Poker, ash rake, and shovel
- Small plate for primary oven draft
- All legs
- All draft and damper handles and caps
- All interior firebrick
- Oven thermometer

Each region of the United States and Canada generally had its own foundries, so in a given area you will repeatedly see a handful of brand names. Because of this, you may be able to replace missing parts by buying a stove with a rotten body but still possessing the parts you require, or by finding a junkyard that has piles of stove parts, a professional restorer who will share his or her cache, or even a venerable hardware store that still has parts for once-popular models. However, if the stove was not made in the region where you found it and vital components are missing or beyond repair, you may have a hard time finding them.

A number of firms do stock replacements. Some are national operations, but many specialize in stoves manufactured within their state. If you can determine the technical name or even describe what is broken or missing, make a phone call to one of these companies. They will probably require the names of both the stove model and the manufacturer. This is best done before the deal for the stove is closed. If you can confirm that the parts are available for less than a king's ransom, it should be safe to buy the appliance.

Cracks in components, such as legs and cooking plates or lids, can be welded electrically with nickel-electrode rods designed to be employed with cast iron. However, this process is quite costly; if possible, have an experienced welder inspect the stove and give an estimate—again, before the stove is paid for.

The most crucial parts of a cookstove are around the firebox and the channels through which the smoke and gases travel before they leave the appliance. When the oven damper is closed, a necessary action whenever you are baking, the smoke will circulate around four sides of the oven. Therefore it is essential to check the oven door and all interior oven surfaces. Push against each to determine if the metal is firm. Do the same with the bottom and back of the stove. If there are holes in these locations, hot embers could drop onto the floor at home and cause severe damage.

Some disreputable restorers use stove cement to fill cracks and then paint it over, in the same way that dishonest used car dealers fix a badly rusted car with body filler. To test for an uncracked stove, tap the metal—all portions of each surface should give off the same sound.

If there is solid metal around a hole, a patch can be welded on, but if the steel close to the perforation is flimsy, avoid buying the stove. When there is a reservoir for heating water on a cookstove, inspect the copper liner. If the stove has been used while it was empty, the liner may be burned out. Check the condition of its seams and remove the liner to inspect the sheet metal beside it. This is a common point where severe rusting occurs.

When the cast portions of the stove are flaky with rust, ensure that a sufficient thickness of solid metal remains underneath. This solid portion must not be paper thin. Most units that have been stored for several years—as is often the case with older appliances—will have a different type of bright orange surface rust. If this corrosion is attacked with an oil-dipped rag, the metal underneath should be solid.

The firebox should be solid and the cast-iron or refractory brick liner present and sound. Few older cookstoves were highly efficient, but there must not be spaces where sizable quantities of air can leak in. If the firebricks are in need of replacement and new ones of the proper shape and dimensions cannot be located, try to obtain a quantity of firebrick cement that can be used, along with a wooden frame, to pour new firebricks within the stove.

Be sure that all doors close relatively tightly and are in working order. A broken hinge may be difficult to repair. If there is a gap between one of the doors and its frame, or if a section of the cooking surface is significantly raised above the other pieces, investigate the cause of this. Either warpage has taken place or something has collapsed.

The grates on which the fire rests should all be in place and in good condition. The more complex kinds are designed to be used with coal. It is essential that a cookstove have grates. The ashes and coals drop from the grate into the ashpan below. (The fire *cannot* be built in the ashpan.) If authentic replacement grates cannot be obtained, a piece of steel at least one-quarter inch thick, with holes drilled in it to allow air to rise from one of the main air intakes near the ashpit, can be substituted. Reinforcing bars (rods of steel used when pouring concrete; available at building centers) can also work. Don't expect either material to last more than a few heating seasons without substantial warpage.

Since steel and cast iron expand at different rates when heated, consult a metals expert regarding what size to cut steel replacement parts.

Once you have ascertained the condition of the appliance and the asking price, ask for a period of time before the deal is closed. If there is a professional stove restorer in the region, contact him and explain what repairs you feel are needed for the unit. Inquire if he believes the asking price is fair for the condition of the appliance, how much he would charge to restore it, and whether the project will be one an amateur can handle. It may be a good idea to get two opinions and estimates.

Moving a Cookstove

When it is time to transfer the stove to your home or the restorer's workshop, the ruggedness of most cookstoves will become apparent. At least two strong people will be needed for even the smallest woodrange, and four healthy individuals will be required to get some cookstoves onto a truck. Be very careful about how the appliance is lifted. If pressure is brought to bear on a component that cannot stand the load, it will snap. If the stove is dropped, serious damage can result to it. Slide timbers at least four inches square under the appliance to allow four people to lift without worrying about damage to the unit or their backs.

Remove all loose and protruding parts, such as top plates and door handles, to lessen both the weight and the likelihood of parts being broken. Tie the oven door shut so that it cannot pop open and, if possible, unbolt the warming closet so the stove will not be top-heavy. If it is not feasible to remove the legs, be careful with them, as the long ones under most ovens break easily.

The safest way of transporting a stove is in a truck that has a solid front to its box. To prevent the stove from shifting when the vehicle is stopping or from falling over when a corner is rounded, set the stove parallel to the cab, against the front of the box. If the truck is open, cover the stove with a tarp before it is tied in, to prevent damage from low branches, stones, or rain. Use plenty of stout rope and test the quality of your knots before the vehicle begins to move. Place cardboard or old blankets between the stove and the edge of the box and insert rags wherever the ropes will touch the stove.

If you have no choice but to use a van or trailer in which a stove cannot be so secured, set blocks in front of and behind each leg and run ropes as high on the stove as possible, to prevent it from toppling over. A cookstove should never be transported on its back, as the firebrick can come loose.

Cleaning

Once the stove has been brought to the workshop, it should be given a thorough cleaning both inside and out so that any flaws that were missed earlier can be detected.

Tackle the interior first. An industrial vacuum cleaner can be handy for reaching into deep corners. The smoke channel under the oven should be carefully cleaned with a long thin ash rake—a rod with a flat piece of metal, approximately one inch by three inches, at the end. If one is not included with the appliance, you may find one at a stove dealer or rural hardware store. This process should be repeated several times during each heating season; check the appliance's condition every two weeks. The cavity is usually reached by removing the manufacturer's nameplate found beneath the oven door.

If the stove has to be completely dismantled to allow repair of major deficiencies, make written notes and diagrams detailing where each component fits. Store parts carefully, placing together those from each area of the appliance.

A thin layer of dirt and grease that has built up on exterior enameled surfaces can be removed by gently using wet steel wool and then a moist rag. If deposits are heavy, the cheapest solvent is kerosene, which should be washed down with water after it has the desired effect. When using kerosene or water on enamel, avoid spilling either liquid on the cast-iron or steel portions of the appliance.

Cast iron encrusted with grease can be cleaned with a paint scraper or putty knife. For removing a sizable quantity of rust from the same material, employ sandpaper followed by steel wool. The coarser the sandpaper, the faster the job will go, but be sure the surface is not scratched.

For regular maintenance of cast-iron surfaces, apply cooking oil with a rag, or wipe wax paper over it. While kerosene, methyl hydrate—ideal for removing surface rust—and domestic cleansers should never be applied to hot enamel because the fluid will be baked into the surface, cast iron should be polished when warm. Oil all cast-iron surfaces each spring to prevent rust from forming during the summer.

The same cleansers and steel wool are also used with nickel plating. If the plating seems intact, do not scratch it while removing dirt or rust. Most cities have plating firms that can rejuvenate these components. Professional stove restorers may be able to steer you to a reputable source. If not, try your luck with the Yellow Pages of the phone book.

Is a Used Cookstove for You?

There are thousands of restored cookstoves in use throughout North America. These can offer many more years of service for, in most cases, not too large an investment. Plain inexpensive models will generally function well but do lack the aesthetic appeal of the "grandes dames." Handy features on any cookstove include a water reservoir; an oven large enough to accept a covered roasting pan; a warming closet above the cooking area, which is effective for keeping food hot; and a handle that allows the main cooking surface over the firebox to be raised as one unit to allow easy loading of wood.

The antique cookstove is especially suitable within an older, restored home. There is no doubt that many of these cast-iron beauties have an appeal and grace lacking in most newer appliances.

FURNACES AND HEATERS

Aging furnaces will not be of use to many contemporary wood burners. Units that classify as antiques were built before the inception of forced-air equipment. The heat is distributed through ducts, far larger in diameter than those used with a forced-air system, that depend on hot air's ability to rise on its own. With many of these, all ducts originate at the furnace. This results in an octopus-like maze of pipes. This style is not easily used unless the needed ducts still exist in an older home. Other older furnaces have only one duct that feeds warm air into a huge grate set into a floor. This type can be employed if the needed grate can be found at a demolition firm or junkyard.

Antique furnaces are generally composed primarily of cast iron. They are extremely heavy and usually durable. They can be a good buy if the home can accept the unit.

A number of styles of antique heaters are available. These include small and large boxes, simple vertical cylinders, massive potbellied models, and elaborate parlor heaters. A heater is usually much easier to evaluate than a cookstove.

Most antique heaters are constructed solely of cast iron. Check the unit's condition. Rust should be only of the surface variety. Consult a welder on whether cracks can be repaired. Since coal appliances often closely resemble wood heaters, be sure that the firebox is large enough to accept a healthy charge of wood. As with any used stove, confirm that all parts are present or replaceable.

Heaters are usually found in the same places as cookstoves.

However, the selection process is more complicated because the size of the appliance becomes a major consideration. While it is not recommended to put a massive cookstove in a tiny well-insulated kitchen, a wide variety of cookstoves can be used in most kitchens, because the cookstove firebox is almost always compact. However, this is not the case with heaters.

Unless a conscious effort is made to improve its efficiency, the antique heater will consume a charge of wood quite quickly. As a result, it is best to buy a secondhand appliance that is smaller than a controlled-combustion model that could be used in the same location.

It is possible to upgrade the efficiency of an antique heater, if the stove owner or restorer is prepared to improvise. Some stoves are designed in such a way that a steel-plate baffle can be easily installed. The seams of most units can be tightened using high-temperature caulking or flexible stove cement. And, with some careful adjustments, the flow of air around the firebox door can be reduced.

The price of used heaters can vary dramatically. A plain unrestored unit could easily be a thousand dollars less than a tall, majestic, fully rejuvenated model.

MODERN SECONDHAND APPLIANCES

Some may wonder why a stove supposedly capable of lasting many decades will be for sale a winter or two after being purchased. It is possible that the stove is a lemon that the original owner is trying to unload on an unsuspecting neophyte. However, there is often a much more honorable reason.

The homeowner may have arrived at incorrect sizing calculations and bought a stove that was either much bigger or smaller than he actually required. He may have acquired a large unit that worked well until he retrofitted his home with a great amount of insulation and a passive solar addition. Or an inexpensive stove purchased as a starter unit may have been judged too plain after a year or two.

The majority of recently manufactured stoves being resold are steel. Examine the seal around the firebox door and the condition of both the firebrick liner and the appliance's walls. If warpage has occurred, the damage should be visible. If some of the steel has changed color, the unit has probably been repeatedly overfired.

Cast-iron appliances have a reputation, which is often deserved, of outstanding longevity. However, cheaply made reproductions are almost always a different story. Some ads will claim that a unit is a "Scandinavian Cast-iron Heater," when in fact the stove only resembles these reliable cast appliances. Learn which cast companies have a solid reputation and check to be sure that one of their names is found on the stove. Inspect any cast heater carefully, as poor operating habits can have rendered it useless after only a few seasons. There should be no warpage or cracks. A mistreated stove may have a baffle or liner plates in need of replacing.

While purchasing an item that is still under warranty can mean something when the guarantee lasts for a year or two, it is highly possible that a stove with a longer warranty can be in rough shape long before the coverage expires. Also, do not believe the seller who claims that the warranty can be transferred, unless he can show you such a statement within the fine print of the warranty. Most guarantees are voided when the unit is sold by the original owner.

Many stove manufacturers have already come and gone within the last decade and, as the years pass, even more will cease to exist. Once a firm goes out of business the resale price of its units will drop, but so will the possibility of finding parts and expert service. It is always best to pay a little more and obtain a well-known brand that is sold and repaired within your region.

An increasing number of stove dealers are accepting quality used appliances as trade-ins on new models. You will likely pay more for a secondhand heater, cookstove, or furnace bought from a dealer than you would if you acquired it from the original owner, but an ethical dealer will examine used units carefully and carry out needed repairs as well as offering a limited guarantee.

PART THREE

Choosing the Right Appliance

After deciding which type of wood heat appliance suits you, it becomes necessary to make much finer judgments regarding the specific unit you will bring into your home. The next two chapters will give you an idea what size of appliance is appropriate for the space you want to heat, what factors indicating product quality, ease of operation, and safety you should look for, and how to decide which manufacturers and dealers to patronize.

9
Size, Quality, and Safety

SIZE

Finding a stove that suits the space you want to heat is the most important step in selecting an appliance.

When properly sized, a stove can be fired at a relatively hot temperature every few hours, keeping the home comfortable and avoiding, for the most part, creosote and emission problems. If the stove is too large, setting a substantial fire will drive people out of the room. The only alternative—aside from buying another smaller and probably less expensive stove—is to use smoldering fires that don't produce much heat and encourage creosote and billowing plumes of smoke. The situation can be compared to having a huge engine in a small car; at most times it must be operated at a level far below where it performs best.

Conscientious dealers recommend smaller stoves even though they make less profit. But some retailers, especially those with a surplus of massive steel stoves, are reluctant to suggest a small unit.

Although the problem of oversizing is more common and serious, buying too small a stove can also lead to difficulties. If a wood stove is the only source of warmth and the unit is undersized, it will either be a cold winter or the appliance will have to be reloaded extremely often.

Sizing Heaters

C. H. Anthony, a highly respected engineer and wood stove seller with stores in Peterborough, New Hampshire, and Westboro, Massachusetts, has prepared a three-part formula for computing the correct size for a stove located in the living area of the home. Originally published in *Wood 'n Energy*, this approach reduces guesswork and dependency on questionable manufacturer- and dealer-supplied figures.

Professionals traditionally use one of four methods for estimating what size of stove will be needed for a particular home. These are the cubic-foot, square-foot, number-of-rooms-in-a-house, and BTU techniques. Anthony opts for the cubic-foot process, since he feels that the square-foot and "rooms" methods are imprecise:

> A room of four hundred square feet with a twenty-foot cathedral ceiling will require approximately twice as much heat as the same room with a standard eight-foot ceiling.... While the BTU method is certainly more precise than the others, it is extremely difficult for the vast majority of stove buyers to relate BTU output to specific home heating requirements.

Anthony does use BTUs per hour for one step within his formula, but the final figure is given in cubic feet.

To determine the rating, Anthony explains that two numbers must be calculated. "These are: (a) a method of computing the average output of any given stove size, and (b) the heat loss per cubic foot for an average house." Many "experts" use only the first part, ignoring the climatic zone and how weathertight the home is.

> Most woodstoves are capable of very large variations in BTU output. However, the average stove user

is interested primarily in a relatively constant output over a reasonable length of time. For the purpose of our proposed rating standard, we have made the following assumptions:

Average weight of air-dried hardwood	—0.015 lbs./cu. in. (26 lbs./cu. ft.)
Average usable BTU content at 20 percent moisture (the average moisture content of seasoned hardwood)	—6,200 BTUs
Average woodstove efficiency	—50 percent
Usable burn time	—8 hours

To find the average BTU/hour output of a stove, first find the wood capacity of the stove in cubic inches by measuring the interior of the firebox (note: usable space only). Length multiplied by width, multiplied by depth, in inches, will give this figure. (Cubic feet can then be derived by dividing cubic inches by 1,728.)

Using these assumptions, and knowing the wood capacity of the stove, you find the average number of BTUs that will be put out by the stove per hour in the following way: Multiply the size of the firebox (in cubic inches) by the average weight of wood (0.015 lbs./cu. in.) This gives you the amount of wood, in pounds, the firebox can hold. Multiply that by the BTU content of hardwood (6,200); multiply that by the efficiency rating of the stove (0.5); and divide the resulting figure by the average burn time (8):

$$\frac{\text{Capacity (in cubic inches)} \times 0.015 \times 6{,}200 \times 0.5}{8} = \text{BTU/hr.}$$

If a stove equipped with a catalytic combustor is being considered, raise the average efficiency figure from 50 to 60 percent, as this device increases overall efficiency between 12 and

17 percent. (This changes the last figure in the numerator above from 0.5 to 0.6.)

While some dealers will claim this first step is not necessary, as manufacturers make available the heat output of their appliances, Anthony does not agree. "Most manufacturers simply do not test their stoves for heat output. I have tested many stoves and in very few instances has the output been close to what was specified."

Step two, the heat loss, must now be calculated. The average 1,500-square-foot home on which Anthony bases his work has 3½ inches of insulation in the walls and 6 inches in the ceiling, a normal number of doors and windows equipped with storm attachments, plus a typical amount of weatherstripping.

He divides the United States into eight climatic regions—his home in New Hampshire is located in Zone Three (see the map below). He calculates that, in his temperature region, the relationship between BTU/hr. production of the stove and the number of cubic feet of the house is as shown in Table 1.

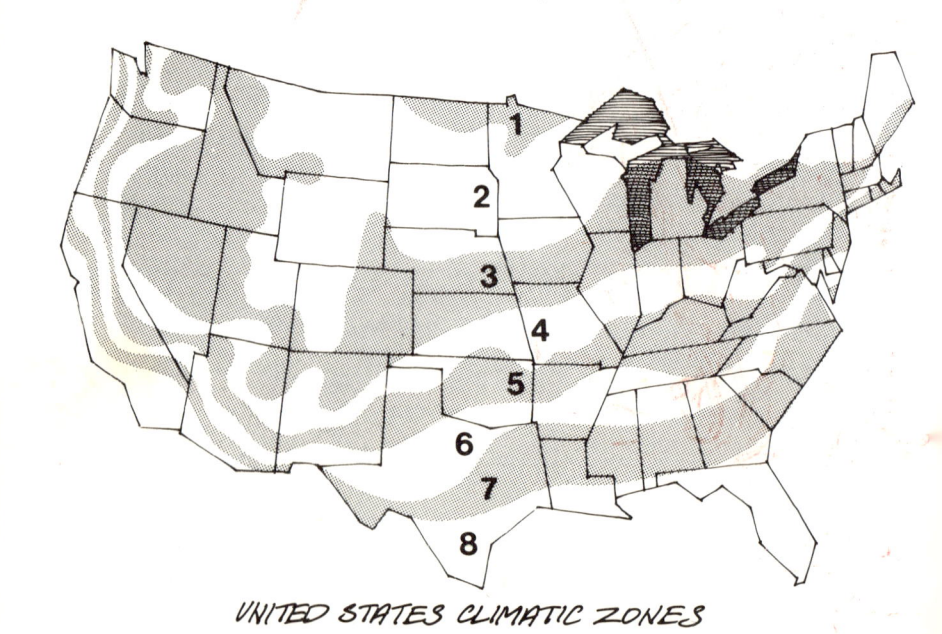

UNITED STATES CLIMATIC ZONES

Table 1
Relationship between average BTU output and cubic foot capacity for Zone Three

BTU/hr. output	Cu. ft. capacity
6,700	3,000
8,900	4,000
11,100	5,000
13,300	6,000
15,500	7,000
17,800	8,000
20,000	9,000
22,200	10,000
24,400	11,000
26,600	12,000
28,900	13,000
31,100	14,000
33,300	15,000
40,000	18,000
44,400	20,000
55,500	25,000

Table 2
Factors to be used to adjust the rated capacity

Zone 1	0.8
Zone 2	0.9
Zone 3	1.0
Zone 4	1.1
Zone 5	1.3
Zone 6	1.5
Zone 7	1.9
Zone 8	2.4

To adjust for the other climatic zones, multiply the number of cubic feet for which the stove qualifies in Table 1 times the factor listed in Table 2. For example, a stove with a capacity of 2 cubic feet (3,456 cubic inches), can put out an average of

20,088 BTUs per hour; this stove could heat, in Zone Three, a space of about 9,000 cubic feet. In Zone One, the same stove could heat a space of only 7,200 cubic feet.

A simple way of altering the formula for a home that is either less or more weathertight than the "average" home is to move the home into another climatic zone. If it is much less insulated than the standard, set it two levels *up* the chart. If it is slightly less insulated, adjust it by one. If the home is better prepared, move it one or two positions *down* the chart.

If you have a fireplace insert that sits well back in the fireplace and does not have an electric blower, move your home up two climatic zones; if the insert protrudes into the room or has a blower, move it up only one zone.

This completes Mr. Anthony's stove-sizing technique, a quite accurate method by which you can examine a stove in a showroom, measure the firebox dimensions, and then make the calculations at home.

Generally, cast-iron heaters and cookstoves are available for all houses. Steel heaters, on the other hand, can usually look after any home but the most compact, as well as small industrial and commercial buildings. Central heating systems—furnaces and boilers—can usually be bought for all but small houses. They can serve commercial and industrial buildings of all sizes.

Once you have arrived at a figure, be quite firm with the dealers you visit. Take along a sketch of your home showing where you foresee installing the appliance, and dimensions of the various rooms. Share your conclusions on which units would suit. Pay attention to the person who listens carefully and makes logical suggestions based on where you want to set the stove and the size of the individual rooms.

Sizing Central Systems

Finding the proper size of central unit (a basement furnace or boiler) requires a different approach from the one just described for stoves located in the living area of the home.

Some people use the hourly BTU output rating given on an existing furnace or boiler, but this method has its pitfalls. First, central system manufacturers are rarely accurate in their estimates. Second, it is common for an oil furnace to be vastly oversized. An experienced dealer will be able to tell whether the BTU rating listed is accurate.

In its January 1981 issue, *Wood 'n Energy* magazine outlines a more detailed approach:

> In northern areas where winters are coldest and central heating units are most popular, a standard house with average insulation will have a heat loss factor of about 33 BTUs per hour per cubic foot of usable living space. The absence of any insulation in the home's walls will double this heat loss factor, while excessive glass may increase it by 0.6 or 0.7. Super insulation found in some new homes today will reduce the basic heat loss factor by nearly half.
>
> To perform this calculation, simply multiply the length of the home's total living area times its width and then its height. The result will be the total cubic feet of the living space. Multiplying this figure by the standard 33 BTUs per hour (or a figure adjusted according to the above guidelines) will indicate the home's nominal design heat loss factor. A central heating unit with a rated BTU hourly output 1.15 to 1.25 times this design heat loss factor should satisfy your needs for solid fuel conservation, efficiency, and warmth.

CAST IRON VERSUS STEEL

There is no clear victor in the debate over whether an appliance should be constructed of cast iron or steel. The durability of cast iron is evidenced by a two-hundred-year-old stove in the Bryant Museum and by the thousands of sixty, seventy-five, and hundred-year-old iron cookstoves and heaters still in operation.

Increasing sales of cast-iron units reflect the public's admiration of the material's aesthetic qualities. Unlike most steel stoves, which are simply black boxes, cast-iron units often have lovely designs molded in and are constructed in fascinating shapes.

With increasing interest in energy conservation, many homeowners are installing double-glazed windows, adding substantial quantities of insulation, and building passive solar additions. These improvements reduce heating demands and concurrently increase the need for compact heaters. Consumers usually find a predominance of cast-iron appliances.

A Toronto dealer, John Creelman, explains that the cast-iron firebox liner used in these models takes up far less space than the firebrick used with most steel stoves. Small steel models tend to have a firebox "the size of a matchbox." Some larger steel stoves have inner measurements comparable to the cast units, but generally steel heater makers have not yet realized that a significant demand exists for small units. It is no coincidence that many of these cast-iron stoves come from Europe, where the majority of houses tend to be more compact than in North America.

The drawbacks of cast iron include its brittleness—appliances made of iron that contains additives are especially prone to cracking or snapping when being transported or installed—and the fact that the quality of the cast iron used in stoves varies more than does that of the steel. Generally, American- and European-made cast stoves are fine products, but those from the Orient, especially Taiwan and Korea, are often inferior imitations of well-known brands.

According to Creelman, these appliances should be constructed of at least "class 20 or 25 grey iron. The heavier class 30, an industrial grade, is very rugged." Joints must be tight and caulked. There should be no pockmarks, ripples, cracks, or uncalled-for ridges in the cast surfaces. The thickness should be at least 3/16 inch, including the inner cast liner, and uniform. The paint or enamel outer surface should be smooth, even, and free of blemishes. Parts, such as legs, hinges, and door handles, should be well built to take punishment.

New cast-iron stoves must be tempered—that is, broken in gradually—and care has to be taken when warming a cast stove that has been sitting idle in an unheated home during frigid weather. Cast iron warps at about the same temperature as steel, but while cast iron will generally flow back into its original shape and steel does not, when permanent warpage does occur with iron, the damage is more serious. A warped steel stove may not be visually appealing, but it is usually usable since its joints are welded. But when a cast-iron appliance undergoes substantial warpage, it is often ruined, as the joints separate.

The steel stove far outranks cast iron in numbers sold throughout North America. This is primarily because steel stoves were noticeably cheaper until recently. However, the cost of steel has risen dramatically and domestic steel and cast-iron stoves are now about equal in price. Imported cast units are more expensive. While the steel stove is rarely as elegant, manufacturers have in recent years added nickel- and brass-plated trim, introduced stove bodies in other colors than basic black, and embellished firebox doors with raised designs.

No one knows just how long a steel-plate stove will last, since this material has come into widespread use in the stove industry only within the past decade. Dealers have found that heavy steel stoves can withstand punishment that will wreck a cast appliance.

Consumers should be wary of purchasing a steel stove with large walls. When heated to very high temperatures, such expanses of steel tend to buckle. Due to this same warping problem, steel doors are rarely used even on steel stoves. With controlled-combustion models, permanent twisting of this component creates serious leaks. Cast-iron doors have become almost universal; if you are considering a steel unit, be sure it has one.

While there are poor quality cast-iron stoves, primarily those imported from the Orient, the high start-up and operating costs of a foundry tend to discourage poor manufacturing in Europe and North America. However, anyone who has basic welding skills and equipment, a source of steel, and a garage can begin producing steel stoves. The investment needed to stay afloat in today's sophisticated market is squeezing out many disreputable firms, but some still remain.

Heavy steel appliances should have quarter-inch-thick steel plate sides and bottom, and a 5/16-inch plate top. Better steel appliances possess top-notch welding, each joint should be free of hollows, tiny air holes, and bumps. Some units made from thin sheet steel have proven durable. The entire interior should be sheathed with firebrick, and braces are needed to keep the walls stiff.

SEALING OF AN AIRTIGHT

Any airtight, or controlled-combustion, model must have tight welded or caulked joints and a door that fits snugly. Check the seal around the door by trying to remove a piece of paper from between it and the door frame while the door is shut. If the paper can be moved, the seal is not sufficient. Some manufacturers invest the time and money required to produce an exact metal-on-metal fit, but many opt for employing a gasket. Avoid those with loose flocking. The seal should be created by design and craftsmanship, not fluffy fiberglass.

NONAIRTIGHTS

Nonairtights are not common, but they can be found. Choices include homemade units put together with a steel barrel and a kit comprised of a door assembly, legs, and a flue collar; older stoves; and a handful of new models. These can be a solution for anyone who wants to purchase a stove without spending a sizable sum on a state-of-the-art unit, who doesn't mind burning substantial amounts of wood (because he has access to inexpensive supplies), and who wants to avoid creosote and emission problems.

THE FIREBOX LINER

Since the firebox walls take quite a beating due to heavy chunks of wood bouncing against them and exposure to high temperatures, it is best if they are lined. Be sure that the liner can be removed for cleaning and replacing in case it needs it.

Steel units generally use firebrick, although a few employ stainless steel or cast iron. Since many stove owners have had difficulties with stainless liners, their use should be avoided unless it is obvious that the manufacturer has taken steps to ensure the material cannot be easily dented.

Cast stoves generally have cast liners. Be sure that the hooks that hold many such liner sections in place are sturdy and substantial enough to keep the liner in place.

SAFETY

Although most stove-related structural fires in homes heated with wood are caused by incorrect installation or operation of the unit, the stove itself can be the cause. Some stoves are safer than others.

There have been cases where a stove door has come open when struck by a log settling within the firebox. Since this could have tragic consequences, search for a door mechanism that locks securely and requires considerable pressure to open. Since gases sometimes build up inside the stove during a smoldering fire, causing flames to shoot out when oxygen rushes in, it is best to have a door mechanism that unlocks in two stages. If flames do "blow back," this design will prevent them from striking the operator's face.

Door handles should have a wood, plastic, or coiled metal grip to prevent scorching of the operator's hand. Maneuver the handle while examining each stove to make sure that your hand won't be brought near the hot walls of the firebox each time you close or open the door.

Since asbestos is a proven health hazard, some experts believe it should not be used as a gasket material around doors. Never use an asbestos gasket that has loose flocking, as it can easily release harmful fibers. For those who wish to avoid asbestos, fiberglass gasketing is widely available.

Some heaters have bolt-on legs that must be tightened from inside the firebox. This design is not a good one. If the unit you are considering does not have legs that are welded or cast into its body, determine how easily you can tighten them. Legs with adjustable pads on the bottom are especially helpful for those who live in older homes with uneven floors.

While many furnaces and boilers and some heaters use a generally fail-safe, electrically operated thermostat similar to that used with oil furnaces, a good number of heaters instead employ a bimetallic coil resembling a spring. Once the thermostat dial is set at a certain position, the coil expands and contracts with the heat of the fire, opening and closing the draft intake regulator as required.

This device is a relatively simple and inexpensive solution to making the appliance more convenient to operate. However, some models are prone to bending out of shape after a few years of use, and occasionally malfunction.

Compare thermostats to determine which are the most rugged. Charles Page, Technical Product Manager for Vermont Castings Incorporated, explains that the device should be easily accessible so that it can be regularly inspected and, if necessary, repaired. He adds that the thermostat must be designed so that if it fails it causes the draft intake control to shut.

Every winter many children are burned when they fall against a hot radiant-type stove. Some heaters, namely the circulators, reduce the surface temperature by using ducts to remove heat and distribute it to the space being warmed. Many of these have an outside metal cover that is safe to touch. Ceramic tile heaters also tend to run cooler than radiant models, but these, as well as the circulators, are generally not as efficient. Thus, someone who buys a stove with this factor in mind might be making a trade-off against performance. A new type of accessory on the market, a portable fence that surrounds the appliance, eliminates the problem without restricting the style of appliance that can be used.

The majority of stove makers do care about safety and have invested the time and money needed to remove hazards from their appliance's design. However, there are manufacturers and importers who do not care about the welfare of their customers. Their units tend to be low-cost models sold by outlets such as hardware and department stores, whose staff members do not know enough about wood heating to realize how dangerous these units can be. Parts may be missing, legs can be of different lengths, and the steel or cast walls are often thin and poorly made. There have been reports of cast-iron stoves, made in the Orient, warping out of shape during the first fire lit in them. This is but another reason for buying a well-known appliance from a respected dealer.

Every unit uses draft controls or draft regulators. These should have two safety features built in. Since the fire could

Wire mesh folding stove guard

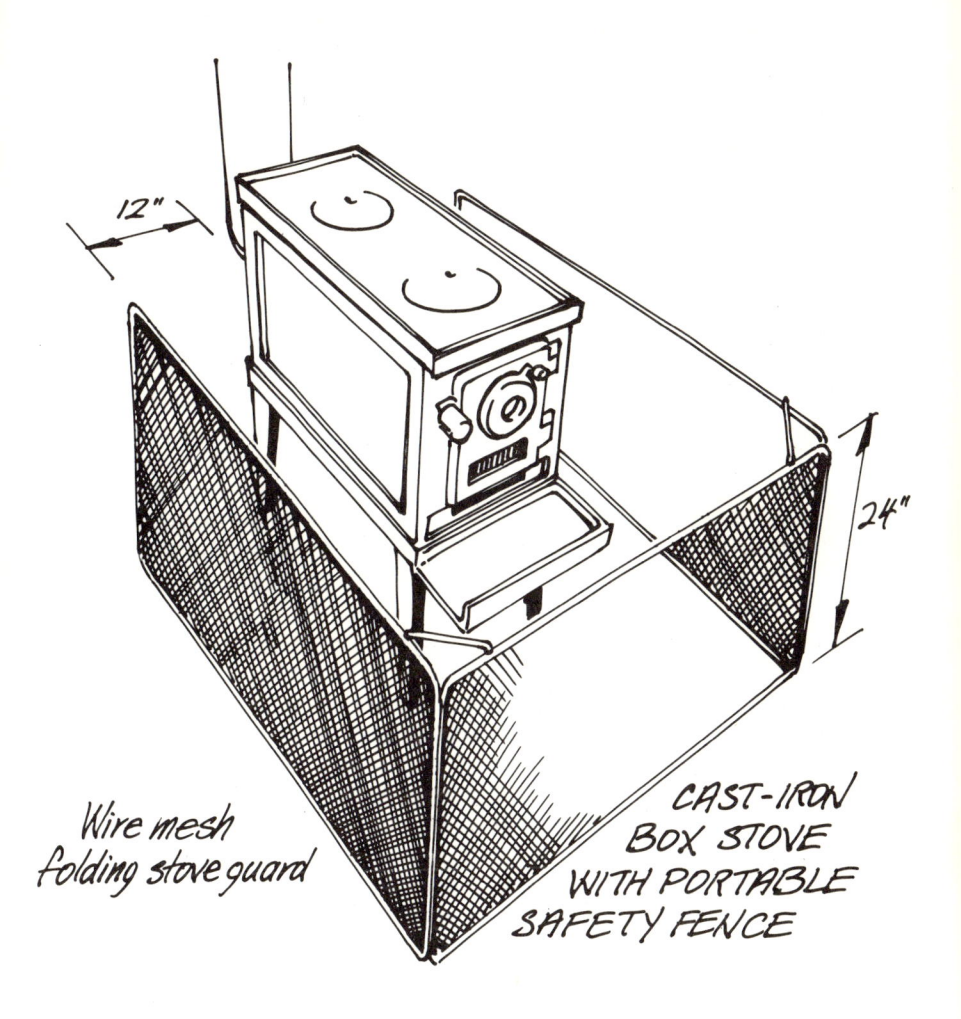

CAST-IRON BOX STOVE WITH PORTABLE SAFETY FENCE

burn out of control if the draft cap or cover fell off, there should be a limit to how many revolutions the cap can be turned. This can easily be checked in the showroom. Additionally, there should be a governor that prohibits the cap from being shut completely. This ensures that some oxygen always reaches the fire, somewhat reducing the possibility of creosote being created.

Examine the stove for protruding parts, sharp corners, and jagged burrs that can be toe stubbers or hand cutters. The appliance should have sleek lines and rounded corners.

STANDARDS

When a stove meets the set of guidelines contained in a "standard," and receives certification or listing from a recognized testing laboratory, questions about its design, safety, and construction will have been answered (as long as the standard is challenging and up to date). While the presence of a certification label does not mean the consumer can take for granted that the appliance is completely fail-safe or that it won't burn his house down, it does demonstrate that the unit is built to a certain level of quality.

In the United States, Underwriters' Laboratories, Inc. (UL) is the main body preparing standards for wood heat equipment. These include UL 1482 for heaters and UL 103 for metal chimneys; other existing and proposed UL standards cover protective wall and floor shields plus all types of fireplaces and wood furnaces.

A great number of laboratories are allowed to test stoves to UL standards. Any stove that passes—known as a listed or certified unit—must have a label affixed that explains who tested it, what standard has been met, and how the unit should be installed. Since states and counties are beginning to demand the mandatory use of listed stoves, check with your local building inspector to determine what regulations are in force. Do this prior to buying the appliance.

CATALYTIC COMBUSTORS

Until standardized efficiency tests are in widespread use, it will be difficult to ascertain which manufacturers have made best use of catalytic combustor technology. The consumer should ask the seller if the stove has been specifically designed to accept the combustor, and the appliance should be carefully examined.

The best combustor units have a sizable heat exchanger for collecting and distributing the additional heat generated. The combustor should be close to and directly above the firebox. There must be a bypass channel to handle excess smoke and gases before the combustor lights off, when the door is opened, and in case the combustor plugs. The selling price should not be more than $150 above that of a similar, noncombustor unit.

EASE OF USE

For the most part, small points make the difference between enjoying a stove and finding it a nuisance to operate and maintain. One example is the firebox door. While the very large doors once found on some North American steel stoves are no longer in widespread use because of warpage problems, the door should be big enough and so shaped that there is easy access to the firebox. When in the showroom, ask the store clerk if he has some chunks of wood you can load into the unit you are appraising.

Consider how easy the ashes are to remove. While some manufacturers claim their units will generate only small amounts of ash yearly, expect to remove ashes *at least* twice monthly from most models. Many units, including a good number of cookstoves and some central heating systems, have an ashpan located under the firebox. While this arrangement is needed when coal will be burned, and can be handy as long as the ashes are emptied almost every day, the pan can be hard to remove safely when it is overloaded.

Most airtight heaters instead allow the ashes to build up in the firebox. When inspecting stoves, take an ash shovel and see how easy it would be to extricate the ashes. Models that don't have an ashpan and that load from the side or front can be annoying because the ashes will have to be removed as often as once a week, to prevent their falling out when the door is opened. A buildup of ashes can also cause blockage of the primary draft intake. Top-loading heaters are better in this regard, since ashes can accumulate for a longer period of time (if the air intake is located high on the firebox, as is often the case with such models).

If the firebox door is on the front or side, check which way it opens, as at times this can be important. Some companies offer a choice of either left- or right-hand-opening doors.

The phrase "available with back, side, or top flue collar" is often seen in promotional literature. On many units, the flue collar can be obtained in the position that would best suit the homeowner's smokepipe and chimney installation. The dealer can often be of help with this decision. Some flue collars can be switched around, while others are permanently affixed. However, manufacturers of the latter type may offer two or three flue collar positions on the same model of appliance.

WARRANTIES

Five years ago, wood stove manufacturers often gave warranties of twenty or thirty years. But if you look around, few of the firms that offered such guarantees are still in business. Most of those who remain have reduced the length of their warranty program. Servicing a two- to three-decade guarantee can be extremely costly. If a firm offers such a plan and then realizes it cannot afford to keep honoring it, the customer may find himself being stonewalled while the stove sits inoperative. Three- to five-year guarantees are now common and perfectly acceptable. Be forewarned that the fine print may tell you that the inner workings of the firebox—the baffle and liner—are not covered, and that the glass used with fireplace models is also excluded.

Think twice about buying an appliance equipped with a warranty that makes the stove owner responsible for shipping the unit to the factory for repair. Having to send a furnace that weighs a thousand pounds across the country may cost more than the unit is worth. Do accept a guarantee that stipulates that the dealer will either handle repairs himself or be responsible for having warranty-honored work carried out.

MANUFACTURERS TO PATRONIZE

Wood stove advertising has become increasingly lavish and professional and is widely seen in magazines and on television. Some companies have been known to spend most of their budget on advertising and little on vital product research and development.

These advertisements will show what the stove looks like, what features it has, whether the unit has a UL listing, and, if it is a local or co-op ad, which stores in your locale are stocking it.

What this presentation will not give is an unbiased impression of how well the stove is constructed and designed, or whether it is a joy or nuisance to operate. To get such valuable information, do your own research and sleuthing and assess word-of-mouth comments. Ask friends and neighbors who heat with wood what appliance they own, whether they like it, and if they are satisfied with their dealer.

One should be wary of supporting small stove companies. To formulate, develop, perfect, and certify a new stove can cost hundreds of thousands of dollars and require two or three years. The stove that was thought up or copied from another last week, built on the weekend, and painted yesterday may be cheaper than the one it resembles, but a close examination may reveal draft intake caps that fall off, pinholes in the welding, a poor door fit, and spaces between the firebrick.

Buy the products of known companies that have been selling wood appliances for several years. Even when such firms introduce a unit, avoid it for a year or two. As with automobiles, new stoves often have bugs that need to be ironed out. Allow someone else the honor of being the guinea pig.

If you are buying your first appliance, do not let the dealer talk you into a unit equipped with every bell, whistle, and combustion-improving device extant. It will take time to learn how to properly fire even a simple unit.

OWNER'S MANUAL

Mastering the operation of any appliance is much easier if you have a proper, illustrated owner's manual. Its value is recognized by testing agencies; every certified appliance must have a thorough guide.

The manual should explain clearly the installation of all parts of the system. It should describe how to use each control on the appliance and how to fire the unit to boost efficiency and avoid creosote problems. All necessary cleaning and maintenance routines should be outlined.

Tips for solving difficulties that can arise during operation should be included. Schematic diagrams, showing each part of the appliance, are helpful for ordering replacement parts.

AESTHETICS

Once the issues of size, material, workmanship, and so on have been dealt with, one final consideration remains—appearance. Before an appliance is hauled home, ask yourself if you can live with it for many years. If it will be installed in the living area of your home, it will be a part of your home's decor. Does it blend with the furniture you own? Will it ruin the effect you have tried to create?

A stove should definitely not be bought for looks alone, and it may not make sense to spend several hundred dollars more than you planned just to acquire a beautiful model, but do remember that even an expensive appliance should pay for itself within three years or so. Spending a bit more money can mean the difference between eventually loathing something and perceiving it as the treasured centerpiece of your living room.

10
The Dealer

Since the wood stove will be providing both independence from uncertain, expensive fossil fuel supplies and a focal point around which winter life can revolve, the search and acquisition process should be fun. However, for far too many people the experience will be a confusing and even unpleasant one.

Finding stoves for sale is not difficult. They are on display in gas stations, outdoor equipment shops, small town hardware outlets, suburban department stores, building supply centers, and those places of commerce that deal exclusively or almost solely in wood heating products.

To find out quickly if a shop is worth patronizing, answer the following questions:

- Are decals displayed that signify that the store owner is a member of professional organizations such as the Wood Heating Alliance?
- From their comments, does it appear that staff members read trade magazines and attend professional seminars and trade shows?
- Are there certificates framed and displayed that show that the staff is taking advantage of the Helping Make It Safe training program offered by the Wood Heating Alliance?
- Does the store keep in close contact with building inspectors and fire departments? While such officials will rarely recommend one store or appliance above

others, they will usually answer questions on whether they are aware of a certain operation and if they feel it should be patronized.
- Does the store seem genuinely interested in educating wood heat users? Does it conduct public wood heat seminars?
- Does the outlet stock wood heat books and magazines plus integral components such as protective wall and floor shields, smokepipe, metal chimneys, and splitting axes?
- Does the shop deal primarily in wood appliances, or are they but a minor sideline?
- Does the store's inventory contain small, medium, and large heaters, woodranges, and fireplace models of both cast iron and steel?
- If the store is selling boilers and furnaces, do staff members have experience in sizing and working with these complicated units?
- Has time and money been spent on creating effective, neat, and well-lit displays?
- Does the dealer carry a sizable stock of spare parts?
- Does the dealer keep records of past customers, and is he happy to share the names and addresses of a few with prospective customers?
- Does the store provide or arrange stove installations and chimney cleaning by qualified, insured professionals?

The outlet likely to score poorly on this checklist is the one with wood stoves displayed along a cramped aisle, surrounded by a multitude of similar lanes lined with a myriad of items. The day you come looking for a stove, the person in charge may be filling in for someone who is sick, or perhaps he was transferred the day before from "Pots and Pans" or "Truck Tires." His prime goal will be to sell the largest and most expensive unit in stock.

It is generally best to do business with someone who makes his or her living with wood stoves. Such people have staked their reputation and bankroll on these appliances and are likely to attain a high rating on the list.

However, this is not to say that every specialty shop is worthy of being patronized. When you walk into many of these outlets, the wide variety and number of units on display may well overwhelm you, even if you have carefully prepared yourself. The quality stores realize how confusing it can be, and have plenty of salespeople on hand. Since you should expect to spend at least an hour and even two or three carefully discussing your needs and examining stoves, it can be disconcerting if one salesperson is working alone on a busy Saturday afternoon.

The clerk who does assist you should be polite, patient, and informed. Don't be rushed or bullied, and don't buy at the first store you visit. Shop around and spend a day or two considering the options before you lay your money down.

The proprietor who wants you as a long-term customer will create a pleasant atmosphere. He may have one or more appliances in operation, supply free coffee and cookies, and provide chairs for waiting or tired customers. He will sell only brands he believes in, and chances are that he won't offer you the best deal. Keeping a trained staff takes money. Displaying a variety of stoves requires costly space. The quality dealer thus has a substantial overhead and won't be in a hurry to discount. Remember this when you are spending an afternoon racing from store to store, burning ten dollars in gasoline trying to save twenty.

Regardless of what some sellers say, you will probably return to the shop once or twice a year even if you make the right choice and pick a superb unit that will endure for many winters. Your wall shield may become damaged, or look too bland to be tolerated through another dreary February. You may need an axe handle, a new door gasket, or a baffle to replace the one that deteriorated.

You will return, and if the store you bought from doesn't have a service department or is no longer around when you need a key part, you may be in trouble. Patronize the person who is approaching the selling and servicing of wood appliances as a long-term profession.

If you feel that you will really need to tap the resources of the dealer in order to make a decision on what you will need, you should visit him out of season when he will have time to spend several hours with you. From August through early November is a hectic time for stove merchants, and even the most helpful staffer may seem distant and abrupt if you drop in for a long session. March through July are good months to shop.

If you wait until snow is on the ground, you may also have a difficult time finding the stove that has caught your fancy. Because sales are not what they were a few years ago, manufacturers are being very careful about how many units they produce. By late October the shelves may be quite bare and you may have to wait weeks to take delivery.

PART FOUR

Installation

11
The Chimney and Smokepipe

The chimney is so common and appears to be so simple in design that most newcomers to wood heat do not realize its importance. As a result, the chimney connected to a wood appliance is often too large, too rickety, or too close to combustibles. The lucky neophyte realizes, after his inferior flue barely manages to contain a chimney fire, why this facet of the wood heat system demands special attention. The unlucky one ends up homeless.

Since controlled-combustion wood stoves became so popular, pressures on the chimney have increased. An unskilled operator can cause thick deposits of creosote to build up within a few weeks. When ignited, this creosote can burn for more than thirty minutes at temperatures exceeding 2,000 degrees. In wood stove terms, this is a veritable holocaust, dwarfing the duration and intensity of chimney fires resulting from the use of nonairtight stoves.

A new generation of extremely durable chimneys is just appearing. The consumer must be aware, however, that these state-of-the-art stacks are not cheap. A more economical approach is to use a well-built chimney capable of withstanding midrange temperatures, and maintain it in such a way that temperatures of 2,000 degrees are never reached.

Even the finest chimney will be susceptible to problems if

it is not suited to the appliance. It is best if the chimney's diameter is no more than one inch larger than the smokepipe collar on the stove; a dramatically oversized flue will encourage creosote. Too small a stack will often cause back-puffing of smoke into the home, since the stove will be capable of producing more smoke than the flue can handle.

Whenever possible the chimney should run up inside the home, so that only the top few feet are exposed to outside temperatures and the elements. This step alone can significantly reduce creosote problems.

The chimney should be close to the appliance; excess smokepipe encourages creosote. It is preferable to locate the appliance where it is most suitable (for radiant models, this is generally the center of the space to be heated) and then install the chimney.

It therefore follows that an existing chimney is not always suitable for use with a controlled-combustion appliance. An older chimney should be carefully scrutinized before being brought back into service.

As the installation of a wood-burning system is considered a structural alteration even if an existing chimney is to be employed, most municipalities require that a building permit be obtained. Some consumers will wish to avoid this step, but the overriding purpose of a building permit is to ensure that work is safely done, not to enforce obtuse ordinances. An inspector experienced in the nuances of wood heating can save your life if a grievous installation error has been committed. If there is not a competent inspector in your locale, contact your fire department or dealer. Having a detailed examination carried out before the first fire is lit is in your own best interest.

To keep both their costs and those of the stove buyer at a reasonable level, some stove dealers counsel people on how to install their own appliance and chimney, making sure that their customers do not take this important task lightly. There are also retailers who provide installations to their customers at a very low cost simply to ensure that the process is carried out correctly. On the other hand, far too many dealers send consumers home as soon as the deal is closed, with few instructions on how to proceed and no offer of professional help.

Do not install your own system if the subject is completely

foreign to you. If you do not have the time to learn, seek out a qualified professional. This person should have some training, either through the Helping Make It Safe program offered by the Wood Heating Alliance, or another course offered by a college or trade organization. A first-class installer will gladly supply references and be equipped with sufficient liability insurance so that damages from any fire that results due to his negligence will be borne by him. A professional should be well read on the latest advances in wood heating and have a working relationship with local building inspectors and fire safety officials. Find out quickly the depth of the person's knowledge by asking detailed questions based on your reading of this chapter. How the person replies should tell you whether or not he is proficient.

THE PREFABRICATED CHIMNEY

Purchasing a factory-built chimney specifically certified for use within a wood heating system by the Underwriters' Laboratories, Inc. (UL), is one method of taking much of the risk out of buying a stack. These are known as Class A, Solid-Fuel, and All-Fuel chimneys.

The majority of prefabricated chimneys are constructed primarily of steel. Three such types, all similar in price, are sold in the United States: air-cooled, solid-insulated, and air-insulated. These come in sections of various lengths that lock together; all needed components such as supports, fire shields, and rain caps are available. Every part must possess a UL sticker, and it is imperative that all components be from the same model line. Parts produced by different manufacturers are not interchangeable. Most of the twenty or so firms selling Class A chimneys in the United States offer a variety of flue diameters, generally ranging from four or five to ten inches.

The air-cooled design contains three layers of steel separated by two channels. The inner liner is stainless steel, the middle layer is either galvanized or aluminized steel, and the exterior is generally galvanized. Air is drawn in just below the rain cap and falls down the outer channel on its own—cold air drops. It then rises along the inner passage to exit at the top. The possibility of heat permeating the stack and reaching nearby combustibles is prevented, because any heat that does reach the first channel is carried upward. However, this cools the flue and increases the potential of creosote being generated. This style of metal chimney should never be used with a controlled-combustion appliance. It is specifically designed for units meant to run constantly at high temperatures, such as zero-clearance and freestanding fireplaces.

The solid-insulated or solid-pack is the most widely sold Class A chimney. Between an inner liner of stainless steel and an outer cover of galvanized or stainless steel is sandwiched an inch-wide column of volatilized silica dust and high-temperature rock wool.

The air-insulated model possesses three layers of steel and two spaces. However, instead of traveling the length of the flue, air is trapped within each section of chimney. Though this design is not as widely used as the solid-pack, it is well regarded by professionals.

Positive features of the Class A chimney include its reasonable price and the fact that an entire chimney can be installed in a few hours. The main limitation is that this is a midrange chimney: The stainless steel liner is ruined if flue temperatures exceed approximately 1,700 degrees.

Although the Class A is known as an "all-fuel" chimney, several cases have arisen in New England where such a unit used with a coal stove for one heating season suffered extensive and permanent corrosion of the liner. Use of a coal stove at low temperatures, and failure to remove the powder that builds up in the flue during the heating season, are generally the causes. Some Class A manufacturers are now recommending that their products no longer be employed with coal appliances. Others have attempted to overcome the problem by glazing the liner with a layer of silicone or using a heavy grade of stainless steel. If you intend to burn coal, and wish to purchase a Class A stack, acquire only such a "corrosion-resistant" model.

There have also been a substantial number of chimneys damaged in transit, often because manufacturers use flimsy shipping containers. A conscientious dealer will try to inspect every section of chimney he sells, but this can prove impossible during busy times of the year. Examine every section of chimney as it is unpacked and immediately return any that are damaged. Some units equipped with a galvanized steel exterior have suffered from premature corrosion. Anyone who resides near salt water or a road that is often covered with salt should opt for a stainless outer casing.

Galvanized steel will also rust if the insulation in a solid-pack model becomes damp. While there have been a few cases of this occurring after the chimney is installed, this generally happens when the sections are shipped in an open truck during inclement weather, or stored in a damp place.

It is also possible for solid-pack sections to suffer from insulation voids, in which a space forms between the insulation and the top of the channel. This creates a dangerous situation, as high temperatures can reach combustibles outside the chimney. These voids can occur when the insulation settles after being freighted a long distance, or because of improper filling during manufacturing. A clue to the presence of a void is a fine powder covering a section when it is removed from its carton. The channel itself can be checked by turning the section upside down and applying pressure to create an opening between the wall of the chimney and the coupler found on the end.

This is not to say that most Class A chimneys are defective; the percentage with such problems is very low. However, while the Class A has performed well for thousands of people and continues to be a competent product, every new owner must realize that it has limitations.

Installation

The prefabricated Class A chimney can be installed in three ways: as an exterior stack that runs up an outside wall of the house, an interior chimney set in a flat ceiling above a stove, and an interior model placed in an angled, cathedral ceiling. Each approach requires a special set of components available from the chimney manufacturer. The stack should always begin within the room containing the appliance. It is not recommended to pass smokepipe through any wall or floor.

A "through the wall" kit is essential for an exterior installation. The main component is an insulated "tee" that accepts

Through the wall installation

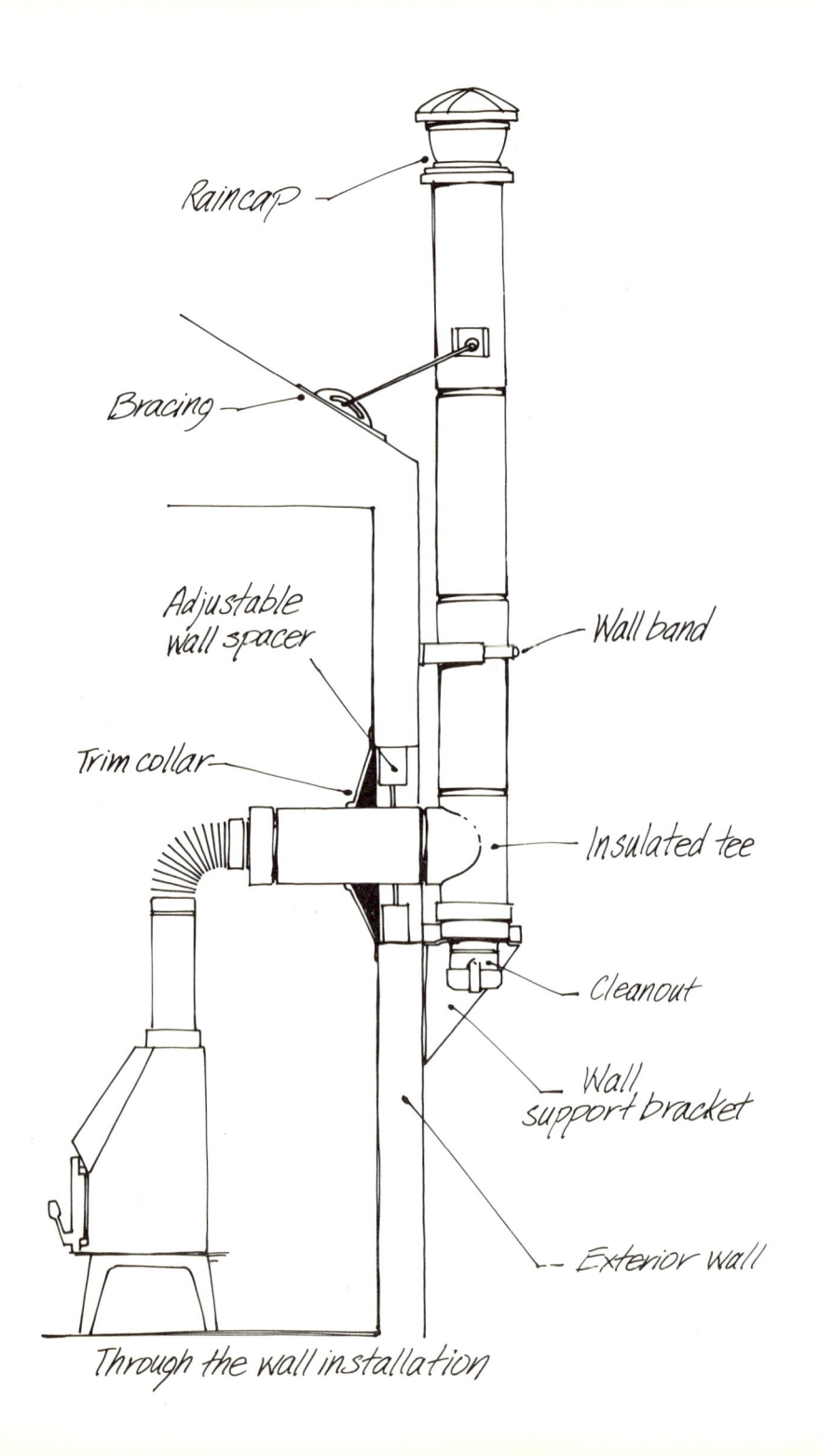

the smokepipe inside the house, acts as the base of the chimney, and contains a cleanout for easy inspection and cleaning of the flue. This tee is secured by a wall support bracket. Also required outside the house are a number of wall support bands that affix the chimney to the house. While many chimney sections simply twist-lock together, others require a locking band at each joint. Inside the house, a wall spacer, trim collar, and finishing collar are needed to allow safe passage of the chimney through the wall, and to connect the chimney and smokepipe.

The primary component of the flat ceiling installation is a "finish support package," located where the chimney goes through the ceiling directly above the stove. Also employed inside are a finishing collar, a cleanout tee made of a single thickness of steel, and firestop spacers that are located above the ceiling support and separate the chimney from combustibles found in the top story or attic. For a cathedral ceiling, a "roof support kit with gimbals" or another type of unit that will fit the slope of the roof is employed. This device supports the chimney and provides proper clearances where the roof is breached.

Every UL-listed chimney must be accompanied by a parts list that details all components required for the specific type of installation you will perform. The chimney must also have an owner's manual that includes illustrations detailing the joining of specific components and installation of the entire chimney. The clearance between the stack and combustibles varies from zero to two inches, depending on the brand. The UL sticker that appears on each component explains what the clearance must be, and the parts are designed to be installed that distance from combustibles. Fires have occurred in such chimneys when airspaces around the metal sections, necessary for ventilation and removal of hot air, have been stuffed with fiberglass insulation. If the chimney is designed to have such spaces, make certain that they exist.

The consumer who has decided to proceed with the installation himself will require a number of tools: tin snips, screwdrivers, hammer, pliers, plumb bob, putty knife, caulking gun, hand drill or properly grounded double insulated electric drill, chisels, 24-inch spirit level, a six-foot tape, a hand saw or

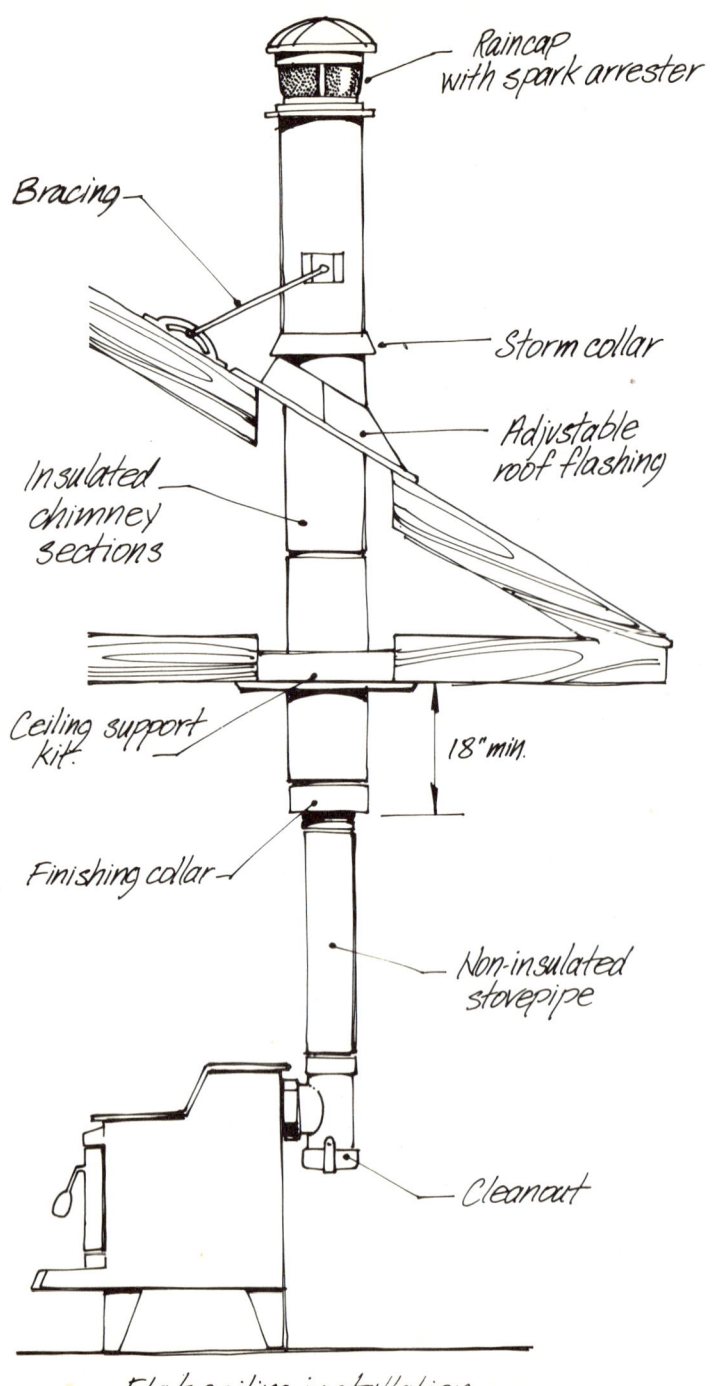

Flat ceiling installation

Roof support kit with gimbals

Segmented collar

Cathedral ceiling installation

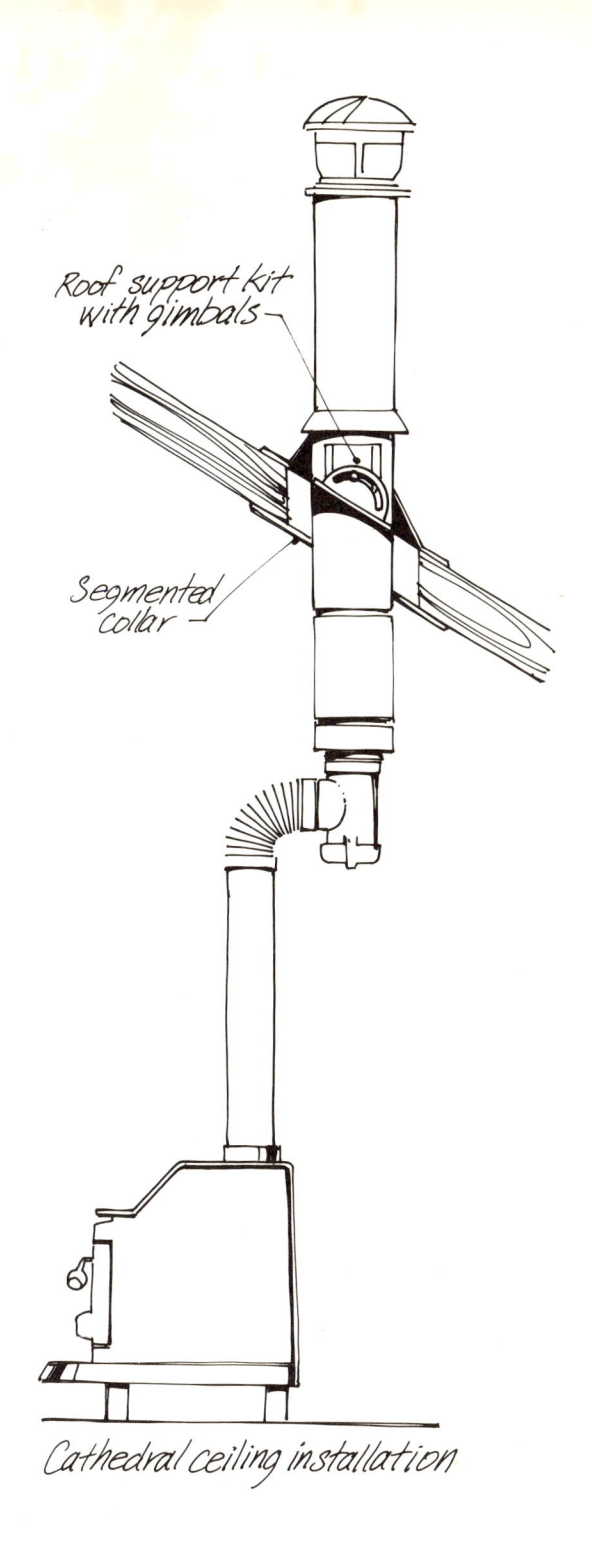

properly grounded double insulated electric saber saw, and metal drill bits. To finish the job after the chimney is in place, waterproofing for the storm collar (of interior chimneys) and roof flashing is also needed. Primer and finishing paint for the flashing are optional.

For the amateur installer, the most complicated step may well be the cutting of a hole in the roof for an interior chimney. Although the owner's manual should cover this procedure, you may want to bring in an experienced carpenter. Never begin to cut a hole without checking to see if electrical wires are present. Unless you are confident of carrying out the task correctly, have an electrician reroute any wires.

All interior units come with an easy-to-install flashing package and some have a storm collar. This is where you will need caulking and waterproofing materials, plus paint if you wish to cover the flashing.

Once the flashing has been laid, and any caulking and paint has dried, check after a heavy rainstorm or with a garden hose to ensure that there is a tight seal. Climb up into the attic and check for dampness. If there is any, caulk again and then repeat the dousing and inspection process. If there is still a problem, bring in a professional roofer.

Chimney Cap

Every Class A chimney must be topped by a rain cap designed to protect the stainless steel interior and prevent insulation within the solid-pack models from becoming wet. Some states, such as California, demand the use of a spark arrester screen with the cap. It can prevent extremely dry vegetation from catching fire, but it will also clog quickly if creosote has formed within the system. It is best to avoid employing a spark arrester unless its use is mandatory or your home has a wooden roof.

Chimney Height

Too low a chimney will cause back-puffing, and too high a chimney can topple over. However, it is best to have the stack as tall as possible. The chimney must rise a minimum of three

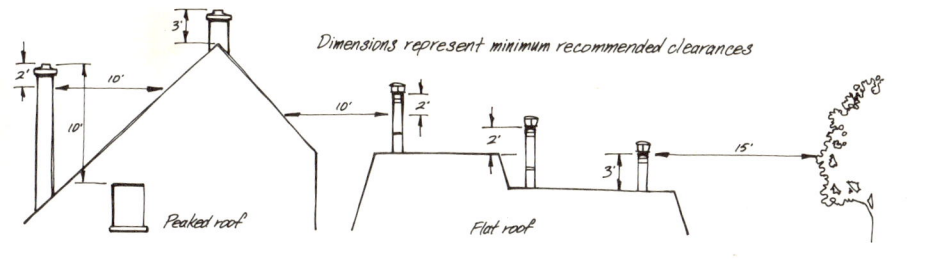

Dimensions represent minimum recommended clearances

Peaked roof   *Flat roof*

feet above where it emerges from the roof, and two feet above any portion of the roof or building within ten horizontal feet. Any chimney that is more than four feet above where it meets the roof must be braced. All Class A manufacturers have such supports available.

If there are branches level with the uppermost point of the chimney, cut them back to provide fifteen feet of clearance. The National Building Code of Canada also has a sensible provision that the top of the chimney be a minimum of ten feet higher than any doors or windows within fifty horizontal feet of the stack.

High-Range Chimneys

The rapid increase in severe chimney fires has led to the development of stronger prefabricated units. Most resemble the Class A chimney from the outside, but use two inches or more of nonsettling insulation (rather than the one inch of silica-rock wool found in solid-pack Class A models), and employ much tougher interior and exterior steel. Others have a solid type of insulation that also acts as the flue's liner. While all of these are larger in diameter and thus require more space when placed inside the house, they are installed in similar fashion to the Class A.

At this time, the UL has not developed a standard for these more rugged stacks and is certifying them only with its UL 103 standard, also used with the Class A. However, the Underwriters' Laboratory of Canada (ULC) has established its ULC S-629M standard, which includes a much more strenuous testing program.

Until the UL comes up with its own more challenging standard, anyone looking for a high-range chimney would do well to obtain one that has both the UL 103 and the ULC S-629M listings.

Another type of high-range stack that has met the requirements of ULC S-629M is quite different in composition. Originally developed in Scandinavia, it is a three-part system that must be erected at the job site, in similar fashion to a masonry stack. An inner liner and an outer casing composed primarily of pumice (volcanic rock) enclose an insulative mix comprised of leca (hollow ceramic pellets) that is combined with mortar. The liners are available in a number of diameters and the entire system can be installed much faster than a traditional masonry chimney. Currently, this is probably the most heat resistant chimney on the market.

None of the high-range chimneys is cheap. The prefabricated units are generally at least half again as expensive as Class A models, and the pumice-leca chimney is even higher in price. However, these do provide a level of security that the Class A cannot match.

THE MASONRY CHIMNEY

When correctly built, the masonry stack is capable of lasting for several decades. But if it is constructed improperly this stack can be an excellent creosote generator. If regular maintenance is not carried out, the chimney's liner can be ruined, as with the Class A, by one severe flue blaze.

Materials

There should be three layers in a masonry chimney: a liner composed of clay tiles, a middle column of concrete, and an outer brick or stone facing. However, when insulation is used, the middle layer is often eliminated. (This is discussed in detail later in this chapter.) These materials are all inexpensive and quite easy to acquire, and can be installed by a conscientious amateur prepared to undertake a project that will likely last more than two weeks and require a great deal of hard work.

The job can proceed more quickly when handled by a mason, but the cost will rise dramatically. Additionally, hiring a professional is no guarantee that the chimney will be erected as it should be, since many are not aware of the special preparations a solid-fuel stack requires. When hiring a mason, be sure that he follows the steps described here.

The key is to have the flue sealed so that cold air is not able to easily penetrate it and creosote cannot leak out. Refractory cement, which will not dissolve in water and is capable of withstanding temperatures of 2,000 degrees, must be used on every joint of the liner. This will probably come as a shock to many masons, who use only the less rugged portland cement or ordinary mortar when they apply a filler of any kind.

To save time and money, many homeowners leave off the stone or brick, resulting in the concrete blocks acting as the exterior. This is not recommended for two reasons: First, the flue will be cooler, increasing the possibility of creosote being formed; second, concrete blocks are quite porous. They attract moisture that can seep inward to the flue, and in cold weather the blocks can freeze. Both they and the tiles can then crack.

The ceramic liner is not a perfect product. The most widely used square and rectangular varieties are available in a limited number of sizes. Thus it is not always possible to match the smokepipe with the proper flue. The eight-by-twelve-inch tile is best for most appliances. The round ceramic tile, which is not easy to obtain, is preferred, since it is easier to clean and because smoke and gases rise more quickly within a round flue. The round tile is somewhat harder to work with, as it can roll off scaffolds and is more difficult to stack than square or rectangular models. The round liners can be ordered from most building supply outlets. A number of diameters are available. The best tile lengths are twenty-four and thirty inches.

You should inspect tiles carefully before buying them, as cracks and other defects are common. They must be transported, stored, and installed with care to prevent further damage.

Additionally, tiles can be destroyed by thermal shock, which occurs when the flue suddenly becomes at least a thousand degrees warmer than the outside temperature, as can happen during a chimney fire. Since the tiles are brittle, their only way of reacting to the resulting stress is to split. The substantially more expensive Scandinavian-made pumice liner is the only high-range flue suitable for masonry chimneys that has so far appeared. For those with more money to spend, the inner pumice liner and insulative leca mix can be employed inside a stone or brick exterior.

There must be careful coordination of the liner and the middle concrete layer. It is best to acquire one-piece cast concrete blocks that fit around the liner. There should be a space of at least three-quarters of an inch on all sides to allow the tile to expand. These cavities should not be filled with refractory cement; only enough of this material should be used to join the liner at each tile joint. The refractory cement must not ooze into the flue and harden either, as this would make the cleaning process difficult. Excess cement should be removed after each tile is set in place.

Some heat will leak out at every joint, even when the proper filler is used. Therefore, the joints of the tile and block must be staggered so that heat cannot transfer easily to the exterior, and on to combustibles. This will also lessen the possibility of liquid creosote flowing from within the chimney out to the chimney's exterior. The easiest way to stagger them is to avoid buying tiles and blocks that have the same multiples; for example, if you use eight-inch blocks and twenty-four-inch tiles, every third block joint will be at the same level as a liner joint. Those who do wish to use the twenty-four-inch tile can cut a few inches (not eight inches) from the bottom one, or begin the tiles below the blocks. (This is done by building up the first block with mortar.)

For each block joint, mortar is used with a mix of three parts sand, one part masonry cement, and a necessary amount of water. Set down only enough to secure the block; be sure that none falls between the block and liner.

Regulations in Canada and the United States differ on how to install two flues within the same chimney. The most widely recognized American fire safety body, the National Fire Protection Association (NFPA), states that the tile liners can be in close proximity as long as their joints are staggered by seven inches, and each flue is completely independent of the other.

The Chimney and Smokepipe 121

In Canada, the National Building Code stipulates that a three-inch-thick masonry wythe be placed between two tile liners. (A wythe is a column or vertical layer of concrete set in place as the chimney is built.) However, if each liner has its own cast blocks, a wythe is not required.

It is best to add the stone or brick exterior layer when the chimney is installed. The NFPA recommends that the stone be twelve inches thick and bricks four inches, since stone is a much better heat conductor than brick. The exterior layer is secured with metal tabs that are placed in the middle concrete block layer at a rate of one per square foot.

Bricks are easier to use than stone since their dimensions are uniform, but their cost has risen dramatically in the last decade. The advantage of stone is that huge quantities are available free of charge in many regions.

If you have never laid stone, have someone with experience help you for the first few days of the project, or read up on the subject and lay a few practice courses. To prevent moisture from seeping inward, cut all joints in the stone (or brickwork) shallow, and cover the entire exterior with a well-known brand of silicone sealer.

If there is neither time nor money to install the exterior as the chimney is erected, you should be sure that several steps are taken to make it easy to add the exterior later. Build the main foundation large enough so that there is a base for the facing. Insert the metal tabs to which the facing is secured as the blocks are set in place, and cover the entire outer surface of the blocks with mortar and silicone.

There is no doubt that the masonry chimney would perform better if an insulative layer were included. While this is done by a few masons, most feel handicapped by a paucity of convenient, easy-to-locate products.

Two insulators, both of which are rendered ineffective when they become damp, are wrap-around asbestos wool and construction-grade vermiculite. Both of these are most easily applied when the concrete layer is eliminated and a 1½-inch-wide gap is left between the liner and the brick or stone. Such a chimney must be extremely well sealed, both on the exterior and in the flue.

Construction Techniques

The foundation of a masonry chimney must begin below the frost level so that it does not heave and twist when the ground warms up in the spring. Also, a soil test must be carried out prior to construction to determine the bearing strength per square foot of the soil. This figure is required to calculate the exact dimensions of the foundation; it must always extend at least a foot beyond the chimney on all sides. Remember to allow for the brick or stone exterior. Information on frost levels, the bearing strength of your region's various soils, and the building of a proper foundation can be obtained from the local building inspector, a mason, ready-mix concrete supplier, or contractor.

The top of the foundation should contain a one- or two-inch-deep cup to catch any liquid creosote that makes its way down the flue, to prevent it from running out the cleanout door. This door should be set just above the pad so that the bottom of the flue—known as the ashpit—can be easily emptied out after the chimney is swept. The door should be large enough for easy removal of the creosote.

Since this door can be exposed to high temperatures, if any creosote lying in the pit ignites while a chimney fire is in progress, it should be cast iron. To lessen the possibility of air entering through this opening and feeding such a blaze, the door must fit snugly into its frame, and there should be no gaps between the frame and facer. Use refractory cement and silicone sealer around the frame. Cast-iron cleanout assemblies should be available through any outlet that sells clay flue tiles and cast concrete blocks. Query a professional mason if your search is unsuccessful.

Since it can be difficult to clean the flue from this cleanout door, some experts recommend the installation of a second door, four or five feet higher than the first. This allows easy insertion of the rods that are integral to the cleaning process. It is best to cut the liner and masonry material directly above this opening away, so that the rods can be easily maneuvered. Instead of having a 90-degree angle where this opening meets the flue, it should be at approximately 45 degrees.

CORRECTLY CONSTRUCTED CHIMNEY

- Bevelled rain cover
- 2"
- Overhang
- 3' min. Ridge
- Flashing
- Cleanout door
- Steel reinforced concrete foundation extends 12" min. beyond chimney on all four sides

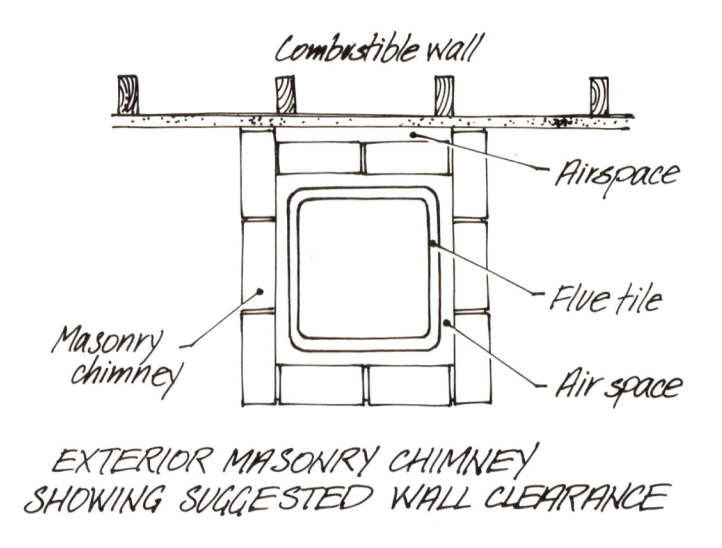

EXTERIOR MASONRY CHIMNEY SHOWING SUGGESTED WALL CLEARANCE

    To prevent a chimney fire from reaching combustibles around the base of the chimney, begin the liner at the foundation rather than a few feet above, as is sometimes the practice, and ensure that combustibles are at least six inches removed from the cleanout door.

    Other clearances between combustibles and the chimney must also be considered. With an exterior chimney, the NFPA regulations state that the chimney can be built right against the home, even if the siding is combustible. However, Canada's National Building Code demands a clearance of half an inch, and some American wood heat experts agree. Jay Shelton suggests in *Wood Heat Safety* (Charlotte, Vt.: Garden Way Publishing Co., 1979) that the chimney be set out half an inch, with the brick or stonework extended on the sides to tie into the house. Space is left between the siding and the closest chimney wall to allow circulation of air.

    Inside the house, there must be two inches between the stack and combustible structural components. However, every floor and ceiling that the chimney passes through requires a firestop that touches the stack. This is simply a noncombustible millboard that covers the bottom of the two-inch opening to prevent a fire from spreading between stories. Two common building products can be used: gypsum board and corner metal lath that is nailed to the wooden framing material and then plastered over for aesthetic reasons. It is highly important that this firestop not be cemented into the facer, as the chimney must be free-floating so that any settling it undergoes will not damage the home.

Baseboard trim and other lightweight wood can come within half an inch of the chimney. However, it must be separated from the stack by a minimum of ⅛-inch of a noncombustible substance. Any style of combustible flooring must have half an inch of clearance; it is not necessary to use a noncombustible object between it and the chimney.

When the stack passes through the room where the appliance will be located, the horizontal connector or thimble that joins the chimney and smokepipe can be quite easy to install. However, if it must run through a combustible wall, extreme caution is necessary.

The thimble must never extend into the flue, as cleaning the chimney would become extremely difficult. It must begin at the inside edge of the tile's breeching or opening (flush with the surface of the flue), or abut the liner.

Two materials can be used for the connector: round ceramic tile or 24 gauge steel smokepipe. The run of pipe coming from the stove fits into this "sleeve." To make inspecting and cleaning easier, do not cement the smokepipe into the sleeve. (If there is a gap, fill it with a fireproof insulative material such as Fibrefrax.) So that smoke cannot leak out around the sleeve, the thimble itself must be permanently built into the stack, then tightly sealed.

If the thimble must pass through a combustible wall, it is best to tear out the wall for eighteen inches in all directions around the thimble, and set in brick supported by heavy-duty framing. If brick is used, heavy-duty framing will be needed to support it. The thimble should always run at least two inches out into the room holding the appliance.

There must be coordination of the diameters of the breeching, thimble, and smokepipe. The thimble must fit snugly around the circumference of the breeching at the flue and accept the smokepipe at the other, while not allowing leakage of smoke and gases.

Once the chimney has been erected the proper distance

INTERIOR MASONRY CHIMNEY

above the roofline, a top cover must be installed around the flue tile. To prevent rainwater from running down the outside of the chimney, it is recommended that an overhang be built that will allow water to fall directly to the ground. From the overhang, the cover is angled upward toward the center. At least two inches of the top tile must remain visible. When the cover has dried, seal it with silicone.

To allow the mortar in the chimney to cure completely, it is best to wet the structure down after a workday is completed and then wrap it in polyethylene. This should be repeated three or four times. For the same reason, the completed chimney should be allowed to sit for a week during hot weather, or two weeks in early spring or late autumn. Then, take another week to break the chimney in. A total of two or three weeks must elapse from when the chimney is completed until hot fires can be built in the appliance.

If you are not in excellent physical condition, do not try to put in eight- or ten-hour days at the beginning of the project. Wear gloves as much as possible, and if you are mixing concrete below where someone else is laying stone, wear a hardhat. Strap on a respirator whenever you are working in dusty surroundings or around asbestos, and use safety glasses if any stone or concrete blocks have to be knocked apart. As construction progresses, it will probably be necessary to use scaffolding. Erect it yourself only if you are completely familiar with the procedure.

When the masonry chimney is built by the homeowner, it is by far the cheapest midrange unit. Using new high-range products such as the Scandinavian chimney will provide an extra margin of safety.

OLDER CHIMNEYS

Employing an existing chimney will reduce the cost of installing a wood heat system. Confirm its suitability for use with a wood stove. Most of the questions that have to be answered center on how safe the stack is, but even if the chimney is in perfect condition it may not be satisfactory if in the wrong place. The smokepipe assembly cannot be fifteen or twenty feet long, so the stove must be set close to an existing chimney. However, this is not always practical, as the stack may be in one end of a long rambling house or in a position that would require the appliance to be in an unsafe spot, such as near an exit or stairway. It is obviously best to determine whether the chimney is properly situated before the evaluation proceeds.

Advice on the practicality of the chimney's location can be obtained from a professional chimney sweep who can also perform the first step in a full inspection—a thorough cleaning of the flue, necessary so that any defects will be easy to spot.

Used Prefabricated Metal Chimneys

When considering whether an existing prefabricated metal chimney is suitable for use with a wood stove, begin by ascertaining whether it is a Class A model listed by the UL for employment with wood appliances. Every component should have a UL sticker. Metal chimneys are also manufactured for use exclusively with gas or oil appliances; these types are not suitable. Confirm that the clearance stipulated on the UL sticker is present along the entire length of the stack.

With exterior models, check that the base under the tee is solid and that all support bands are in place. These should be found approximately every ten feet, with the highest one located near the roofline. With chimneys situated inside the home, guarantee that the support holding the chimney is in good condition and that all needed radiation shields are in place.

The cleanout opening on the chimney should be in fine shape. If air can leak in, use a block of wood and a steel-headed hammer or a rubber-headed auto-body hammer to close the gaps. The cup or door should be held snugly in place.

Inspect the outside of the chimney for corrosion, dents, and any deterioration at the top of each section. This last condition appears when there is an insulation void. (These voids can also be checked for by running a hand around the upper few inches of each section while the appliance is in operation. If one portion is considerably hotter than another, insulation is missing.) Any sections with voids should be removed.

If there are substantial creosote stains on the exterior, or if the chimney cap has begun to turn blue, the chimney has been abused. Discoloration of the cap is caused by extremely high temperatures that have probably also damaged the flue itself. If the chimney is an air-circulator model, be sure that the intake and exit ports at the top of the chimney, just below the cap, are not blocked. (Remember that such a model is not thought to be very practical for use with a wood appliance.)

From either the top or the cleanout, make a thorough visual inspection of the flue. Every Class A liner should be perfectly round; if a portion has collapsed, the damaged sections should be replaced. If rust flakes were removed with the creosote when the chimney was swept, there is likely to be a serious corrosion problem that can also render the chimney useless.

Having the chimney sweep assist with the entire inspection is recommended. He will be able to help you decide which damage is reparable and which permanent.

Older Masonry Chimneys

Begin checking an old masonry chimney with the exterior. The foundation must be solid. Check that the chimney is not leaning. Chimneys that begin on an upper level of the home and are supported only by a wooden stand are not safe. There must be a cleanout door for access to the flue. Check to be sure that the door has not warped and that there are no leaks around the frame. You may wish to obtain a new cast-iron assembly. When a cleanout is not present, chances are that the chimney was not designed for use with a wood appliance. However, if the chimney is otherwise acceptable, a cleanout can be built in one wall of the stack.

An outside chimney should be at least half an inch away from the house, and the aforementioned clearances around an interior chimney must be present—two inches to structural members, and half an inch with flooring and trim. Inspect the thimble, ensuring that the correct installation is in place.

Stains on the brick or stonework are evidence that a great deal of creosote was generated by past homeowners, and that refractory cement is not found at every liner joint.

The inspection of the masonry chimney's interior must be carried out carefully. This can be done from the top or, using a mirror, from the cleanout or breeching. A sunny day should provide all the illumination required within the flue, but if the weather is overcast, use a flashlight or light bulb dangled down from above.

There are a number of defects to look for. A major one is an unused breeching. Such openings can be extremely dangerous, as past homeowners may have simply covered them with a thin metal cover, now hidden under wallpaper or paneling. During a serious chimney fire, very high temperatures could seep out through this and transfer to combustibles. Expose any breechings and seal them in a safe manner with mortar and brick or stone.

The chimney should have a proper clay or concrete liner that covers the entire interior. Most older stacks have a poured concrete liner. If there are gaps, hot spots could be caused on the exterior. If you cannot confirm if pieces are missing, have a look at the creosote removed from the flue. If it contains concrete or clay, the liner is deteriorating. It should be fixed before the stack is put back in service, as more chunks could fall and block the flue. Make sure that the flow of smoke is not being obstructed in any way.

As a final precaution, a professional chimney sweep can perform a smoke test. The top of the flue is blocked and a scented smokebomb is placed in the ashpit. The entire exterior of the chimney is then examined for fissures. If there are minute leaks, they will be revealed by the scent. This procedure should not be attempted by an amateur.

Chimney Relining

Once the inspection is completed, it is time to decide if the chimney is salvageable. Fortunately, a number of quality relining products are appearing on the market. One approach is to use the inner liner and leca mix of the Scandinavian chimney. The liner sections are notched and lowered from the roof. This procedure requires an experienced mason and a flue with a quite large diameter.

There are also a handful of British relining products that are being installed by chimney contractors, masons, and sweeps

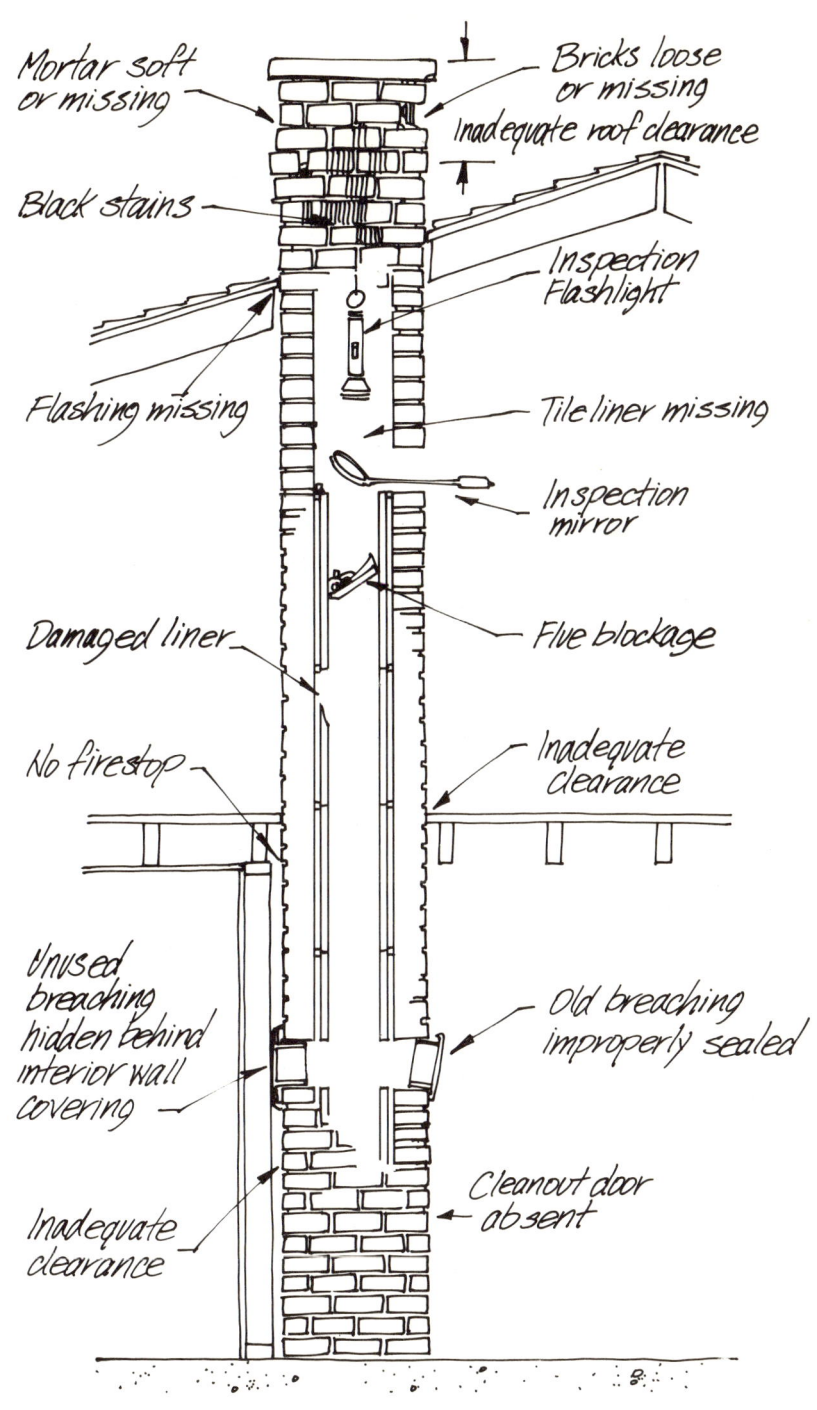

DEFECTIVE CHIMNEY

in this country. The main component is a diaphragm that is lowered, while deflated, into the flue. Attached to it are a number of brackets that hold it out from the walls. After the bottom of the flue is sealed and the diaphragm is inflated, a special masonry mix is poured around it. After twenty-four hours, the diaphragm is deflated and removed. All of these methods are quite expensive, but they can restore an otherwise worthless flue.

A number of companies sell stainless-steel smokepipe as relining kits. While these are cheaper, they have drawbacks. They can be used only in an arrow-straight flue while the other devices can be employed even in chimneys that curve near their summits. These steel reliners contain only one quite thin layer of material, while the other models are thicker and help to insulate the flue. Finally, the stainless steel might last only a few years, but the masonry units should endure for generations.

Many neophytes consider connecting their appliance to a flue that is already serving another stove or furnace. The UL states that any appliance it has listed must have its own chimney. This is the best policy to follow. If you are determined to feed two appliances into the same flue, have at least twelve vertical inches between where the two units enter the chimney. If you are connecting a wood appliance and another type of heating unit, the wood stove must always be on the bottom.

While it may be a painful decision to make, there will be times when an older chimney is simply not usable, even if a new liner were to be installed. For the safety of your family, do not take a chance—replace it with a new chimney.

THE SMOKEPIPE

All too often, flimsy smokepipe is purchased as an afterthought following the acquisition of the chimney and appliance. What consumers who scrimp do not usually realize is that many chimney fires also affect the smokepipe. It turns bright red, twists, groans, and—if the metal is thin—can burn out and allow the dangerously hot creosote to fall onto floors and rugs.

The only smokepipe that should be used is constructed of oxidized black, enameled, or stainless steel of at least 24 gauge. The thicker 22 gauge is even better. Lighter models are not

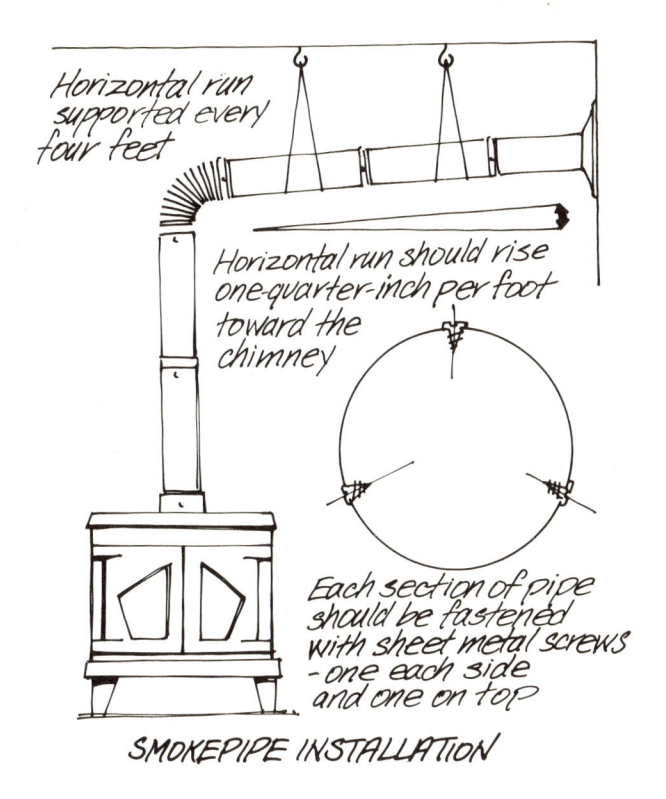

[Figure: Smokepipe Installation — Horizontal run supported every four feet. Horizontal run should rise one-quarter-inch per foot toward the chimney. Each section of pipe should be fastened with sheet metal screws - one each side and one on top.]

acceptable and shiny galvanized pipe is not recommended, as it releases toxic zinc fumes when heated to high temperatures. Most respected wood stove stores stock the proper types; the oxidized black pipe is by far the most common.

The next step is to ensure that all joints contain three self-tapping sheet-metal screws. These prevent the pipe from coming apart accidentally, especially when put under stress during a chimney fire.

Creosote comes in many forms. Most remain inert after being created, building up within the chimney or smokepipe. However, the liquid type will spread. Those who have tried to remove stains left behind on floors and rugs know how damaging it can be. (Ammonia is best for removing such stains.) Install each pipe section with the crimped, female end down, so that liquid creosote is able to flow easily through the smokepipe system and into the stove, where it will probably be consumed. To provide additional protection against spillage, place all sections so that their seams are on top.

For the pipe to fit snugly inside the appliance's flue collar, the diameters of the pipe and collar should be identical. Some stoves have holes drilled in the collar to accept screws. If these are not present, make your own with an electric drill and the proper bits. When the pipe must have a larger diameter where it connects with the chimney, install an adapter as close to the stack as possible.

The connection between the masonry chimney and smokepipe has already been detailed. For joining the pipe and a Class A stack, each chimney manufacturer generally has its own design. Ensure that this joint is secure and that the pipe is attached in such a way that liquid creosote will run into the pipe and not onto the floor.

Years ago, when buildings were poorly insulated, it was common to set the stove as far from the chimney as possible and join the two with yards of smokepipe. Since the stoves used in those days were poorly sealed and burned wood quickly, this approach made sense, as a great deal of heat was reclaimed via the pipes. However, controlled-combustion appliances and much higher insulation levels have made this technique obsolete—and foolhardy.

The smokepipe assembly's maximum length should be eight feet, and if it can be made substantially shorter, so much the better. A long horizontal run is more dangerous than a lengthy vertical one, as the former will allow creosote to collect much more easily. If a horizontal pipe system does run for eight feet (or, against all professional advice, longer), there must be a support every four feet. Employ the perforated strapping often used with hot water pipes, or another type of strong metal band that will not transfer much heat to the combustible material into which it is screwed or nailed.

It is also essential that the assembly not contain more than two elbows, as each slows down the flow of smoke and gases. The NFPA prefers an elbow that allows the smoke to curve gently around the corner rather than making a sharp 90-degree turn. However, some of these elbow models allow liquid creosote to leak out. Have the seller recommend a satisfactory compromise selection.

Make inspection and cleaning of the pipe network easier by installing, instead of an elbow, a tee containing a cleanout door, at the end of the horizontal or vertical run closest to the chimney.

There is debate over whether the pipe should rise when it runs horizontally toward the stack. The NFPA suggests an elevation of ¼ inch per foot of pipe. Jay Shelton and some other experts believe this is not necessary. The rise may slightly simplify cleaning of the pipe and allow liquid creosote to move toward the stove more easily. It is important that the pipe never drop between the final elbow (or tee) and the chimney.

Whenever smokepipe shows any evidence of corrosion or general deterioration, replace it immediately. Stainless steel pipe, although it is substantially more expensive than the black type, will endure much longer. Expect the latter style to last five heating seasons at the most. If there are any fires within the smokepipe system, the life expectancy will be greatly reduced. Poor quality pipe should be changed after one or two seasons.

A product gaining in popularity is double-wall, air-insulated smokepipe with a stainless steel liner. It keeps the flue gases quite warm and cuts in half the clearance usually required between the pipe and combustibles—the NFPA-recommended clearance between standard smokepipe and combustibles is eighteen inches. The double-wall pipe can therefore be very handy with many stove installations. As the next chapter will describe, it is simple to reduce the clearance between radiant heaters and combustibles to less than eighteen inches with the use of heat shields. But unless action is taken to also reduce the pipe's clearance, it is not safe to do so.

Other methods of decreasing the distance include a shield that is placed around the portion of the smokepipe facing the combustible and secured by the screws at each joint, and a protector that is affixed directly to the wall or ceiling.

Use of such a protector is not as desirable as the other methods of reducing clearances. First, a wall or floor shield is conspicuous, and, second, it must cover a wide area, as the

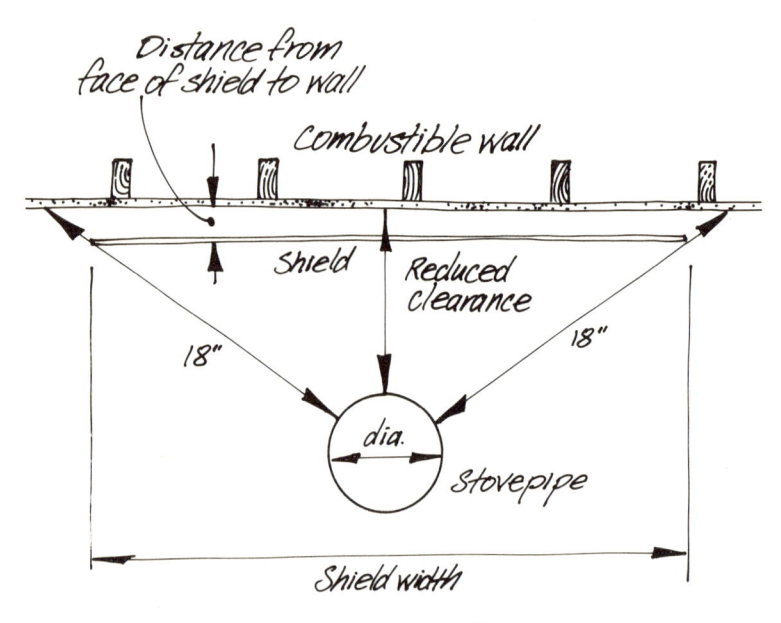

Figure: Diagram showing clearance between smokepipe and combustibles. Labels include: "Distance from face of shield to wall", "Combustible wall", "Shield", "Reduced clearance", "18"", "18"", "dia.", "Stovepipe", "Shield width".

CLEARANCE BETWEEN SMOKEPIPE AND COMBUSTIBLES

NFPA believes that further protection is needed in addition to that set directly in front of the smokepipe. It insists that the shield extend out on each side a distance of eighteen inches from the point on the smokepipe that is closest to the combustible. The shield should also be set an inch out from the wall to allow air to circulate behind it and carry away excess heat. Details on what materials can be used and how to secure a wall shield are found in Chapter 12, Installing the Appliance.

As mentioned previously, smokepipe should never pass through a combustible floor or wall. While exceptions must not be made for floors, it is possible, if no other solution is available, to run the pipe through a wall. It is recommended to have this handled by a professional, and to design the set-up so that all portions of the smokepipe can be easily observed.

A commonly used device that is *not* safe is a small metal thimble that provides only three inches of clearance around the

Table 3
NFPA guidelines for reducing clearances from smokepipe

Minimum thickness of protective material needed (must extend outward as described in text)	Minimum clearances (in inches) from the smokepipe	
Without protection	18 inches	9 inches
1) ¼ in. asbestos millboard with 1 in. airspace.	12	6
2) 28 gauge sheet metal on ¼ in. asbestos millboard (no airspace).	12	4
3) 28 gauge sheet metal with 1 in. airspace.	9	4
4) 28 gauge sheet metal on ⅛ in. asbestos millboard and with 1 in. airspace.	9	4
5) ¼ in. asbestos millboard on 1 in. mineral wool batts with wire mesh or equivalent (no airspace).	6	4
6) 22 gauge sheet metal on 1 in. mineral wool batts reinforced with wire or equivalent (no airspace).	3	2

pipe. However, a huge thimble that allows eighteen inches all around is satisfactory. Also acceptable are an opening cut into the wall that provides eighteen inches of clearance in all directions and a brick protector that puts eight inches between the pipe and combustibles. Obviously, this last device will be quite heavy and demand substantial support. None of these is easy to install or visually subtle, but they will work.

There are some accessories that are placed inside the smokepipe. These include dampers, hot water coils, ovens, and the probe of a thermostat used to measure the temperature within the pipe. (There are other thermometers that contain a magnet and simply attach to the exterior of the pipe.) Except for the thermometer, these are difficult to install and usually unsuited for use with a controlled-combustion appliance. Once you have ascertained that the unit is safe to employ within your system, have a veteran woodburner, stove installer, or sheet-metal worker assist you.

Finally, although it is probably self-evident to most readers, it must be pointed out that smokepipe can never be used as a chimney. When installed outdoors, it will cause severe creosote problems, and the pipe is simply not rugged enough to endure the rigors experienced by a solid-fuel stack.

WHEN QUALITY SMOKEPIPE and a chimney are set in place correctly, they will require little attention aside from regular inspections and cleaning. On the other hand, inferior or poorly installed components can be a constant source of worry and danger to the residents of a home. The choice of how to proceed lies with each woodburner.

12

Installing the Appliance

When the wood heat appliance finally arrives, there is generally excitement and impatience—most people are eager to achieve instantaneous energy independence. However, the stove should be installed slowly and carefully.

WALLS AND CEILINGS

For the majority of appliance buyers today—those who acquire a certified unit—the process of determining how to safely install the stove is quite simple. When the UL or another organization tests the appliance, it stipulates at what distance from combustibles it can be installed. This information—known as the listed clearance—is included on the listing plate found on the unit, and within the owner's manual.

Other numbers that can be important are the basic NFPA clearance, which must be followed with unlisted stoves, and the reduced distances that can be attained with the use of various heat shields composed of noncombustible materials. (Generally the listed clearance is less than the NFPA distance. However, there are exceptions, such as with some fireplace-heaters.)

The standard NFPA clearance figures are listed in Table 4.

At first glance, some of these distances may seem excessive. It is true that even the hottest fire in a stove will likely not

Table 4
Minimum clearances to combustible materials (without protection) for all types of appliances*

| Type of appliance | \multicolumn{4}{c}{Minimum clearances (in inches) from the surfaces of the appliance} |

Type of appliance	Top	Sides		Rear	Front
Cookstoves and water heaters without refractory brick lining in firebox.	30	36	18**	36	36
Cookstoves and water heaters with refractory brick lining in firebox.	30	24	18**	24	36
Circulating heaters	36	12		12	24
Radiant heaters	36	36		36	36
Manually loaded furnaces	18	18		18	48
Boilers and automatically stoked furnaces	6	6		6	48

* Except for some certified units, follow instructions on listings plate.
** Denotes side of cookstove farthest from the firebox.
Information from NFPA 89M, "Heat Producing Appliance Clearances 1976."

ignite a wall three or four feet away, but there is an exceptionally good reason why these clearances must exist—pyrolysis.

When wood is repeatedly exposed to the relatively low temperature of 200 degrees and then cooled, it undergoes a chemical change. First, water is evaporated; later, volatiles such as phenols, wood alcohol, and acids are consumed. Eventually, the wood closest to the source of heat is transformed into pyrophoric carbon, which is highly dangerous as it is able to spontaneously ignite and burst into flames.

Pyrolysis is not confined to wood heating; a shorted wire in an electrical system or the hot water pipes used with any boiler can also cause it. Pyrolysis can occur within a few months of the appliance's being installed, or after many years. It is difficult to detect, but the threat is terribly real. The person who ignores the NFPA and UL numbers and places his stove nearer to combustibles than it should be is courting disaster for himself, or an innocent family that buys the home some time later.

Installing the Appliance 141

It is therefore essential to know what lies behind every surface around the appliance. If you did not construct the home yourself, try to examine the inside of walls, floors, and ceilings. Locating blueprints or querying the builder or a former owner are other approaches. Realize that a noncombustible surface is no guarantee against pyrolysis. Plaster, stucco, brick, stone, or ceramic tile will not protect wood inside the wall when the stove is installed too close.

This is not to say that the stove cannot be safely moved nearer than the NFPA or certified clearance stipulates. For many years, the NFPA has published a list of building materials that can be used as shields to reduce the distances. These include two thicknesses of asbestos millboard (⅛-inch and ¼-inch), mineral wool batts, and two gauges of sheet metal (22 and 28). Different clearances can be attained by employing these singly, in tandem, or with a one-inch-wide airspace between the shield and the combustible wall or ceiling. During the first few years of the current wood heating renaissance, amateurs and professionals alike attempted to have their installations conform. However, it is now apparent that much of the NFPA lineup of materials has become obsolete.

The reasons for this obsolescence include aesthetics, availability of materials, and health safety. Mineral wool was formerly in extensive use as an insulator. In recent years it has nearly disappeared from building supply outlets due to the ever-increasing popularity of fiberglass. Mineral wool batts are thus hard to find and, when employed with wire mesh, as was once common, result in a far from attractive installation.

Asbestos is of course condemned by the medical profession as a cause of lung cancer and other respiratory diseases; there is no doubt that the fibers can be debilitating when inhaled. Fire safety officials readily admit that asbestos can be a health hazard, but, at the same time they do believe asbestos millboard can be safely used. They recommend that it be cut outdoors, away from buildings, animals, and water supplies, with the sawyer and any helpers wearing a respirator. They further suggest that all edges be covered when the material is installed so that fibers cannot escape.

It may be true that asbestos millboard can be employed without risk, but such a hue and cry has been raised over asbestos that the majority of retailers no longer stock any products containing it. The person determined to buy asbestos millboard may have a hard time locating it. (Millboards made of a ceramic material instead of asbestos are becoming quite common; these are safe.) While asbestos cement board is thought by some experts to be more rugged than the asbestos millboard and to present no more of a danger, it is not recommended by the NFPA.

There are no problems with sheet metal, aside from the fact that it can buckle if used in too large a sheet or when improper supports are present. Sheet metal remains an integral component in many commercial and homemade shields. The other NFPA recommendation—the one-inch-wide airspace—has also emerged as being a key element in most proper shield installations.

When the shield is correctly set out from the wall, the top and bottom are two inches removed from the ceiling and floor respectively, and the sides are left open, air can circulate freely behind the shield. The shield functions similarly to the air-circulating type of Class A chimney, with the space making it possible for any heat that builds up to be carried away.

The consumer who is willing to spend money for a commercial, aesthetically pleasing wall (or ceiling) protector that does not contain asbestos has a continually expanding selection to choose from. Additionally, the risk of buying an unsafe or poorly made product is reduced by the existence of a UL certification program. Materials used to create these shields include venetian-blindlike slats of metal, sizable pieces of sheet metal, ceramic tiles within steel frames, plus compressed ceramic fibers and metal shavings. According to *Wood 'n Energy* magazine, models that use an exterior covering, an inner core, and a metallic backing are preferred.

At the time of writing, a confusing situation exists, as most of the UL-listed shields contain substances not recommended by the NFPA. It is expected that the NFPA will eventually recognize UL-certified substances, but until this takes place some building inspectors may not allow the use of UL shields. Before purchasing such a protector, consult the local permit issuer.

Information on how the clearance can be reduced with a UL protector is found in the instruction manual that must ac-

1" Airspace between shield and wall

All dimensions indicated should be regarded as minimum clearances

36"
1"
36" BOTH SIDES
6"
Floor shield
6"
18"
12"
2"

2" Airspace between bottom of wall shield and floor

PROPER WALL AND FLOOR CLEARANCES

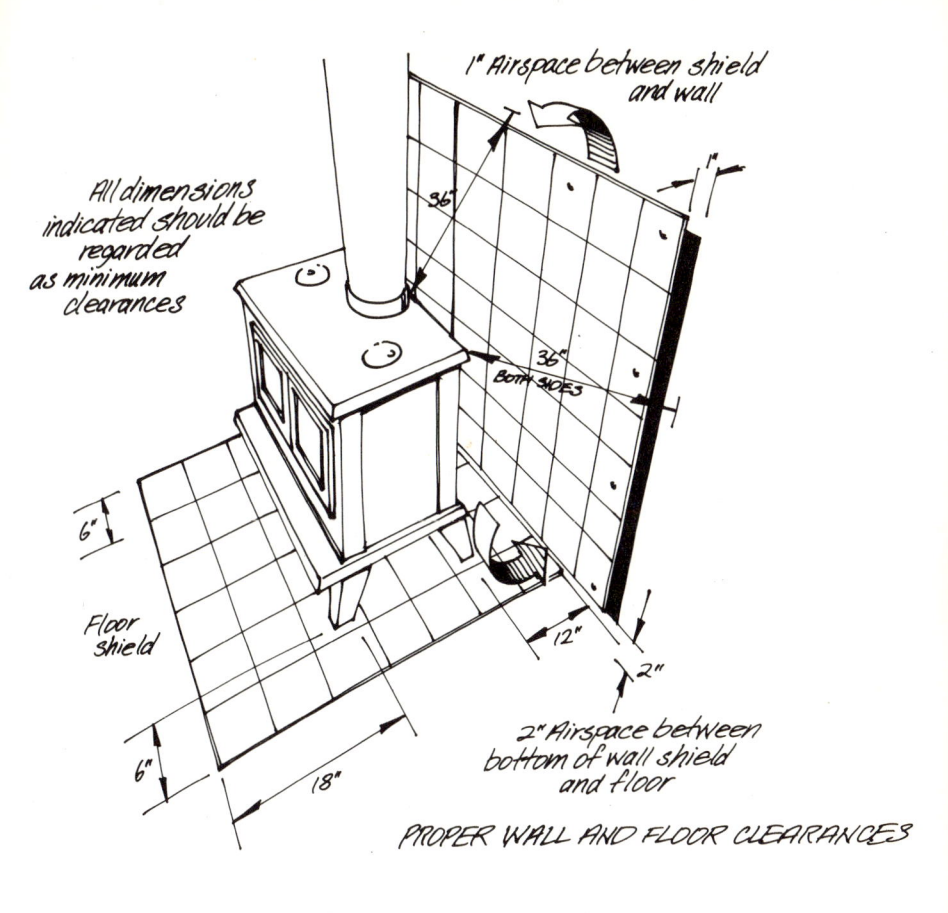

INSTALLATION OF COMMERCIAL SHEET STEEL AND CERAMIC TILE WALL SHIELD

...to avoid heat transfer to wall, shield mounting screws should not be placed directly behind stove...

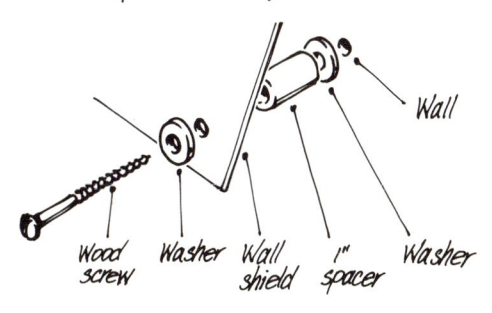

Wood screw — Washer — Wall shield — 1" spacer — Washer — Wall

Table 5
NFPA guidelines for reducing clearances from cookstoves, hot water heaters, circulating heaters, and radiant heaters

Minimum thickness of protective material needed (must extend outward as described in text).

Minimum clearances (in inches) from the surfaces of the appliance.

Without protection	top	sides & rear	sides & rear	sides & rear
	36	36	18	12
1) ¼ in. asbestos millboard with 1 in. airspace.	30	18	9	6
2) 28 gauge sheet on ¼ in. asbestos millboard (no airspace).	24	18	9	6
3) 28 gauge sheet metal with 1 in. airspace.	18	12	6	4
4) 28 gauge sheet metal on ⅛ in. asbestos millboard and with 1 in. airspace.	18	12	6	4
5) ¼ in. asbestos millboard on 1 in. mineral wool batts with wire mesh or equivalent (no airspace).	18	12	6	4
6) 22 gauge sheet metal on 1 in. mineral wool batts reinforced with wire or equivalent (no airspace).	18	12	3	2

company the product; it is common for the distance to be cut down by two-thirds. Be forewarned that some widely available shields do not possess UL certification. These contain unsuitable materials such as cardboard and gypsum board. The latter, which is also known as Gyproc and Sheetrock, is thought by many to be fireproof. However, because its main fire retardant is water, extended exposure to high temperatures dries out the material and renders it useless as a protector.

For the homeowner who wishes to prepare his own shields,

a number of approaches can be taken. The easiest materials to use are 24 gauge sheet metal and 22 gauge aluminum, spaced a full inch from the combustible. To produce a safe, visually pleasing unit, cover the shield with a suitable color of high-temperature stove paint and have a sheet-metal shop roll the edges. These two substances reduce the clearance by two-thirds for walls and 50 percent for ceilings—as long as the airspace is present. (Since heat rises, excess temperatures close to ceilings will not be as easily dissipated by air circulation.)

To suspend the shield from the combustible surface, use inch-long pieces of copper pipe, ceramic insulators employed with electric fencing, or proper spacers that can be purchased from some stove dealers. It is important that the protector not be secured directly behind or above the stove, as excess heat could be transferred to combustibles. Place screws only along the outside edges of the device. If there is nothing solid in the wall or ceiling to attach the screws or nails to, use a lag shield behind each fastener. Ensure that it is noncombustible. It is best to place metal screening with gaps of less than ¼-inch along all edges of the shield to prevent objects from falling behind the unit.

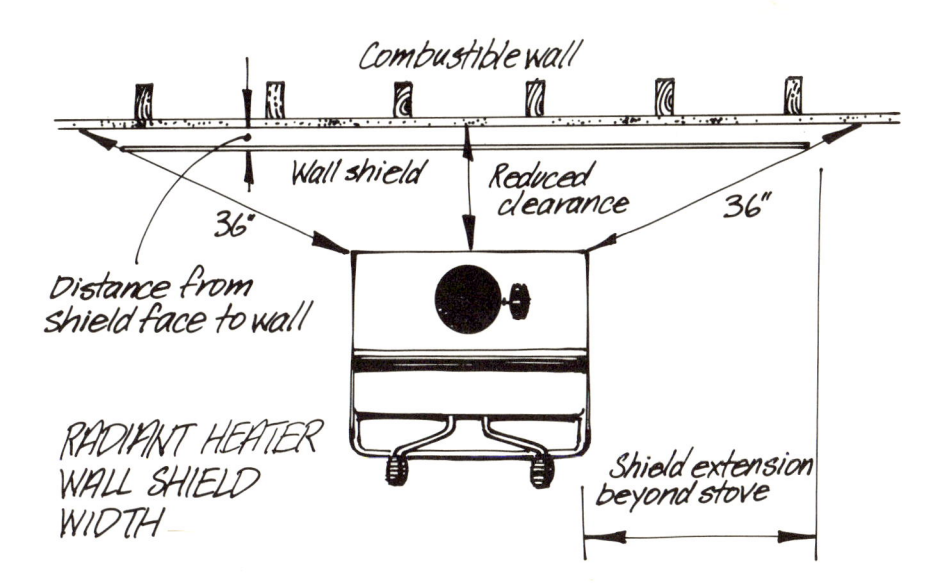

Brick wall shield

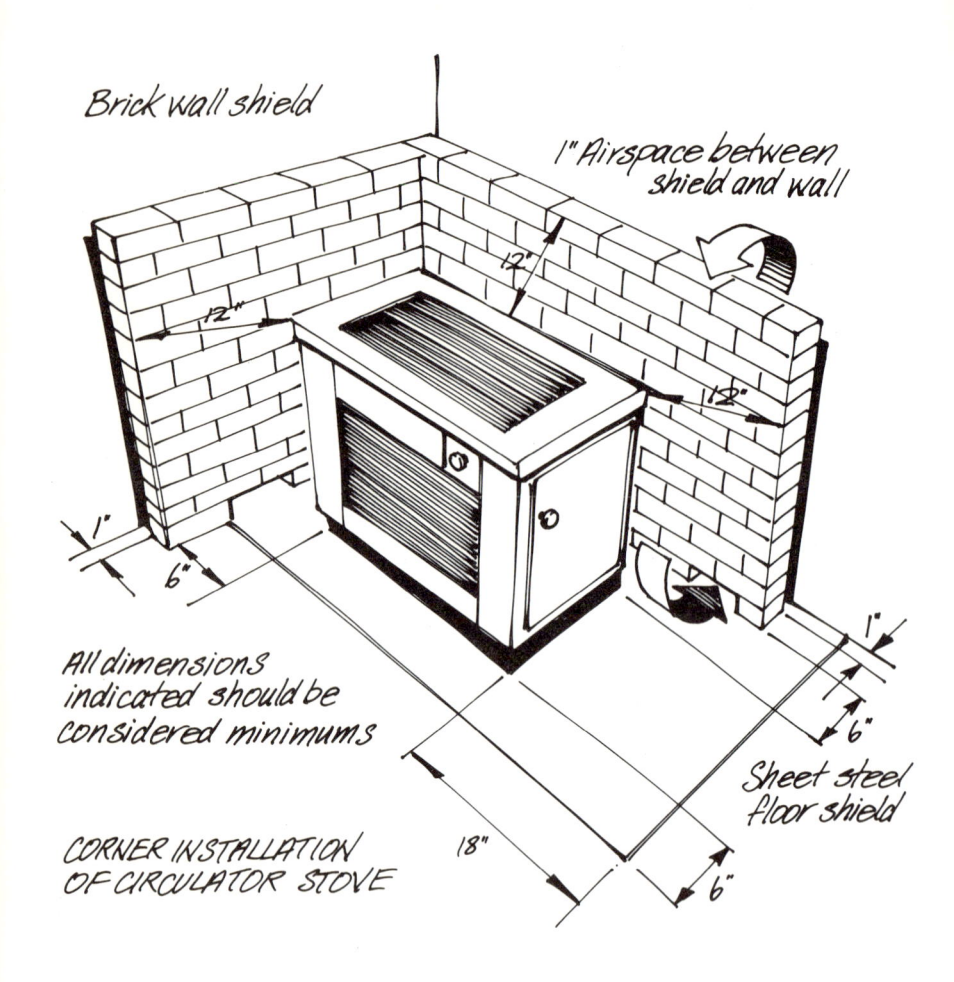

1" Airspace between shield and wall

All dimensions indicated should be considered minimums

CORNER INSTALLATION OF CIRCULATOR STOVE

Sheet steel floor shield

As with the wall protector used with smokepipe, these devices must extend out quite a distance to the sides. The rule is that the measurement to each edge of the shield, from the point on the appliance closest to it, has to be equal to the basic clearance demanded by the NFPA. So, even if a radiant heater can safely sit twelve inches from a wall, the measurement to each side of the protector from the near corner of the stove must be thirty-six inches. (The same approach is used with the top of the shield; at the bottom, there should be, as previously described, two inches between the unit and the floor. The same space is left when the shield is high enough to approach the ceiling.)

Installing the Appliance 147

A solid brick shield can also be constructed. However, before such a project is begun, check that the floor is strong enough to support the substantial weight. Stone can be employed but, while four-inch-wide bricks will suffice, eight to twelve inches of stone are required. When the shield is set out an inch, and proper ventilation is available along all edges, the distance can be reduced by 50 percent. It will be easier to provide the necessary ventilation holes along the top and bottom when bricks are installed than it would be with stone. If this shield is being erected in the corner of a room, it can be self-supporting, but if the protector is a straight unit, it must be tied into the wall with one metal tab per square foot. Otherwise, it could topple over. Do not allow mortar to harden between the protector and the wall.

FLOORS

According to the NFPA, the floor shield must extend eighteen inches beyond any side of the appliance containing doors, and six inches past all others. The expansive protection in front of openings is required to prevent hot coals and sparks from damaging floors and rugs. (See page 143 for illustration of floor shield.)

Jay Shelton suggests, in his book *Wood Heat Safety*, that these NFPA recommendations are not always sufficient. He prefers to see the covered area in front of the doors on a fireplace-heater extended twenty-four inches, the protection along the solid sides of radiant heaters increased from six to eighteen inches, and the portion of the floor shield behind the stove reach back to the wall. He does believe that six inches is sufficient with the solid sides of circulators.

The thickness of the floor protection required varies with the distance between the bottom of the appliance and the floor, and whether the stove contains a built-in shield under the firebox. Always consult the owner's manual.

The NFPA thickness guidelines are as follows for unlisted stoves. With eighteen inches of vertical clearance, a 24 gauge sheet-metal pad of the proper dimensions is sufficient. With six to eighteen inches, quarter-inch-thick millboard covered by the sheet metal is necessary. (Shelton prefers one of two other methods—the sheet metal under two inches of sand or gravel contained by a frame, or the use of a layer of four-inch-thick concrete blocks. These are laid with all holes parallel to one another. The blocks are not joined, and the holes must remain open on the ends to allow circulation of air. It is best to use them together with the sheet metal. The blocks are set only under the appliance, and the sheet metal extends the correct distances.) The NFPA feels that heaters having less than six inches of space need the same sheet-metal-block arrangement.

With furnaces and boilers that have the firebox located at least eighteen inches above the floor, 24 gauge protection extending beyond the appliance on all sides is needed only when the unit sits on combustible flooring or joists. Follow the manufacturer's directions closely. The few furnaces and boilers that have legs more than four inches in height need quarter-inch asbestos millboard and the 24 gauge sheet metal. (The NFPA states that central system floor protectors must extend out the same distances as those set under heaters.)

With downflow-type furnaces, the four inches of block are stipulated; those units that lack legs and do not allow flames and gases to come near the appliance's base require the blocks and sheet metal. Finally, furnaces and boilers that have high temperatures attained in their base must use two layers of four-inch clay tiles plus a section of 3/16-inch-thick steel plate. The holes on the two layers must be perpendicular to one another.

When the NFPA recommendations regarding the distances that the shield must extend out from the stove are followed, it is generally easy to purchase a suitable UL-listed floor shield. (The UL has separate testing programs for wall and floor models.) The floor devices often possess a sheet-metal top and a ceramic or metal underpad. There are also metal pans that are filled with mortar that is then covered with ceramic tiles. This type of shield is quite pleasing visually.

Since many of the commercial models are not available in quite large dimensions, it may be necessary to prepare a homemade protector when the consumer wishes to follow the guidelines suggested by Shelton. A sheet-metal shop willing to work with asbestos can prepare a shield—for units with a vertical clearance of six to eighteen inches—that has millboard of the proper thickness topped by 24 gauge sheet metal that is rolled over on the edges to save feet and shoes from being cut, and to cover the asbestos. It may be possible to acquire a large sheet of ceramic fiberboard that is noncombustible; it can be substituted for the asbestos millboard.

For the same type of appliance, another protector can be created by having a metal shop construct a shallow pan of 24 gauge metal with sides at least one inch high. Pour in three-quarters of an inch of mortar. If you wish to have a shallow top of flat stones, set them in the wet mortar. When you want to employ ceramic tiles, allow the mortar to dry overnight. Then apply adhesive that is heat resistant to at least 1,200 degrees Fahrenheit, followed by the tiles. It is best to prepare such a heavy shield where it will be used, as it will be very difficult to move.

In *Wood Heat Safety,* Shelton outlines three simple floor pads for appliances with legs of at least six inches. All use a 24 gauge sheet-metal bottom and a frame constructed of two-by-four lumber. The first has four-inch-wide bricks (set on their sides), stone, or concrete, which is either "mortared, sanded, or just close-packed." The second contains two inches of small-size gravel, and the third possesses the same thickness of sand plus "a noncombustible overlay or cover." The last two function best when a pad comprised of an 8 × 8 × 4" block, or something similar, is set under each leg.

FURNACE DUCT CLEARANCES

As was discussed in Chapter 6, more space is required between combustibles and the ducts of a solid-fuel furnace than is needed with an oil-fired appliance. The latter's ducts are generally installed to allow two inches of clearance in the first six feet out from the plenum, and no clearance after that. With the ductwork of a wood or combination wood-oil furnace, the minimum is eighteen inches over the plenum and with the first three feet of duct (unless the unit has certification that allows reduction of the distance needed over the plenum), six inches in the next three feet, and one inch after that. (It is often impossible to suspend the ducts eighteen inches from combustibles. Table 6 shows how the clearances can be reduced.) The ducts that rise from the basement to circulate heated air throughout the upper levels of the house cannot begin to turn upward within six feet of the furnace. They must have 3/16-inch clearance on all sides, or consist of two walls that have this amount of space between them.

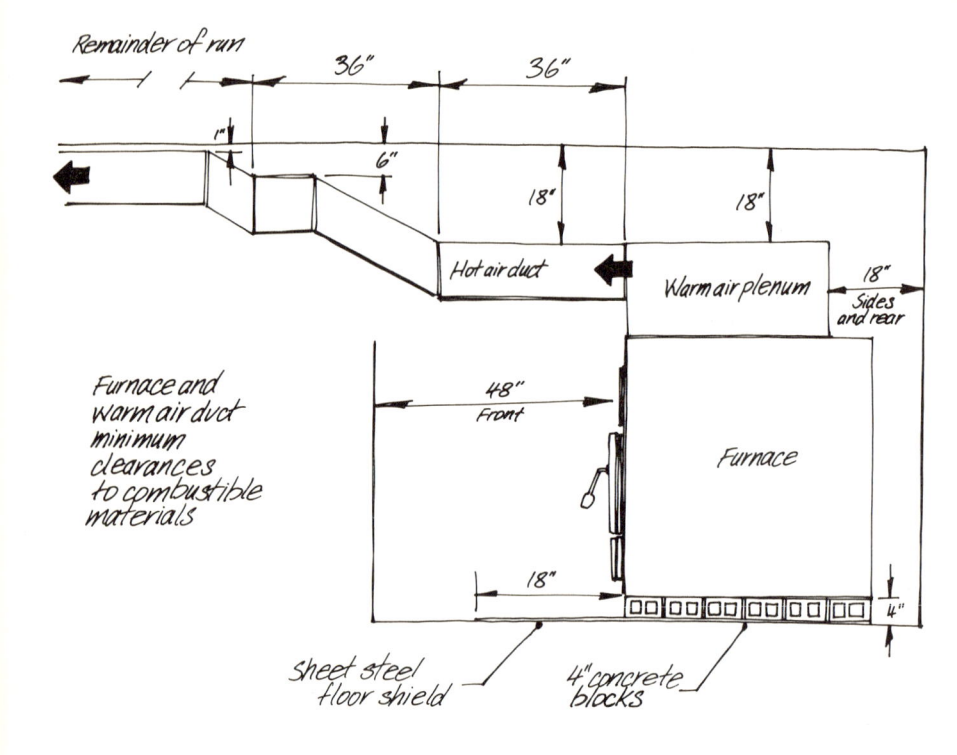

    Remember the previous recommendation that any furnace or boiler be installed by a professional. Be sure that he realizes that the ducts must be set as discussed. Also check that an add-on furnace is put in following the directions laid out in Chapter 6. Before the installer is paid, have the building inspector give the complete system a thorough perusal. Such a full examination should be carried out before any appliance is first fired.

Table 6
NFPA guidelines for reducing clearances from furnaces, boilers, heating ducts, and plenums

Minimum thickness of protective material needed (must extend outward as described in text).

Minimum clearances (in inches) from the surfaces of the appliance, plenum, or duct.

Without protection	top 18	sides & rear 18	top 6	sides & rear 6
1) ¼ in. asbestos millboard with 1 in. airspace.	15	9	3	2
2) 28 gauge sheet metal on ¼ in. asbestos millboard (no airspace).	12	9	3	2
3) 28 gauge sheet metal with 1 in. airspace.	9	6	2	2
4) 28 gauge sheet metal on ⅛ in. asbestos millboard and with 1 in. airspace.	9	6	2	2
5) ¼ in. asbestos millboard on 1 in. mineral wool batts reinforced with wire mesh or equivalent (no airspace).	6	6	2	2
6) 22 gauge sheet metal on 1 in. mineral wool batts reinforced with wire or equivalent (no airspace).	4	3	2	2
7) ¼ in. asbestos millboard (no airspace).	18	18	4	4
8) ¼ in. cellular asbestos (no airspace).	18	18	3	3

WOOD APPLIANCES AND HOME INSURANCE POLICIES

There is no clear-cut answer to the question, "How will a wood stove affect my insurance premiums?" The thousands of home insurance companies active in this country have diverse opinions on wood heat. A few do not insure any home containing a solid-fuel appliance; some invoke a higher premium, but many do not.

It is essential to phone or write your insurance agent when the installation is nearly complete. If the appliance is certified and a building permit has been obtained, most representatives will simply wish you luck and perhaps add that your premium will be increasing. (When the equipment you wish to buy is not listed, it is best to contact the agent before you complete the purchase.)

If your annual rate will be increasing between 10 and 25 percent, grin and bear it, realizing that it may well go higher if you don't do your part toward ensuring that Americans heat properly with wood. If the premiums will be escalating by 25 to 100 percent, start shopping around. This size of increase is not common.

Some agents will inform you that an inspector from the insurance company will be paying you a visit. This should not be cause for alarm as long as the instructions of this book, the manuals of the system's various components, and the building inspectors advice have been followed.

If the representative is not notified, there is a structural fire, and the wood heat system is determined to have been the cause, you may have a hard time collecting your claim and finding another company willing to insure you.

PART FIVE

Operation

13
Starting a Fire and Keeping It Going

With most appliances, it is best to build a fire in several stages. Begin with paper or wood shavings (not sawdust). The paper should be squeezed into fairly tight balls—use four or five pieces. Place them in the center of the firebox, a few inches back from the loading door. On top of the paper or shavings, set eight or ten slender sticks of kindling. Cedar is the best, as it is easy to split and ignites easily, but pine or another softwood will do. Be sure that whatever wood you employ has been seasoned for a minimum of eight months; a year is even better.

If the design of the firebox allows, place the sticks tepee-style, with the top ends criss-crossing and the bottoms spread out around the paper. If the firebox is too narrow to allow this, set the kindling parallel to the firebox's length and on top of the paper. The tepee method is best because the sticks will not fall off to the side when the paper is consumed, as they can if set flat on top.

There are some downdrafters that turn the pile over, having big logs on the bottom, followed by kindling and paper. Read the owner's manual and follow its firing instructions. The procedure described here is recommended by most manufacturers.

Once the kindling is prepared, open all drafts on the appliance fully and make sure that there are no combustible objects on or near the unit. Bizarre treasures can be unearthed if you have young children or pets.

Even the veteran woodburner has days when a fire simply won't catch, but do not rush or take shortcuts. Wait until everything has cooled and start over with new paper or shavings. The cause of your problem can be unseasoned kindling or damp paper. Another factor can be ashes that have risen until they have blocked the air intake, starving the fire. The ash-emptying chore can be delayed a few days by pushing the ashes away from the draft intake each time wood is added.

Some stove operators use flammable liquids to help get a stubborn fire under way. This is extremely dangerous as the inebriated woodburner, who mistook naphtha for the less volatile but still potent kerosene, can testify. He blew his cookstove's lids through the kitchen ceiling! Although you may consider using such substances when you cannot get a fire rolling, do not be tempted. Even the experienced person can have a serious explosion, and these flammable liquids are hard on the firebox liner and smokepipe, due to the intense temperatures they create. It is also risky to burn, within an enclosed firebox, garbage and artificial or newspaper logs. This is especially true with a catalytic-combuster equipped unit, as plastic or foil can ruin the device.

It is safe to use one of the solid, commercial fire-starters. These save kindling, simplify the starting process, and are available from most stove dealers and hardware stores.

When the small kindling is burning nicely, add more wood. If you have a good selection and quantity of fuel, use a few larger pieces of softwood for this second stage, and then employ small hardwood (if such species are found in your region). As the hardwood ignites, increasingly bigger pieces can be injected. However, it is important not to rush this final step. It can take as long as half an hour to establish the fire.

One major cause of creosote is a cold flue. When you add massive logs or restrict the inflow of air too soon, the chimney will not have warmed up sufficiently. Even more time than normal will be required if your chimney is located on the outside of the house, or if an interior flue has not been employed for several days. Besides encouraging the formation of creosote, a fire slowed down too quickly will release significant quantities of pollutants, and the fire may not be well enough established to last. It is a shock to come home after being away for a few hours and walk into a frigid home when you are expecting a cozy, warm one. A check of the firebox will usually reveal that the heavy pieces of wood are virtually intact.

When placing new fuel on coals remaining from an earlier charge of wood, follow the same procedure, opening the draft intake wide and leaving it there until the new blaze is set.

Heaters with a full Scandinavian baffle have a "front-end combustion design" that burns the logs from front to back. The coals must be pulled toward the firebox door before wood is added. Again, consult your owner's manual for the manufacturer's recommendations.

When coals are present, it is possible to go for days without using matches to ignite the wood. This is preferred, since valuable kindling is conserved and because the start-up phase employing paper and the kindling produces a substantial amount of pollution. Try to time recharging of the appliance so that coals are always present and, if possible, leave them behind whenever ashes are removed.

Although some manufacturers are mending their ways, far too many still advertise that their controlled-combustion stove is "convenient," retaining a fire for ten, twelve, or even more hours. The only way to obtain such burning times is to have the draft control nearly closed. Some labor may be saved, but generation of creosote and pollutants is almost guaranteed, and the efficiency of the appliance is greatly reduced.

Instead of having smoldering fires constantly, build quite hot blazes with a limited number of large chunks of wood. If your schedule allows, such charges should be made every two to four hours. The safest solution for woodburners who work all day and want to sleep through the night is to have small, hot fires whenever possible. Everyone burning wood should have such a blaze each morning, and there is no reason why the same procedure cannot be followed during evenings and week-ends. These fires not only use wood efficiently, but also burn out creosote that accumulates while the draft control is turned down. It will take a few weeks to learn the proper draft settings. Different strategies are needed for the small, hot fire that lasts three or four hours, and the slower blaze that will endure through the night. You will know that you are on the right track with the latter when a perusal of the firebox in the morning reveals a thin layer of glowing coals. You do not want to see only ashes that signify that the fire burned very quickly, or an immense heap of coals and remnants of the logs, showing that the air intake was too restricted. If you are a neophyte, you may want to install a thermometer that indicates whether the interior of the smokepipe is warm enough. There are two styles; one adheres to the pipe with a magnet, and the other has a probe that is inserted inside. Although the latter type is more difficult to install, it is far more accurate.

The stove owner must also learn to vary his firing procedures with the seasons. In midwinter, small charges of wood will be needed several times a day, but in spring or autumn this would overheat the home. Many operators use a great amount of wood and allow it to smolder, hoping to receive the small quantity of heat required. But this type of fire generates startling deposits of creosote. The safest spring and fall technique is to continue with compact fires, but to simply construct fewer each day. Having a hot blaze first thing in the morning should eliminate the overnight dampness and keep the house warm until the sun gets higher in the sky. A second fire, set after dark, can warm up the dwelling before bedtime. Obviously, the same procedure should be used during wintertime thaws.

The veteran woodburner learns that there are other ways to control the fire besides adjusting the inflow of air. These include the species of wood burned, the thickness of the pieces, and the quantity of wood loaded.

Neophytes sometimes get into trouble by overfilling an appliance and leaving the draft open too long. If the walls of the stove begin to glow red and the area around it becomes unbearably hot, shut the air intake almost completely and remain in the room until the rate of burning has slowed and temperatures have dissipated. Never charge a stove with a sizable quantity of wood, leave the draft ajar, and go to bed or leave the house. Until you are familiar with how your appliance performs, fire it only when you can be nearby.

If you are reading this in January or February and have been firing your stove for several months with the draft control nearly shut, do not begin to use small, intense fires without cleaning your wood-burning system from top to bottom. Otherwise, the first such blaze you build may be all that is needed to ignite the creosote deposits that have almost certainly formed within your smokepipe and chimney.

USING A COOKSTOVE

While most other kinds of appliances have only one or two air intake controls, the majority of cookstoves possess five or six drafts and dampers. Initially, it is common for the neophyte operator to be puzzled.

The three most important draft controls are usually located low on the end of the appliance that contains the firebox (this is the primary firebox draft); at the back of the cooking surface (this is usually a sliding cast-iron knob that controls a plate that sends smoke either around the oven or up the flue); and a smokepipe damper.

Other drafts are commonly found on the ashpan door under the firebox, in the upper portion of the end containing the firebox, and to the right of the bottom of the oven. This last device is used only if the stove possesses a water reservoir.

All drafts must be open to start a fire, except the reservoir lever. Within any cookstove is a system of shaker grates. These must be cleaned of ashes before a fire can be ignited. On most woodranges this is accomplished by using a special crank and turning the two or three rods found under the firebox.

Once the fire is established, the drafts can be manipulated in a number of ways, depending on the purpose of the blaze. If you wish to simply warm a damp house on a spring morning and then boil a pot of tea or coffee, place a few pieces of softwood in the firebox and leave the drafts open until your needs have been fulfilled. The fire can then be allowed to die.

Oven draft control

Check draft

Main firebox draft control

Smokepipe damper

Water reservoir draft control

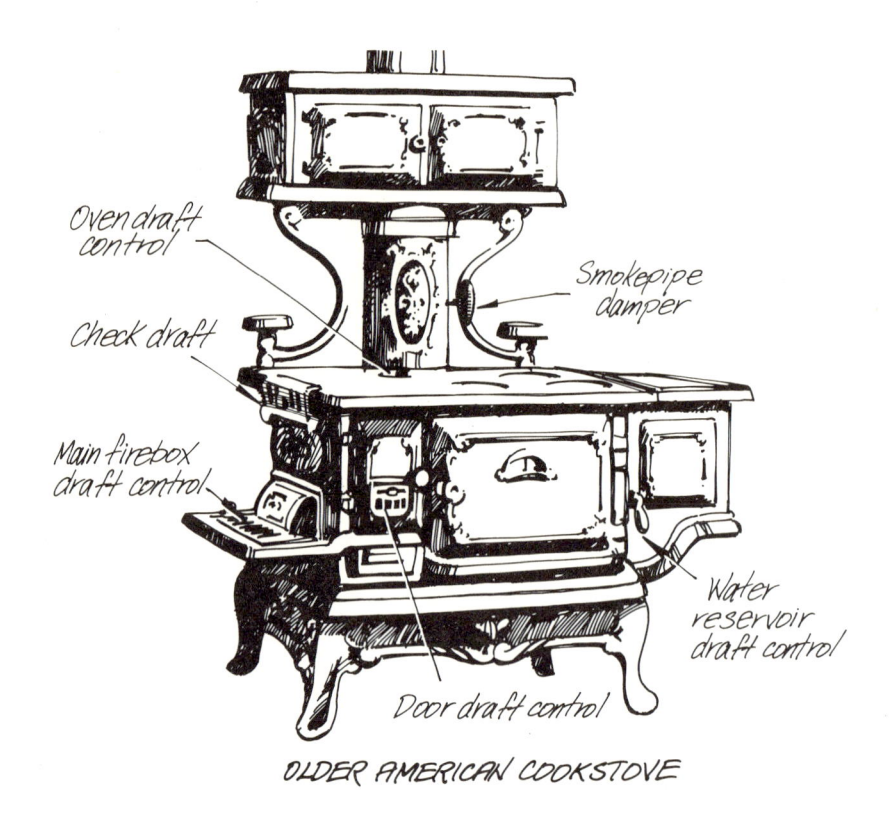

Door draft control

OLDER AMERICAN COOKSTOVE

    For baking and winter heating, move the oven draft toward the closed position (the right on most models) and use split hardwood so that the fire will endure. To increase the oven temperature, partially close the smokepipe damper. This action will warm up the body of the stove and the oven quickly. The oven can be brought to an even higher temperature, if your baking fire falters, by dropping in some softwood, opening the main firebox draft, keeping the oven draft nearly closed, and shutting the smokepipe damper even more. There is a limit to how far the smokepipe damper can be closed. When the stove begins to smoke, that level has been reached.
    For baking, it is best not to depend on the thermometer found on the outside of the oven door, if your appliance is an

older model. The thermometer is often the component of a cookstove that breaks down first, especially if the range has been moved several times. Use a portable model that can sit on the oven racks.

The hottest area of most cookstove ovens is the upper left corner, near the firebox. Since the heat distribution is not uniform, baking must be rotated. How often a pan should be turned depends on the oven temperature and the baking time. For the same reason, be careful where a portable thermometer is placed. The average temperature is probably found exactly in the center of the oven, away from both the top and the left side.

To distribute heat around the water reservoir, the lever beside the oven is usually placed in a horizontal position. Additionally, the oven draft must be at a closed setting.

Different temperatures on the cooking surface can be found by moving the pot or pan around. The hottest spot is generally over the back of the firebox. Water can be brought to a boil quickly by removing one of the lids or plates and setting the pot down into the hole so that its bottom comes in direct contact with the fire. Woodranges usually have one lid that is a trio of rings to hold three sizes of cooking pots. Before using a pot, rub soap on its bottom to facilitate removal of the soot that will adhere to it.

Once you have used a cookstove for a month or two, you will likely be able to make it obey your every wish. Older couples who have owned a cookstove for many years will be a great source of knowledge.

HUMIDITY

It is common for the interior of an older home to become very dry after a few days of wood burning. One way of curing this is to run an electric humidifier or vaporizer several hours a day. Keeping the air slightly damp is best for everyone's health and will prevent wooden furniture from splitting and the structural wood of the home from becoming tinder dry.

A few heaters have a built-in humidifier tray. This can be a useful accessory, curing the problem without the use of electricity. Another method is to keep a pot or kettle filled with water on top of the appliance. This works well but does have drawbacks. If the outside of the pot becomes wet, surface rust will form on the appliance and, if the stove is a toploader, the pot has to be removed each time the fire needs tending.

AIR CIRCULATION

The best wood appliance will be useless if the heat it generates cannot reach a portion of the space that needs to be heated. However, before buying electric blowers and installing cast-iron ducts, remember that an appliance will often do a better job of warming an area than may be expected. If possible, do not spend money or make permanent alterations until the stove has been used for a couple of weeks.

It does make sense to design a new home specifically for being warmed by wood. Steps that facilitate easy circulation of heat include limiting the number of interior partitions, building a first-class chimney as close to the center of the house as possible, and making the home compact rather than rambling. If such a dwelling is super-insulated, as all new homes should be, it will require a smaller appliance than older homes of the same dimensions.

In decades past it was often necessary to install ducts between the first and second floors, as a staircase was not sufficient for carrying heat to the poorly insulated upper level. Today, few homes will need such ducts as more insulation is used in attics. However, it may still be necessary to push heat to outlying rooms on the main floor.

Blowers within fireplaces and heaters can help, as can small electric fans designed for this purpose, which are easily affixed to door frames. A simple passive method (not requiring electricity) is to place a register in the wall between two rooms. But before such an alteration is made, talk with members of your local fire department. They may recommend against making certain renovations. A hole cut in the wrong location could enable a blaze to spread quickly.

Stuffy upper stories and cathedral ceilings that trap hot

air can be cured with a multispeed electric ceiling fan equipped with long wooden or metal blades. While it will prove uncomfortable and energy inefficient if done every day, simply opening a window can solve an overheating problem that occurs but a few times each winter.

14
Maintenance and Fire Safety

THE ANNUAL INSPECTION

In the days before controlled-combustion appliances came to the fore, it was traditional to clean the chimney and smokepipe twice annually—between heating seasons and once during the winter, preferably during a thaw. If a competent sweep lived nearby, it was common to have him handle these chores, since his services could be afforded when they were required infrequently.

Today some poorly operated wood heat systems require cleaning every two weeks or at least once a month. To hire a sweep this often is beyond the economic reach of most homeowners. However, having such a professional give close scrutiny to the complete wood heating system once each year is recommended.

Many experts suggest having this annual checkup early each autumn, but there are several reasons why the spring is a better time. Ashes left in a stove for several months can begin to corrode any metal they touch. Since the appliance should therefore be thoroughly cleaned before being mothballed for the summer, it makes sense to concurrently do a complete inspection. It is also best to have the stove worked on when you are aware of what parts are acting up and in need of attention.

When components do have to be replaced, it can take

several weeks to get them, especially if the unit is imported and parts you desire are out of stock in the United States. If you order in April or May, chances are that you will have what you need long before it is time to put the stove back in operation.

There are both ethical and dishonest sweeps. The recent surge in demand for this service has brought untrained and unscrupulous men and women into the marketplace. Search for a sweep who has liability insurance, certification from a chimney sweep school, and any required local licenses. He should be prepared to agree on a fee before the job is begun and provide references if they are requested. For further information on this and every facet of cleaning the entire wood heating system, *Be Your Own Chimney Sweep* by Christopher Curtis and Donald Post (Charlotte, Vt.: Garden Way Publishing Co., 1979) is highly recommended. If you clean your own chimney most of the year, watch the sweep closely; you should be able to pick up a great deal of useful information.

The sweep should tighten all of the appliance's bolts and check the condition of legs and moving parts such as hinges, door handles, draft mechanisms, and thermostats. The firebox liner should be inspected; when it is composed of firebrick, cracks and gouges need to be repaired with refractory cement. If it is cast iron, fissures and other signs of deterioration should be looked for. Respect the sweep's judgment; if he feels that something is not reparable and should be replaced, do so.

If the stove has a baffle, examine it carefully. If it can be removed, the area behind and above it should be cleaned, preferably with a stiff, steel-bristled, hand-held brush and a vacuum cleaner. The sweep should have an industrial-type vacuum; do not allow your residential model to be used for this.

Ashes should be removed and dry sand added if the quantity that should be present in the bottom of the firebox has become depleted. (The use of sand is recommended by many manufacturers.) With cookstoves, all cavities should be carefully cleaned. Whenever rust appears inside or out, it should be sanded down with steel wool or sandpaper, then wiped with an oil-dipped rag.

The asbestos or fiberglass gasket employed with a great

number of appliances should be inspected. If it is deteriorating, replace it. Have the sweep run his hand along its entire length; burrs or lumps should be sanded down by someone wearing a respirator. Have a look at your owner's manual before the sweep arrives. Other maintenance procedures may be suggested.

Electrical components such as blowers and any wires that show signs of being damaged by overheating must be replaced. Any wood or combination furnace should be serviced every year not by a sweep but by a licensed furnace mechanic.

Smearing the exterior of a stove with a light film of cooking oil is recommended except for painted or enameled surfaces, if the unit will be stored in a damp area. When the stove will be kept where it is directly exposed to the weather, cover it with a tarp or a sheet of polyethylene. Place a box of kitty litter under the stove to absorb condensation that forms under the tarp, and leave the unit's doors ajar. If the stove will remain installed, have a very small fire once a week to evaporate any moisture that forms. (This must not be done if the chimney top will be covered.)

Have all wall and floor shields examined. If any sections have come loose, refasten them in exactly the same location. Measure all distances between the stove, smokepipe, and furnace ducts and all shields and combustible surfaces, to ensure that nothing has shifted. If the stove is removed for the summer, do this adjusting once everything is set back in place during late summer or early fall.

While it is obvious that much of the stove inspection is simple and can in fact be handled by the stove owner, it is recommended to have a sweep do it at least after the first heating season. Having observed him, the operator should then be able to perform this portion of the annual checkup.

However, if the appliance is an open fireplace or an insert, the inspection is trickier. These contain their own chimney, which the sweep should examine after every heating season. Additionally, most fireplaces have a damper that makes cleaning the flue much more difficult, and the direct connection used with many inserts lends yet a further degree of complexity to the procedure. Instead of doing a haphazard job and perhaps damaging your back trying to shift a heavy insert, hire a professional.

THE SMOKEPIPE AND CHIMNEY

During the annual inspection, the sweep should move the entire smokepipe assembly outdoors, with paper or plastic bags taped to the ends so that soot and creosote cannot fall onto rugs or floors. If previous suggestions were followed, the smokepipe should be short enough that it does not have to be dismantled to facilitate carrying and cleaning, but if there are elbows or straight runs of more than a few feet, break it down at every second or third joint. Each pipe section should be thoroughly cleaned and then inspected both inside and out. Quality smokepipe is not expensive, so immediately replace any piece that is showing even the slightest evidence of wear. Once the pipes are clean, all screws must be tightened.

Before the inside of the chimney is tackled, a professional sweep will carefully inspect every portion of the exterior, giving special attention to the foundation or base, the cleanout, the strength of supports and bands used with metal models, and the condition of the stainless or galvanized steel, brick, stone, or block that comprises the exterior.

THE EQUIPMENT

A professional sweep carries a sizable arsenal of brushes and rods capable of handling almost any residential chimney. He understands, as must the homeowner buying his own equipment, how vital it is to match the brush carefully to the flue. Before a brush is purchased, the interior of the chimney should be carefully measured. The brush must fit tightly, being neither too wide, which will not allow the bristles to push against the chimney walls with the pressure needed to remove hard, stubborn creosote, nor too narrow, which is even more ineffective.

While some sweeps may resent the loss of business represented by the homeowner who buys his own equipment, the realistic professional will do everything he can to make sure that the homeowner buys the right gear. In fact, some sweeps sell brushes and rods.

Steel brushes are most commonly used. Square, rectangular, and round models are available with either round or flat bristles. The latter type tends to be more expensive. While many pro-

CHIMNEY-CLEANING EQUIPMENT

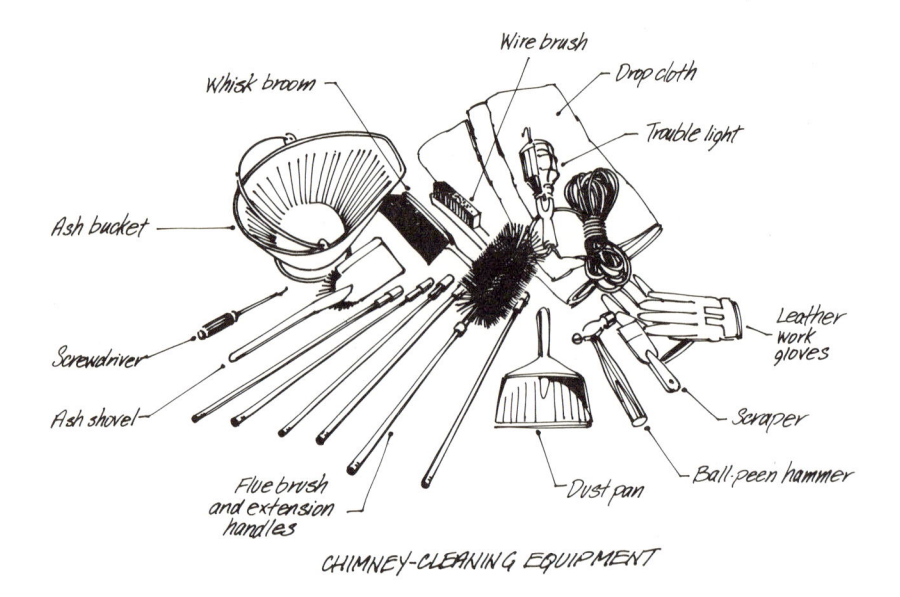

fessionals believe that nylon or bassine brushes are not as suitable, some metal chimney manufacturers stipulate their use. Always buy brushes from a sweep or wood stove dealer and insist on a brand that carries a guarantee.

For the rods, which allow the sweep to apply a great deal of pressure, *Be Your Own Chimney Sweep* recommends fiberglass models with a diameter of 0.35 inches and pipe thread fittings. The authors believe that three-foot rods are practical and suggest that ownership of the equipment be shared with a friend or neighbor. Since each stove owner will need the brushes for a maximum of perhaps a week annually, this makes a great deal of sense.

CLEANING THE FLUE

It is safer to clean a chimney from inside the house, but some flues are built in such a way that this is impossible. When working inside, tape a paper bag over the cleanout to prevent dust and soot from dirtying the home. Have only a narrow slit to accept the rod. It is also a good idea to lay down an old sheet or newspapers under where you will be working and walking. Soot can cause bad stains in rugs.

Cleaning from the top of the chimney will sometimes provide the sweep with a better view of what needs to be done, but it can also be treacherous. Never wear shoes with leather or worn soles; do not walk across a wet or snow-covered roof unless you are experienced at it; and check the strength, slickness, and steepness of any roof before putting your full weight on it. Use a safety belt and rope attached to a solid object if possible. You can tie a rope around most masonry chimneys, but steel stacks are not strong enough for this.

Do not take unnecessary risks. If you feel that the cleaning of your chimney is a task you cannot handle safely, hire a sweep each time it needs attention. If you find yourself having to pay him frequently, this may be the incentive you need to operate the system in an efficient manner that discourages creosote.

If the chimney has a cap and a spark arrester, both should be carefully cleaned with a hand-held steel brush, as a spark arrester clogged with creosote can restrict the exit of smoke. A professional sweep will use his time on the roof to perform other chores for the homeowner, checking roofing materials and the flashing around the chimney. For an extra fee, most will handle any patching that needs to be done.

The actual cleaning process is quite simple when the proper equipment is used. The brush and first rod are pushed either up or down the flue as the case may be. As this and subsequent rods disappear into the chimney, the next one is attached. It is on the downward stroke that most of the cleaning is done; the first trip should remove most of the creosote and soot, but it is best to brush downward once or twice more.

When the sweeping has been completed during the spring inspection, the interior should then be carefully scrutinized. (The problem areas that should be looked for were discussed in Chapter 11.) Once it has been determined by the sweep that the flue is healthy, a fine-mesh screen should be placed across the top of the flue if there is no spark arrester. This will keep birds, bats, and other creatures from using the chimney as their summer home. Be sure to remove this screen before autumn.

Some woodburners try to scrimp when cleaning the chimney by employing improper tools. Small fir trees, rugged chains dragged against the walls, sacks containing something heavy and bulky enough to fill the entire lateral dimensions of the chimney opening, and even live geese are used. The last one described is inhumane, and none is as efficient as a chimney brush. Additionally, a chain can do severe damage to both metal and masonry chimneys.

WHEN TO CLEAN

Examine the smokepipe and chimney *every week* as long as wood is burned regularly, and if the stove is fired occasionally, inspect the flue a minimum of once a month. When the creosote has accumulated to a depth of one-quarter inch on the walls of the flue, it is time to clean.

If you have installed a cleanout, checking the chimney's condition is easy. Simply remove the cleanout cup or open the door, on a sunny day, and peer upward. With chimneys that have thick walls or a small cleanout door, it may be necessary to use a mirror.

Clean the smokepipe whenever the chimney is being looked after. Except for the annual inspection, it is usually not necessary to dismantle the pipe sections completely and take them outside. While it will not work as well as a chimney brush, and is capable of damaging the pipe if swung too hard, a rubber hammer (used in auto-body shops) tapped softly against the outside of each section can remove any light, dry creosote. However, this procedure will not dislodge hard, glasslike deposits. Inspect the pipe after it has been cleaned and, if such stubborn creosote is still present, take the pipe down and use a chimney brush.

Sections of pipe that contain a damper, hot water coil, or another accessory will clog up with creosote quickly. They should be given special attention each time the pipes are cleaned.

As has been stated, it is normal to clean a system two or three times a year, and abnormal to do it once a month or even more frequently. Usual causes of excess creosote are green wood, too long a smokepipe system, an improperly operated appliance, a cold chimney, and too tight a home, which will result in a shortage of oxygen. A cure for the last problem is to install a duct that will bring in outside air.

The green, unseasoned lumber found within the walls of a brand-new home can be another source of moist air. This problem should clear up on its own after the first heating season.

If you delay cleaning a dirty chimney, the system will remind you that it needs attention. Smoke will pour out of the stove on occasion, and it will become difficult to get a hot fire burning. The tendency then is to build a bigger fire, but often this is all that is needed for the creosote to catch fire. The burning of garbage and excess paper can also ignite a creosoted chimney.

CHEMICAL CHIMNEY CLEANERS

Some stove operators try to avoid the hard work and expense of cleaning a chimney properly by using chemicals that are claimed, by their manufacturers and some wood heating professionals, to either remove creosote completely or facilitate the cleaning.

There is ongoing debate over the worth of these compounds. During 1980, Jay Shelton carried out a battery of tests at his New Mexico laboratory. Writing in the Canadian magazine *Harrowsmith*, he concluded,

> The (four) particular brands of chemical chimney cleaners we tested did not exhibit any substantial effectiveness in our tests. We used both oak and pine, seasoned wood and green wood, cool and hot fires, and normal and high doses. We looked for prevention of creosote buildup, the disappearance of creosote, the falling down of creosote flakes, and changes in the creosote's brushability. Although some of these phenomena were observed, they were equally as strong in the untreated systems as in the treated ones. Thus the effects were not attributable to the chemicals but rather to factors common to all the systems, such as temperature. Hot fires tend to dry and loosen many creosote deposits.

There are some chimney sweeps who do feel that the chemicals are worthwhile, making the creosote easier to brush away. But even such proponents agree that chemical chimney cleaners should never be solely depended on. Every chimney must be physically cleaned whenever it becomes at all dirty.

HANDLING THE ASHES

Handling of ashes should always be done with caution, not because of the ashes themselves, which are relatively harmless, but due to the likely presence of hot coals that can remain in the ashes for a few days or a week after the appliance has been in use. As stated earlier, it is best to leave the coals in the stove but, short of sifting the ashes, there is no way to set aside every glowing ember. The owner's manual will usually give some indication of how often the ashes will need to be emptied.

An ashpan-equipped appliance is more convenient because the ashes, which build up beneath the firebox, can be dealt with any time, even when a fire is burning. With stoves that allow the ashes to lay right in the firebox, the fire must die down before the ashes are accessible.

Never set the ashes in a cardboard box or even a metal container and then leave them in a room or shed. Do not dump them under a porch. Always use a sturdy steel pail with a tight-fitting lid, a small shovel, and thick gloves. Although the ashpan used with some units can itself be used to carry the ashes outdoors, it is safer to place the ashes in a metal pail right at the stove. An overflowing ashpan can spill coals or dirty ashes onto carpets or floors.

Establish an ashpile outdoors, well away from buildings, paths, and driveways, and make sure that the ashes are always dumped there. They can be used in the same way as lime to balance soil that has become too acidic, but it is best to mix them into a compost pile so that they are diluted. If ashes are dumped directly onto a garden, they should be plowed under to a depth of about eight inches. Some plants, such as blueberries, thrive in acidic soil, so don't sprinkle wood ashes nearby. Consult gardening books for further information.

For those who still use a privy, ashes are great for keeping the odor down. Dump in a cupful daily during hot weather. Be sure that only coal-less ashes are used, or your beloved outhouse could go up in flames. Many people carry a sack of dry ashes in their vehicle during the winter. There are few substances better for providing traction on icy surfaces. If you wish to safely store dry ashes, keep them in the metal container, which must be set outside on sand or stone where it cannot cause a fire.

Whenever the ashes are emptied, give the appliance, shields, and smokepipe a fast inspection. Tighten loose bolts, examine the shields, and check to see that the smokepipe is secure where it enters both the appliance and chimney.

CLEANING HOT WATER SYSTEMS

Any system that heats water within a wood-fired appliance will require periodic cleaning. The philosophy on how the system should be flushed is changing. The manual prepared for the Tarm boilers states: "Coils are cleaned with hydrochloric acid. It is a dangerous procedure that should only be attempted by a qualified and experienced person." However, the authors of *Be Your Own Chimney Sweep* explain that this approach has been made obsolete by a commercial product known as Nutek 500. They advise that it is not easy to acquire and suggest that an industrial boiler sales or service firm be contacted.

These authors describe how the homeowner can safely clean the hot water system himself:

> You will need a short piece of flexible tubing with a fitting that matches the upper connection of the coil, two buckets, and an end plug that matches the lower fitting of the coil (or water jacket). These fittings are outside the stove. When you have collected these things, begin by closing the valves that lead to and from the domestic water supply, then uncoupling the top fitting of the coil and attaching the section of flexible hose. Fill the hose with water, and put the end in a bucket of Nutek 500 solution. Raise the bucket high enough to set up a siphon and disconnect the lower coupling. You want the water to drain out of the coil and into the second bucket, sucking the Nutek 500 into the coil.

When the coil is filled with solution, seal the lower coupling with the end plug. Light a fire in the stove. The fire is necessary because the Nutek 500 does not act as a cleaning agent until heated. Maintain a fire just hot enough to boil the solution for four to six hours, remembering that expansion and boiling will push the nonacidic solution out of the upper coupling and back into the bucket. If you use plastic pipe or hose, beware of overheating the plastic. If the plastic goes too soft, wrap a cold wet towel around the hose and connection.

At the end of the boiling period, remove the plug from the lower fitting and drain the solution, replacing [it] with fresh water via the siphon technique. Heat this water to boiling and redrain, replacing it with fresh water. Continue flushing with cold water until you feel comfortable reconnecting the domestic water. (You are actually safe after the second flush.) Despite the biodegradable claim, take the used solution and dump it outside where it cannot contaminate open water.*

If you prefer not to do this yourself, ask your sweep if he will handle it. When the system is being used solely with the wood appliance and only during the traditional winter heating season, cleaning the pipes once yearly—during the spring inspection—will be sufficient. However, if solar or electrical components are employed to make the system usable year round, it should be cleaned every six months. If you believe that the flow of water is being impeded between cleanings, flush more often.

INITIAL PROBLEMS

It is not uncommon to have a few kinks to iron out when your wood heating system is first put into service. If your appliance is

---

* *Christopher Curtis and Donald Post*, Be Your Own Chimney Sweep (Charlotte, Vt.: Garden Way Publishing), p. 41.

not receiving enough combustion air, it will smoke. A primitive cure is to open an outside door slightly. More permanent solutions include removal of some weatherstripping near where the appliance is located. Loosen a section at a time until the smoking stops. You may also install a duct that routes air from the outdoors directly into the stove.

Smoking will also take place if the draft controls are shut too quickly or tightly. When smoking suddenly begins as you are adjusting the draft control, simply reopen it until the smoking ceases.

Even smoking that occurs when the loading door is opened can usually be eliminated or at least drastically reduced by opening all drafts or dampers a couple of minutes before you wish to service the fire. If you do not want the blaze to burn at full power, turn the draft controls down again once the new wood is well past the smoldering stage.

If smoke puffs out of the appliance on windy days, your flue may be too short. The easiest solution can be to install a special chimney cap designed to increase flue draft. A more difficult and costly approach is to lengthen the chimney. If you have a metal factory-built unit and wish to do this, remove the rain cap and add another section of chimney. If the height of the chimney above the roof goes beyond four feet because of this, braces will be required. It is obviously a major project to build a masonry stack higher. There is a much simpler solution if a tree is the cause; remove any branches that are obstructing the flow of air around the top of the flue.

If the appliance begins to smoke on a calm day, and this continues regardless of the weather, it is likely that the flue is becoming clogged with creosote.

If your smokepipe is larger than the diameter of the flue, you will have grave problems. This is why it is so important to take the chimney and flue collar measurements into consideration before the system is purchased and installed.

If you have two flues within the same chimney and smoking is occurring, the easiest and most visually pleasing solution is to place a rain cap over both flues, with a partition between them. A second is to make one flue several inches higher than the other.

If you cannot solve the problem on your own, bring in a chimney sweep or contractor who has experience with "smokers." If he makes sizable changes to the system, have it reinspected by the official who originally examined it.

CHIMNEY FIRES

If you are awake when a fire begins in the smokepipe or lower chimney, you may realize immediately what is happening, whether or not you have experienced the situation before. A rumbling sound will come from the chimney and the smokepipe will begin to crackle and perhaps turn red. Sometimes a blaze can begin in the upper part of the chimney and be well under way before anything is heard. A clue will be the odor of burning tar from the liquid tars found in creosote.

Commercial chimney fire alarms are available that can act as an early warning system should a fire start during the night. Be sure that the model you are considering is adjustable, and that it can be set as high as 1,200 degrees. Those that sound at 600 degrees can be counterproductive, as they scare the stove operator into running the appliance at too low a temperature.

If a chimney fire has started, roust everyone out of the house and call the fire department. If you need immediate assistance, telephone a neighbor. If it is safe to go near the appliance, close all drafts and dampers. When there is less oxygen to feed it, the chimney blaze's ferocity will diminish. If you have two appliances on the same flue, close the draft controls of both. Also keep all doors and windows closed.

Attempt to extinguish or at least decelerate the fire in the appliance. Shutting all drafts will have helped. If it is possible, reach in quickly with a poker and knock the logs apart, but remember that when you have the firebox door open you are feeding the chimney fire. Never dump water on the stove or into the firebox, smokepipe, or chimney. It will have little effect on the blaze but can cause these components to warp. The best solution for quelling the appliance fire and concurrently attacking the chimney blaze is to throw in a quantity of baking soda (which should be kept nearby) or use a commercial chimney fire extinguisher. Never throw in salt, which can cause severe corrosion and, even more serious, emit chlorine gas when heated.

If you have installed the entire system correctly, with safe clearances from all combustible materials, a short run of smokepipe equipped with screws and stove cement, and a proper chimney, you should be able to make it through a chimney fire with little worry, but, it is hoped, having learned a lesson. If you haven't done things properly, you may not be so lucky.

Keep an eye on surfaces close to the appliance, smokepipe, and chimney, and if any begin to smoke, apply wet towels. If you do not have a spark arrester on your chimney, have someone watch the roof, especially if it is made of cedar shakes. Sparks and flames will be shooting into the air and it may be necessary to wet the roof down.

Have enough hose that you can at least make an attempt to contain the fire, should it spread before the fire department arrives. As the power in your home should be turned off if a fire becomes serious, wire the water pump on a separate circuit, if you possess your own water system.

Above all else, it is essential not to panic. You can hurt yourself by doing something foolish such as grabbing red-hot smokepipe or stumbling around on an icy roof. Stay calm and proceed at a steady, unexcited pace. When the fire is extinguished, inspect the entire system for damage and check all combustibles close by to ensure that nothing is smoldering. Clean out any remaining soot and creosote before the appliance is again used.

FIRE SAFETY

Coping with a fire is much easier if the emergency departure from a home has been prepared for. Drills should be held regularly so that every member of the family knows what to do and where to exit if a fire breaks out. If your home has two or more stories, be sure that each family member has an alternative route down from upper-level rooms in case a stairway is blocked. Decide on one spot well away from the building where everyone will rendezvous. A landmark such as a big tree is easy for small children to remember. Make sure that everyone understands it is essential to remain there and not try to reenter the home.

If you have young children, an older person should stay with them at all times.

If smoke becomes thick before you are able to escape, crawl along the floor, since smoke rises. A wet towel or shirt held over the mouth makes breathing easier. Do not open any interior door if the handle is hot, as the fire is likely to be right behind it.

Anyone living in a remote location should store blankets, a spare set of vehicle keys, flashlights, a first-aid kit, plus clothes and shoes for each family member, in a barn or garage far removed from the house, so that they will have essential supplies if they must leave the house while wearing only nightclothes. It is also wise to post emergency phone numbers and directions on how to reach the home from the nearest fire station next to every phone. You can panic when a fire breaks out, and if a babysitter or guest who is unfamiliar with nearby streets and roads is the only adult there, such instructions become even more essential. Have the local fire prevention officer inspect your home at least once a year. Take notes and follow through on any suggestions made.

VISITORS

Wood appliances are fascinating to urban residents who consider them a rustic novelty. Once you install a stove, you will find that most visitors not familiar with wood heating will be instantly instilled with a pioneering fervor. Such interest is welcome, but it can be dangerous. When visitors offer or even demand to help, be sure they cannot do themselves or your appliance and home any harm.

Their assistance will be greatly appreciated when wood has to be hauled or stacked, a chimney cleaned, or an appliance moved. One chore that almost always attracts the newcomer is wood splitting. Spur the person on, but show him how to perform the task properly and safely. Lend him gloves, shin pads, and safety boots if he hasn't brought his own.

Be hesitant about allowing a neophyte to tend your stove. If you are hiring a babysitter for the evening, service the appliance before leaving and instruct the person not to touch the appliance unless it becomes too hot and the draft control needs to be turned down. It is even safer to let the stove go out and use auxiliary heating if the home is so equipped.

SMOKE DETECTORS AND FIRE EXTINGUISHERS

Most wood heat appliances will smoke at least occasionally. If you have a sensitive smoke detector located very near the stove, the frequent buzzing will become a nuisance.

It is possible, however, and recommended to use smoke detectors within wood heated homes. There are two basic kinds—photoelectric and ionization. The former style can be hung in the same room as the appliance, but only if it is several feet away. The recommended locations are near stairways and in halls adjacent to sleeping areas.

The better detectors have a loud alarm, come with a warranty, and possess a system that allows you to instantly check if the device is working. Buy a model that is UL certified; they are available in many retail outlets including hardware, department, and safety equipment stores.

It is also a good idea to have at least one UL-listed chemical fire extinguisher handy to each appliance. It should be mounted on a wall, to the side of the stove farthest from an exit, in case anyone becomes trapped by a fire. Inspect the extinguisher's pressure gauge periodically to ensure that it is in working order.

THIS CHAPTER HAS BEEN INCLUDED not to scare, but simply to warn about the dangers that can ensue if a wood system is not installed, operated, and maintained correctly. Burning wood is not usually a game of chance—most people encounter disaster because they are flirting with it.

PART SIX

Fuel

15

Bringing in the Wood

When a wood stove is installed, trees suddenly take on new importance. Until then, most people take them for granted, having a hard time identifying even the predominant species found around their home.

The two general categories of trees are the hardwoods (deciduous) and softwoods (coniferous). Hardwoods are most readily identified by their broad leaves shed each autumn, softwoods by their needles that generally remain year round. It is the hardwoods such as the oaks, ashes, beech, maple, and hickory, that are the finest American fuel woods. This is mainly due to their high density, or specific gravity, and the lack of pitch and gum, both of which are present in softwoods. Table 7 shows how the density of trees affects the amount of heat they are capable of delivering.

Stove owners who live where there are bountiful supplies of hardwood use softwoods such as cedar, pine, balsam, and spruce mostly as kindling, but in some areas people have no choice but to employ softwoods as their primary fuel. The loose composition and lightness of these woods do suit them, when seasoned, to starting fires. On a pound-for-pound basis, they burn hotter than hardwoods, but much more rapidly.

Thus, hardwoods are preferred, but the local situation will govern what is available. Find out what species are best in your specific area by asking your wood appliance dealer, other woodburners, or the nearest office of your state's forestry department. There are a number of ways of obtaining fuel wood. The cardinal rules to remember are: The more labor you do personally and the closer you go to the forest, the cheaper the wood will be. Only the wealthiest woodburners will be able to heat their

Table 7
Density of trees and heat produced

Species	Relative density	BTUs per air-dry cord
Hardwoods		
Shagbark hickory	.72	32,800,000
Black locust	.69	31,400,000
White oak	.68	31,000,000
Bitternut hickory	.66	30,000,000
Chestnut oak	.66	30,000,000
American beech	.64	29,100,000
Laurel oak	.63	28,700,000
Northern red oak	.63	28,700,000
Rock elm	.63	28,700,000
Sugar maple	.63	28,700,000
Yellow birch	.62	28,200,000
White ash	.60	27,300,000
Southern red oak	.59	26,900,000
Black walnut	.55	25,000,000
Oregon ash	.55	25,000,000
White birch	.55	25,000,000
Black tupelo	.50	22,800,000
Southern magnolia	.50	22,800,000
Water tupelo	.50	22,800,000
American sycamore	.49	22,300,000
Silver maple	.47	21,400,000
Sassafras	.46	21,000,000
Yellow poplar	.42	19,000,000
Red alder	.41	18,600,000
Eastern cottonwood	.40	18,200,000
Black willow	.39	17,800,000
Quaking aspen	.38	17,300,000

Table 7 (continued)

Species	Relative density	BTUs per air-dry cord
Softwoods		
Tamarack	.53	24,100,000
Western larch	.52	23,700,000
Douglas fir (coastal)	.48	21,900,000
Bald cypress	.46	21,000,000
Red pine	.46	21,000,000
Mountain hemlock	.45	20,500,000
Western hemlock	.45	20,500,000
Alaska cedar	.44	20,000,000
Pacific silver fir	.43	19,600,000
Lodgepole pine	.41	18,600,000
Eastern hemlock	.40	18,200,000
Ponderosa pine	.40	18,200,000
Sitka spruce	.40	18,200,000
White spruce	.40	18,200,000
California red fir	.38	17,300,000
Western white pine	.38	17,300,000
Balsam fir	.36	16,400,000
Eastern white pine	.35	16,000,000
Subalpine fir	.32	14,600,000
Western red cedar	.32	14,600,000
Northern white cedar	.31	14,100,000

The theoretical heat production of any species can be calculated by multiplying the density by three figures. These are: 62.3, which converts grams per cubic centimeter into pounds per cubic foot; 85, which is the number of cubic feet of solid wood often found in the average cord (80 and 90 can also be employed); and 8,600, which is the average number of BTUs in a pound of oven-dry wood. (Obviously, the heat potential will be 10 to 25 percent less with unseasoned wood.)

The densities used in the above chart are listed in the Woodburners Encyclopedia, *written by Jay Shelton. He in turn found them in the* Wood Handbook, *published by the Forest Products Laboratory, and the* Agricultural Handbook #72, *published by the U.S. Department of Agriculture.*

homes all winter with split wood delivered by a dealer. Most stove owners will have to combine hard work, ingenuity, and foresight.

BUYING YOUR OWN WOODLOT

The person looking the farthest down the road, who wants a lifetime guarantee of energy independence, will consider buying his own woodlot.

There are obvious pros and cons to this approach. Many will believe it is much cheaper to buy wood each year than to fork out several thousand dollars for property. In a strictly monetary sense, they are correct. Buying a woodlot only to allow the free cutting of fuel wood annually is not cost effective. However, the person who is thinking of acquiring a country retreat, who would like a place to escape to, and enjoys challenging physical work will do well to buy property with a sizable forest containing the species of trees suited to use as fuel wood. It is not necessary to have a square mile of woods—the right five to ten acres can keep a family in fuel forever.

The ideal forest for the woodburner is one that is high and dry, with access roads already in place. The more remote the property, the cheaper the asking price will be, but if it is terrain favored by mountain goats, you will need expensive equipment or workhorses to draw out your wood. If you do want to buy a small tract specifically as a woodlot, look for something in close proximity to either your home or retreat. The expense of gathering your own fuel will escalate rapidly if you are spending a fortune in gasoline making long trips solely to haul wood.

It is not essential to begin with a parklike woodlot full of majestic, mature, straight trees. In fact, such woodlots will likely be far beyond the economic reach of most consumers, as they contain extremely valuable marketable timber needed for lumber, furniture, and countless other wood products. Additionally, burning such wood as fuel, when first-rate timber is becoming scarce, is a waste of an important natural resource.

Unless you have the finances and ambition to become a timber baron, be content with a second-, third-, or even fourth-growth bush, one that has already been logged. These may not be as picturesque as mature forests, but they will be affordable as well as possessing a huge quantity of potential fuel wood. This is not to say that you should purchase something containing only low-grade trees; the wise person will look for a tract with enough marketable timber that he can eventually recoup at least a portion of his investment.

Once you have located a few properties that are accessible, close to home, and in your price range, start comparing them. If you intend to use the land for recreation purposes, aesthetics should be a concern. Is it scenic, with a few lookouts and perhaps a small stream? If you have any plans to live there eventually, find out if the road is serviced in the winter, how close schools, stores, and hospitals are, and whether electricity and a telephone can be easily and inexpensively obtained.

In assessing the woodlot itself, determine whether the forest is even- or uneven-aged. An even forest is one where nearly all trees are of similar height and diameter. They have grown up following a fire, where there was once a field, or where clearcutting—a logging technique by which all usable trees are harvested simultaneously—was employed. The uneven-aged bush is one that has been a woodlot for an extended period of time. Here are found saplings, maturing and prime trees, and dying or dead ones.

The uneven-aged bush is a much better investment for the family making a long-term purchase, as trees will always be available for cutting each year, as long as the forest is properly maintained. With an even-aged bush it tends to be feast or famine—a great many trees become mature all at once, and it will then be a long time before sizable trees grow.

Once a woodlot is acquired, it is best to plan its future carefully. If the road system to and within the bush is poor, improvements should be made. An inventory should be prepared that lists the quantity, location, size, health, and species of the trees. Making a map and color-coding it to show where the various types of trees are situated can be very helpful.

Seek professional assistance with this project. The forestry department of most states will offer the services of experienced woodlot appraisers either at no charge or for a small fee. In the New England states, assistance with the costs involved in building roads is also available. Private foresters who specialize in helping landowners develop woodlots are also active in many regions.

In the even-aged forest, the trees that should be kept for timber production are obviously the straighter and stronger specimens. Fuel wood will come from the diseased, crooked, stunted, overmature, and damaged trees. These should not be removed all at once, as the remaining trees may be exposed to too much sunlight and wind, causing sunscald, unwanted sprouting, and windfall. It is also best to spread out this weeding process so that fuel wood is available over several years.

With the uneven-aged forest, the initial clearing is a little more difficult, because all the healthy trees are not the same size; some will be perhaps two inches across, while others can have a diameter of two or three feet. The state forester can be of great assistance in helping decide which trees should stay, which are suitable for fuel wood, and which are ready to be sold commercially. Take a day before you intend to fell trees and select in a slow, deliberate manner; this is an important chore that should not be rushed. Once you start wielding a chain saw, the adrenalin rushes and you can find yourself making rash, later-regretted decisions. A tree can be cut down in a few minutes, but it may need a lifetime to be replaced.

The woodlot owner who is interested in eventually cutting sawlogs should allow the selected crop trees to grow relatively close together. Such trees provide the long straight timber desired in hardwood species for veneer, railway ties, and furniture making and, in softwood, for lumber. The tops or crowns should intertwine. This is recommended because the trees must fight for light and, as a result, they develop long clean boles free of branches.

Once the initial cleaning out is done, the trees can be left alone for a few years. When the crowns become too interwoven, it is time to return and cut more trees to give those that remain the exposure to sunlight that they require.

The sugar maple, for making maple syrup, requires a great deal of sunlight. The trees must be a fair distance apart.

If the number of marketable trees ready for harvesting

each year is small, the owner will find it profitable to cut the trees himself and sell them to a mill. Logging operators will gladly enter a bush if a sizable quantity of mature, high-grade trees are to be found there.

This process, although profitable, can do serious damage to a woodlot if poor techniques are used. Overcutting can turn a healthy uneven-aged forest into a devastated disaster zone, housing only scarred saplings and seedlings. Mechanical skidders can cause erosion and other ecological damage. A great quantity of treetops, brush, and poor quality logs will be left on the forest floor; these will have to be used within two or three years. For that period there will be a surplus of fuel wood, then supplies will be meager during the years it will take for the woodlot to replenish itself.

If you do have a good number of trees to sell, try to find a logger who works with horses rather than a skidder. Hire a forester to help you and the logger select the trees to be harvested; allow only mature specimens to be cut. Before the logger and his crew move into the bush, sign a contract with him that stipulates that only marked trees can be cut, that only horses will be used, that the slash and treetops will be cut into small pieces, and that the logger will be fined for every infraction. Some loggers will not accept such a contract; these are the characters you don't want in your bush. If you cannot visit the forest once or twice a week while the logging operation is under way, have someone who lives nearby act as your watchdog.

Owning a woodlot is obviously not for everyone: The acquisition can be costly; you will likely have to buy equipment and spend many hours of hard, dangerous work to put most forests in shape. However, a woodlot will also provide the independence and satisfaction that no other method of garnering fuel wood can match.

GOVERNMENT FUEL WOOD PROGRAMS

In response to an ever-increasing demand for fuel wood, many states and the federal government have established programs to supply low-cost wood from publicly owned lands.

Since the details of these programs vary from state to state and region to region, it is best to consult the nearest office of your state forestry department or the U.S. Forest Service.

The cost of the fuel wood will probably be low, but expect limits on the number of permits given and on how many cords can be obtained. Additionally, because successful applicants are usually required to fell marked, standing trees themselves, or pick up eight-foot-long logs from a rural depot, a chain saw and truck or trailer will likely be needed.

BUYING FROM A LOGGER

Anyone who lives within fifty or sixty miles of logging operations and has the space to temporarily accommodate a towering pile of timber can purchase the same fuel wood used by many dealers—cull logs. These are crooked, oversized, and rotten-in-the-center sawlogs cut by a logger and judged unsalable as commercial timber. Rather than leave them to rot, as was formerly the case, many loggers now deliver truckloads to woodburners. (Since some loggers do not own this waste wood, it is a good idea to check with the property owner after a cutting operation is complete.)

If you live in a densely populated neighborhood, nearby residents may resent the mammoth heap of logs and the substantial amount of chain sawing that will ensue. Also, expect your lawn to be badly damaged if that is where the logs must be dumped. Do not plan to burn such wood soon after it arrives. Any logger who has a thriving market for cull logs will be selling them, totally unseasoned, only a few days after they are felled.

Whatever the drawbacks, buying a truckload of cull logs—eight or more full cords of wood—can be a real bargain. It is the cheapest way to have unprepared wood delivered right to your door.

The timber industry can also supply slabwood, the thin pieces with bark on one side that are cut from a log before it is sawed into lumber. Slabwood used to be free for the taking, but expanding chip and fuel wood markets have curtailed this practice. It is dangerous to burn large heaps of slabwood in a heater, since they can reach a high temperature. But softwood pieces, when seasoned and split, make excellent kindling. Both softwood and hardwood chunks work well within the small firebox of a cookstove.

SCROUNGING WOOD

If you have a truck or sturdy trailer, you can sometimes find free fuel wood in or close to a city. Some people burn wooden freight pallets, which are often given away when damaged. However, these too should be used only in small quantities. Large branches are trimmed and entire trees cut down by highway, power company, and telephone crews, land developers, and tree surgeons. If you see logs lying by a public road or in a bulldozed area, find out who the owner is and ask permission to remove them. Taking wood without someone's approval is no longer being looked on lightly by police departments and property owners, as tree rustling has become a serious problem.

Another procedure is to telephone likely government departments and private firms and ask what they do with their wood. Chances are that employees take it home for their wood appliances, but you may get lucky.

Some regions have been badly hit by the Dutch elm disease and other ravaging pestilences. Scores of dead trees line many roads. A municipality may give you permission to cut trees that lie on its road allowances. If you notice such trees on private property, approach the landowner; he may be glad to have such trees cut.

There are surprising amounts of free wood available. To obtain such caches requires a truck or trailer and speed. When you notice a new pile, act quickly, as chances are that you are not the only person after it.

BUYING FROM A DEALER

While fuel wood purchased from a dealer strikes a mighty blow to hopes of heating for less money than is required to operate an oil, gas, or electric system, some people have no choice but to buy at least a portion of their winter's wood from a dealer.

If you break a leg and lack friendly neighbors who will rally around, the dealer can be a lifesaver if you depend on wood to heat your home. If you misjudge the number of cords needed during your first winter with a wood stove, move to a new locale as the snow begins to fly, or need only a few armloads annually for a fireplace, even the high prices posted by most fuel wood dealers will look reasonable.

However, as with every facet of wood heating, there are ethical sellers of fuel and those who ought not to be trusted. If you can recognize the various tree species and can tell seasoned wood from that cut yesterday, it should be safe to acquire wood from an itinerant dealer at a farmer's market or suburban shopping center parking lot. However, if you lack such expertise, deal with a major seller listed in the Yellow Pages of your phone directory. (Check out even these firms with your local Better Business Bureau or consumer protection agency.)

Buying an illustrated tree guide is one way of learning how to distinguish the bark patterns of the various species. Spending time in the woods with a forester or veteran woodburner is another. Carry wood for a friend or neighbor until you can tell the difference in weight between green and fully dried chunks of the species. Examining the ends of logs is another method. Seasoned wood will be gray rather than white and will have cracks or checks. However, the weight technique remains the most foolproof.

Remember that a full cord measures eight feet long by four feet wide and four feet high. It should be stacked that way, not in a heap. Also check how tightly the pieces are piled, as a disreputable dealer will work in a great number of substantial air spaces.

As stated earlier, wood is cheaper the closer you go to the source. You will reduce the cost substantially if you drive out of the city and buy in a small town or rural area. You must of course include the cost of gasoline. Country sellers often advertise in city and suburban newspapers and post notices in grocery stores and laundromats.

Finally, if you must buy wood from a retailer, you can lower the price by splitting the "rounds" yourself and by purchasing the largest quantity of fuel wood you can store. (Wood is split not only to allow it to fit into those appliances with small loading doors but also to accelerate the seasoning process.)

When a stove owner uses wood cut from his own property or obtained inexpensively through a government program, there is no doubt that wood fuel is much less expensive than natural gas, oil, or electricity. However, when wood is bought from a dealer, this is often no longer the case.

Knowing how to compare the prices of wood and conventional fuels can be a great help to the person for whom the switch to wood is purely economic. Lewis T. Hendrick, a Minnesota forester, described a very simple method in *Wood'n Energy* magazine. His formula depends on knowing the unit cost of the conventional fuel—the price per thousand cubic feet of gas, gallon of oil, and kilowatt hour of electricity. This figure, which can be easily obtained from your conventional-fuel supplier, is then multiplied by the quantity of the fuel needed to generate one million BTUs of energy (1,430 cubic feet of gas, 10.9 gallons of heating oil, and 293 kilowatt hours of electricity) to determine the cost per million BTUs of the conventional fuel.

Then turn to Table 7 (page 184) and calculate how many million BTUs of energy can be had from a cord of the wood you will be burning. Multiply this figure by the cost per million BTUs of the conventional fuel you would otherwise be using to find how much a cord would cost if it were priced at the same level as the conventional fuel. For wood burning to be cost effective the cord must cost less than the amount arrived at.

Say, for example, you could buy heating oil for $1.25 per gallon, but you intend to buy a cord of white birch to heat your home. According to Table 7, a cord of white birch will deliver 25 million BTUs; at $1.25 a gallon, a million BTUs from heating oil would cost $13.62 ($1.25 × 10.9); 25 million BTUs would cost $340.50 (25 × $13.62). So the cord should cost less than $340 (in most parts of the country wood still costs much less than this) for it to be economically feasible to heat with the wood.

16

The Harvest

If you are sufficiently committed to wood heating to purchase a high quality appliance, chances are that you will eventually begin collecting as much of your own wood as possible. Otherwise, you will not be able to afford to fire the stove regularly unless you are wealthy.

Gathering your own fuel, even if it means cutting up heavy branches that fall onto a neighbor's lawn during a storm, involves coming into contact with the tools of the trade—axes and chain saws. Working with trees and logs is a dangerous task. From the outset, it is essential to treat the woods and your equipment with the utmost respect.

Harvesting wood becomes safer and easier as you gain experience. After you have cut down many trees, you will learn what *should* happen. But differences in the grain and health of the tree, the terrain, composition of the surrounding bush, and the weather make the felling of trees an ever-changing event.

If possible, begin by working with a veteran woodcutter. Go out in the bush with this person. Observe, help, and ask questions. Have him explain why a tree is being knocked down in a specific direction. Learn to be aware of the little things that tell an old-timer where a tree should fall. Then start your own felling career with small-diameter trees. Once you have perfected the three most important cuts, you can safely approach a stately large-diameter specimen with confidence.

Never overwork yourself, especially if you are not accustomed to hard physical labor. Professionals in industries such as mining, construction, and logging know that fatigue can cause serious errors. Put in a good day, but don't overdo it. If you are not in the best of shape, don't be embarrassed; pace yourself and increase the length of your workday gradually.

WHEN TO HARVEST

An argument could easily be sparked among a gathering of woodburners by asking them to agree on the best time of year for cutting fuel wood.

Some would contend it is best done in late winter when snow levels in the bush are decreasing and the days are often sunny and relatively warm. Wood burns best when seasoned for twelve months, so winter cutting allows the wood plenty of time to rid itself of moisture. (It is not recommended to cut wood during the winter for use days later; burning such very green wood is dangerous.)

A drawback to winter cutting is transportation. Even as spring approaches, you may need snowshoes to get around in the forest. Unless you have access to a team of horses or a tractor with tire chains, hauling wood out of the bush while snow remains will be difficult.

One solution is to cut and split the wood in winter, stack it in a clearing to allow seasoning to begin, and transport it later when the snow has melted and roads are firm. This method results in more pieces of wood to transport but, as it dries, the wood loses weight and thus becomes easier to move. Also, newly cut wood splits best in winter, as both the cold and wetness of the wood make it simpler to knock apart. It is important that the wood be stacked where it will be exposed to direct sunlight.

If you do cut in winter and return in spring or summer to pick up the wood, take your chain saw along. You may find that you can harvest a foot or two of prime trunkwood that was buried beneath the snow when the trees were originally cut down.

It is not a good idea to leave your stacked piles of split wood in the bush for an extended period of time if there is a possibility of people helping themselves to the fruit of your hard labor.

Cutting in the summer and autumn is made easier by the

absence of snow and soggy roads. Drawbacks to cutting in high summer are the heat, which can be very hard on you and the saw, and the countless species of bugs that inhabit the woods. Autumn is a good time, especially if you are a year ahead with your fuel supply.

HOW MUCH WOOD TO CUT

If a home was previously warmed by a conventional fuel, a quite accurate figure can be arrived at, using the second part of the Hendrick formula outlined in *Wood 'n Energy*.

Begin by computing the actual number of BTUs burned the previous winter. (If that winter was milder than usual, pick one that more accurately reflects the amount of heat that will likely be required.) This calculation is arrived at in two steps: First, multiply the total number of units consumed (available from the fuel supplier or by adding up figures on invoices) by the numbers of BTUs theoretically available from each unit (.7 million per each 1,000 cubic feet of gas, 91,700 per gallon of oil, and 3,413 per kilowatt hour of electricity).

Next, use Table 7 (page 184) to find the theoretical quantity of BTUs available in a cord of the one species you will be primarily burning. Multiply it by the efficiency of the wood apliance. (Hendrick uses 55 percent, so the number of BTUs available from the cord would be multiplied by 0.55.)

Divide this answer into the number of BTUs delivered by the conventional fuel-fired appliance and you will know how many cords will be required to replace the conventional fuel. It is always best to prepare at least two extra full cords each winter in case the weather is worse than usual or you end up with more poor quality wood than you expected.

If your home is brand new or previous heating records are not available, consult your wood heat appliance dealer or neighbors who heat with wood. They should be able to give you an accurate estimate.

PROPER CLOTHING AND EQUIPMENT

The right clothes and safety gear make bush work more comfortable and, most important, much less risky.

Safety Boots

Safety shoes or boots with steel toes and nonskid soles in good condition are essential. Worn soles can cause a saw operator to slip at a crucial moment. Steel toe protectors can save a foot from being crushed by a falling log or from being cut by a whirring chain-saw blade.

For spring, summer, and fall, all-leather work boots are ideal. In winter, leather-upper, rubber-bottom boots with felt liners are inexpensive and warm.

Pants

Wear long pants even on a hot day. Your legs will not be scratched, and mosquitoes will be cheated out of a feast. Clothing will take a beating while you are in the bush, so use old, comfortable, cheap garments. For ease of movement, the pants should not be too tight, and for safety reasons they should be neither loose nor baggy.

It is a good idea to wear pant suspenders while working in the bush. Pants can become soaking wet from damp underbrush; suspenders will keep heavy, wet pants secure far better than a belt.

Shirts and Jackets

Since bare arms will be lashed and pricked, wear long-sleeved shirts. When working in the winter, wear several layers that will allow unrestricted movement. Heavy parkas or long coats are impractical, as they impede the easy motion of the arms, which is essential when wielding a chain saw.

Gloves and Mitts

Protection for the hands is a must. During hot weather, a pair of leather work gloves will suffice, but in the winter you will desire something heavier. Examine the selection of rugged gloves and mitts available in hardware and clothing stores. When operating a chain saw, you will likely want, on your trigger hand, something lightweight that can be replaced by a heavier glove when the cutting is finished. Since you will also be picking up chunks of wood repeatedly, use gloves with which you can easily grip large objects.

Safety Gear

There are individuals who refuse to wear ear plugs, safety glasses, and the other accoutrements used by safety-conscious loggers; they are asking for trouble. For felling trees, wear a comfortable, tight-fitting hard hat; add a liner for cold weather. When bucking or splitting wood, a snug wool cap will keep your head warm and hair clean. Avoid dangling tassels and scarves that can become caught in a chain saw; if your hair is long, tie it back.

If you work only occasionally with a chain saw, a lack of ear protection can lead to prolonged ringing in the ears. If you cut wood regularly without noise barriers in your ears, permanent damage can ensue. For the weekender, cotton batting in the ears will suffice, but sound leakage does occur. Ear plugs or safety headsets are far superior. They can be bought from industrial equipment and safety supply firms and from some chain-saw dealers.

Puncture-proof pads for arms and legs are becoming popular. Examine the various models available and pick those that impede movement the least.

Safety Glasses

When a chain saw is operating, wood chips and sawdust particles are in the air almost constantly. When using a sledge and steel splitting wedges, there is danger of flying metal. One of the better approaches is a safety helmet that contains earmuffs and a mesh shield that covers the entire face. Safety goggles offer good protection as well, but they can be awkward and fog up easily. Safety glasses are more comfortable and are available for a reasonable price.

Hard Hat, Hearing and Face Protection

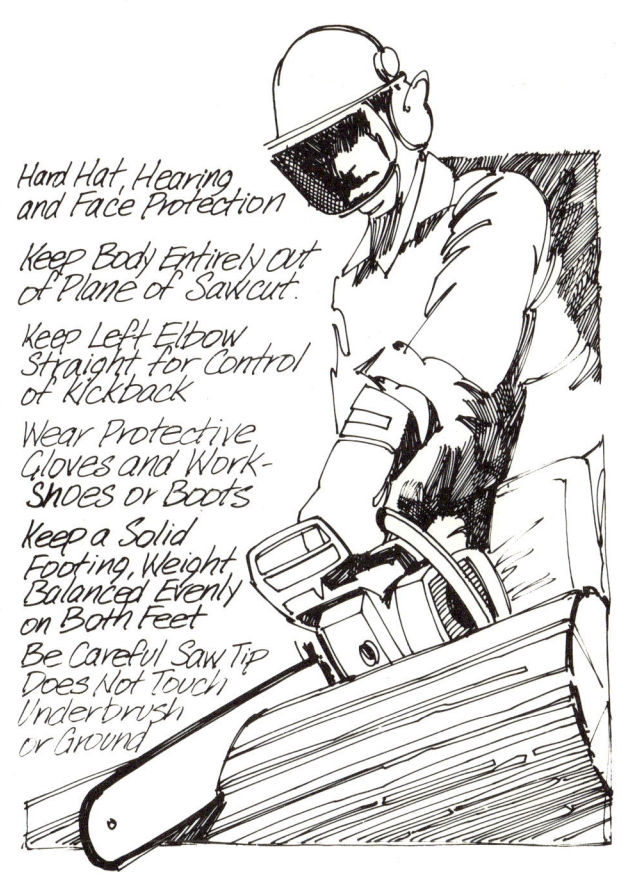

Keep Body Entirely out of Plane of Sawcut.

Keep Left Elbow Straight for Control of Kickback

Wear Protective Gloves and Work-Shoes or Boots

Keep a Solid Footing, Weight Balanced Evenly on Both Feet

Be Careful Saw Tip Does Not Touch Underbrush or Ground

SAFETY EQUIPMENT AND STANCE FOR USING A CHAIN SAW

IN THE BUSH

When leaving for a day of wood gathering, be prepared. Besides your chain saw, you should carry a sizable knapsack loaded with a chain-saw wrench, an extra spark plug, two chain files, wedges of various sizes, a set of socket wrenches for minor repairs, a bush axe, plus extra gas, and chain oil. Also recommended are a sledgehammer or maul for splitting logs, and a peavey (or the similar cant hook) that makes rolling over a log quite an easy task. A first-aid kit is another useful accessory; accidents can happen in the woods far from a hospital or doctor's office.

It is best for at least two people to work together, because of the weight of felled trees and as a safety measure. If you cannot avoid cutting wood alone, notify a friend or neighbor where you will be and what time you expect to return.

FELLING A TREE

Before the tree to be toppled is attacked with the chain saw, a thorough study must be made of the tree and the immediate area around it. If the tree leans or has more branches on one side than another, the direction of fall can be affected. Such faults can be determined by walking slowly around the tree and peering upward. Be especially careful of dead top wood; if large pieces—affectionately known as widowmakers—come loose with the vibrations caused by the sawing and increasing rocking of the tree, they can kill. If the tree looks too dangerous, leave it. If it is a hazard where it stands, have an expert remove it.

Be cautious of hollow and rotten trees, as they can be very complicated to cut. It is hard to recognize hollow specimens just by looking at them, unless there are holes in the bark. But once you begin to cut, the bar of the saw will move forward at an incredible rate. Fungi or obvious exterior decay are telltale signs of a rotten tree, as are dark brown sawdust and the same easy movement of the saw.

Avoid cutting uphill. The grade can make it difficult to gauge the lean of the tree, and it is hard to work on a hill, especially when the ground is wet. Trees cut up onto a slope can fall or slip back toward the cutter.

Two escape routes, heading off approximately 90 degrees apart, from the back of the tree, should be identified and memorized. If the tree begins to plummet before you expect it to, a safe quick exit can be made.

Decide where the tree will be felled. Few trees grow completely straight—a lean of some amount is usual. Without heavy logging equipment, it is virtually impossible to set a tree down farther than 45 degrees from its natural fall line. The task is always simplified if you can topple the tree in the direction it is already leaning.

Three factors will influence exactly where you should try to place the tree. The first, most important consideration is nearby trees and their branches. Try to find a hole where the tree can drop without getting hung up. The tree that falls cleanly will be safer than one that wedges itself firmly against another. The second is ease of transporting the wood. Remember that you will have to move the felled pieces, and that almost all unseasoned wood is heavy. The third is the wind. If a gale is blowing, don't cut! The direction of the fall could be tragically altered by a strong gust.

When starting a chain saw, always follow the procedures laid out in the owner's manual. The technique of starting a saw while holding it in the air with one hand is foolhardy even for experts. Pull the cord only when the saw is on the ground and firmly gripped. Before cutting begins, make sure that all helpers and onlookers are far enough removed that wherever the tree comes down they will be safe.

The proven method of felling a tree requires three cuts. This system usually prevents splitting of the trunk and allows the saw operator to aim the tree by creating a hinge, which, in similar fashion to the one on a door, guides the tree in the direction you wish it to go.

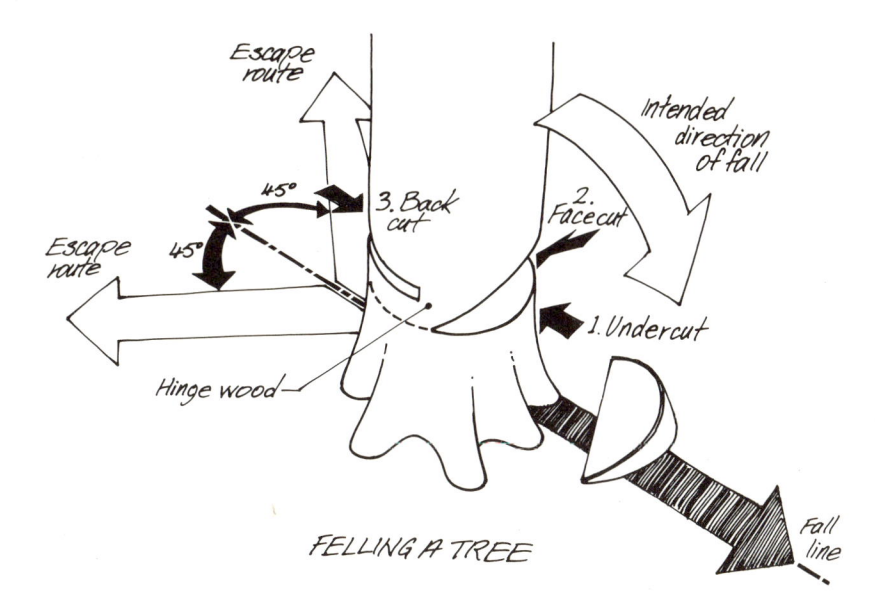

FELLING A TREE

The Undercut

The initial action with the chain saw, the undercut, is made on the front—the portion toward where you want the tree to fall. The center of this cut should correspond exactly with the intended fall line, and it should be made as close to the ground as possible. This avoids wasting wood in the thickest portion of the tree and makes later work such as skidding much easier. However, the undercut should be above the tough root swell and high enough to avoid hitting dirt and rocks with the chain.

It should also be as parallel to the ground as possible. If it is angled, the tree will tend to fall in the direction of the low end of the cut. This parallel stroke should go in no further than one-third of the tree's diameter. If made deeper, there is a risk of the tree falling backward. Additionally, it is vital to have the undercut penetrate the same amount on both sides of the tree. If it does not, the tree could break off prematurely or fall off to the side. Using the middle part of the chain's bar, and not the tip, will lead to a straight cut.

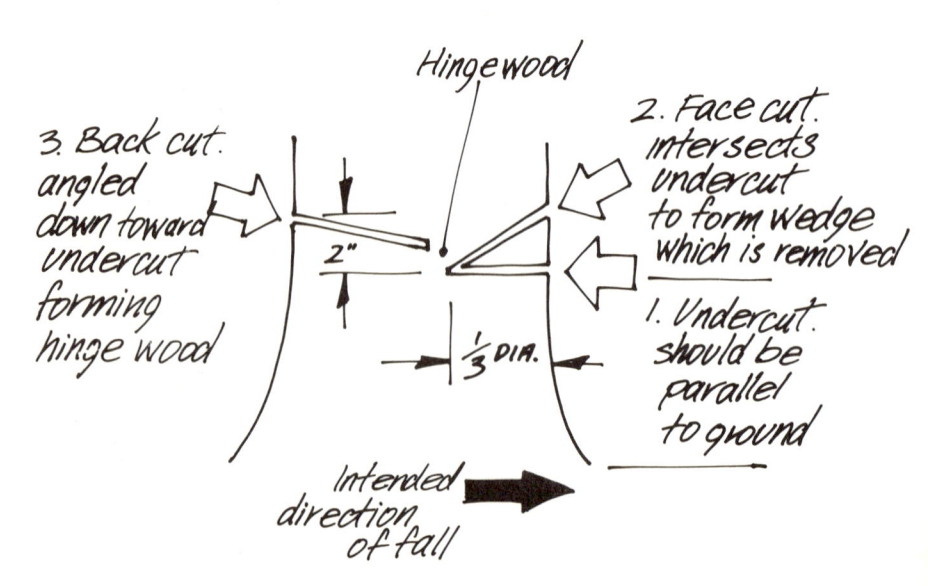

Hinge wood

3. Back cut. angled down toward undercut forming hinge wood

2"

⅓ DIA.

2. Face cut. intersects undercut to form wedge which is removed

1. Undercut. should be parallel to ground

Intended direction of fall

THREE BASIC CUTS REQUIRED TO BRING DOWN A TREE SAFELY

The undercut is obviously important, as it lays the foundation for the toppling of the tree. To do it properly requires practice.

The Face Cut

The face cut is made a few inches above the undercut, at an angle to it of approximately 45 degrees. Ideally this stroke should meet the back of the undercut and remove a triangular-shaped piece of wood. This enables the tree to begin to fall before the final stroke, the back cut, is finished.

The Back Cut

The back cut completes formation of the hinge. As its name implies, it is made on the rear of the tree, away from the direction it will fall. This cut is begun two or three inches above the level of the undercut and descends so that it will meet the undercut or be above it. When the back cut is carried out correctly, the tree should begin to loosen as the cut is made, before the saw reaches the undercut. The operator pulls the saw out, turns it off, and makes a quick exit as the tree starts to fall. This is where prior scouting for escape routes will pay off. Never stand directly behind a falling tree, as it can split or spring back much more quickly than you can move.

If the saw does come near the undercut, the back cut has been made too high, and the tree could come back toward the feller. If the mistake is realized while the back cut is in progress, the operator should start over.

Holding a Side

The technique of holding a side, and the use of wedges—sometimes used concurrently—are aids to making a tree fall precisely where you want it. To hold a side, leave the hinge wider on one side than on the other. Carried out during the back cut, its purpose is to restrain the tree on the thick side as it begins to fall, pulling the tree in that direction.

Wider side of hinge hold's back fall

Hinge wood

Undercut

Back cut

Intended direction of fall

Lean of tree (natural fall line)

HOLDING A SIDE

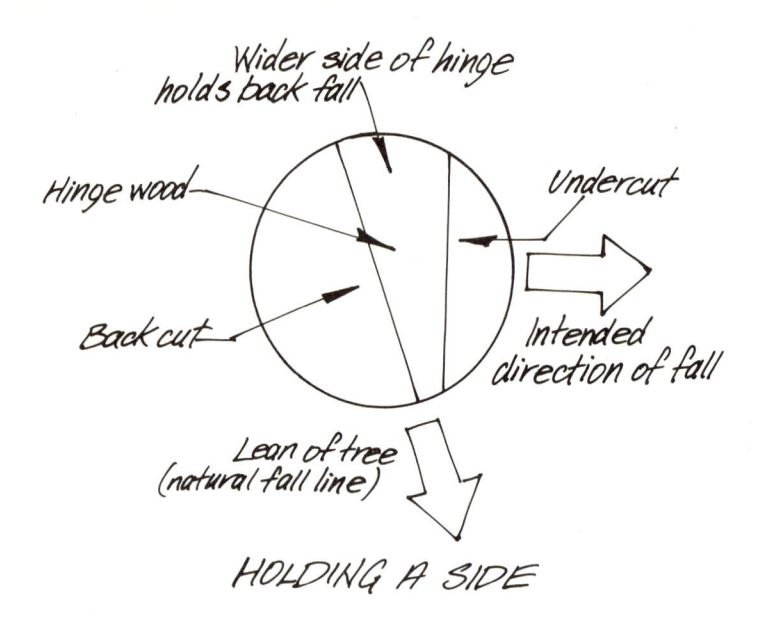

For example, say that the tree is leaning toward a clump of cedars. As you stand at its back, the hazardous clump is on your right. The back cut is made so that the hinge is thicker on the left side. As the tree starts to go over, it would be pulled to the left, avoiding the clump. This procedure should be tried initially on small-diameter trees.

Wedges

Wedges can be great aids for both the person who does not have a great deal of experience and the veteran who is up against a challenging tree. They are especially useful with large-diameter trees that can pinch the bar of the saw. For felling operations, the finest ones are made of plastic, hardwood, and light metals such as magnesium and aluminum. The heavy six- and eight-pound steel splitting wedges would wreak havoc if touched by the saw's chain.

A key function of the wedge is to fell the tree once the back cut comes near the undercut. For the greenhorn, wedges make it safe to stop, remove the saw, and finish the cut by driving in one or more of them. Their placement depends on the task they are required to perform. If it is a simple matter of finishing a correctly placed back cut, the wedge should be set directly at the center of the incision. If a pair of wedges are to be brought into play for the same purpose, they should be equidistant from the center.

When it appears that the tree will not fall where you have aimed it, or if you are unsure that the holding-the-side procedure is going to perform as it should, a wedge can be used to direct the tree in the intended direction. Unlike holding a side, which pulls the tree, the wedge pushes; it should be placed 180 degrees from where you want the tree to topple.

Returning to the example described earlier, where the clump of cedars is on your right as you stand behind the tree and you wish the tree to fall to your left, the wedge should be placed on the right side of the back cut. Drive it in with a series of light blows delivered by a sledgehammer or the back of an axe. If struck heavily, it is liable to pop back out.

PROBLEMS

Difficulties that even an old-timer encounters include loosening a cut tree that is hung up in a standing one, freeing a pinned saw, and dealing with a tree or branch being held under pressure.

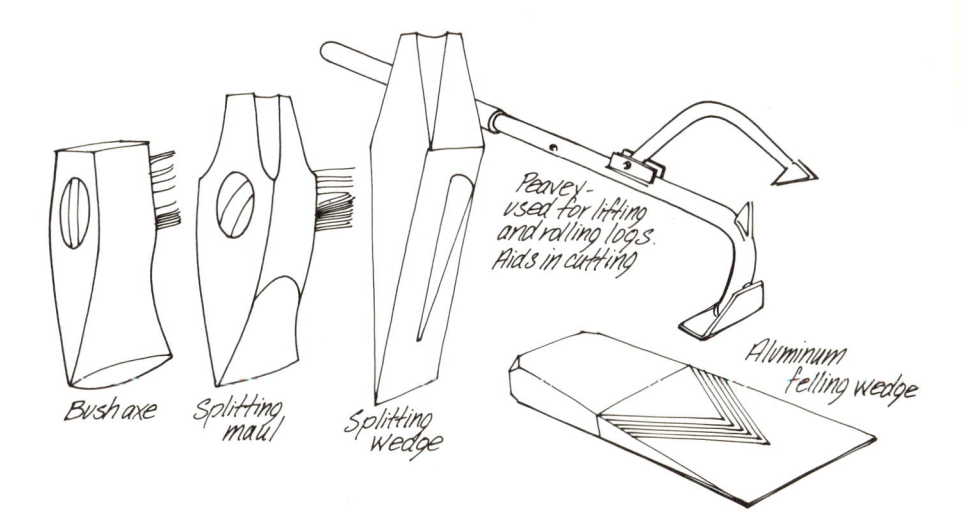

Bush axe Splitting maul Splitting wedge Peavey—used for lifting and rolling logs. Aids in cutting Aluminum felling wedge

Loosening a Hung-Up Tree

When a tree that has been sawed becomes entangled in a neighboring one, the safest remedy is to use a long chain or cable attached to a truck, tractor, or team of horses. The cable should be stout and in excellent condition, and bystanders should stand extremely far back from the action, as the chain can snap and fly to one side or the other.

The person who lacks such paraphernalia can use other techniques. All demand extreme caution. Sometimes a tree becomes stuck while still sitting on the stump and attached at the hinge. The solution is to finish the back cut and simultaneously have helpers apply pressure, by pushing the tree, to roll it away from where it is caught. Watch your feet when the tree crashes off the stump.

If this does not work, or the tree is sitting on the ground, try rolling it with a peavey. One or two of these tools should be placed near the bottom or butt of the tree. Do not stand behind the butt, as the tree can kick back as it comes free.

A third solution is to shorten the tree by cutting off part of the trunk. Both the cut itself and the force with which the butt will hit the ground will help to free it. Start your cut from the top or back of the tree. Once you feel the tree begin to close in on the saw, remove it immediately and complete the process from underneath. Again keep your feet away from the spot where the tree will slam into the earth.

If none of these approaches succeeds and the half-downed tree is a hazard, have someone who possesses the proper equipment remove it as soon as possible.

A Trapped Saw

A saw sometimes becomes caught while a tree is being felled. If this happens, you have learned a lesson—wedges should have been used. Try to insert one after the fact; if you cannot get it in where you need it, enough of a gap can usually be created by starting a good distance away and carefully opening the crack. This requires two or three wedges. Be careful, as it is possible to bring the tree down, and not in the direction you want it to fall.

If wedges will not liberate the saw, make another full series of cuts above the old ones with another chain saw or a two-person manual model.

When the saw becomes stuck in an already downed tree, pressure from underneath will usually free it. This can be done with a peavey or a long steel rock bar. Alternatively, a wedge can be inserted into the top of the cut, or another full swath can be made nearby.

A Tree under Pressure

When a tree falls and forces another into a bent position instead of snapping it, a dangerous situation is created. You can try rolling the downed tree away from the trapped one, but be sure that no one can be hit if either tree flies into the air. Call in an expert if you do not feel you can manage this safely; cutting a sprung tree can be a deadly business.

With small saplings and branches that are being held, a saw cut on the outside of the bend will usually cause the wood to crack. If you try this on the inside of the curve, the saw will become stuck. Although such thin vegetation can look innocent, proceed carefully.

CUTTING YOUR OWN FUEL WOOD from the stump is the cheapest and probably the most satisfying approach. But it can be exceedingly perilous. Stay calm, be sensible, and don't work when overtired. Avoid getting into a situation beyond your experience and control. Most wooded regions have foresters and veteran loggers. They respect the power of a tree and will usually be glad to give advice or lend a hand when it is asked for.

17
Bucking up Wood

Woodburners most commonly use a chain saw to buck up fallen trees, or purchased logs, into "rounds" small enough, when split, to fit into a furnace, heater, or cookstove. While this process is much simpler than cutting the tree down, there are a few techniques that need to be mastered.

If the section of tree is light enough to lift, place a round under it, then rest one end of the log on the ground so that, with the round acting as a fulcrum, the other end will rise into the air. This allows the wood to be bucked up with ease. By placing the round so that it will roll, you can push the round farther in as the log becomes shorter. This procedure works best if you have a helper sit on the log being cut—near the end touching the ground—to prevent it from moving. Never allow the saw's chain to hit the earth after cutting a log. Large pieces of bark placed under where you work will save wear and tear on the chain.

Using two rollers or sawhorses will not work, if you cut from the top, since the top of the log will be forced inward, pinching the saw's bar. This succeeds only when the log is sawed from underneath.

If the log you are cutting is too heavy to lift, even when cut into relatively short lengths, make all necessary cuts on the top and then, using peaveys, roll the log over 180 degrees and complete the cuts.

In times past, trees were often used as part of a fence, so before any bucking is done examine the log for old nails, fence

BUCKING TECHNIQUES

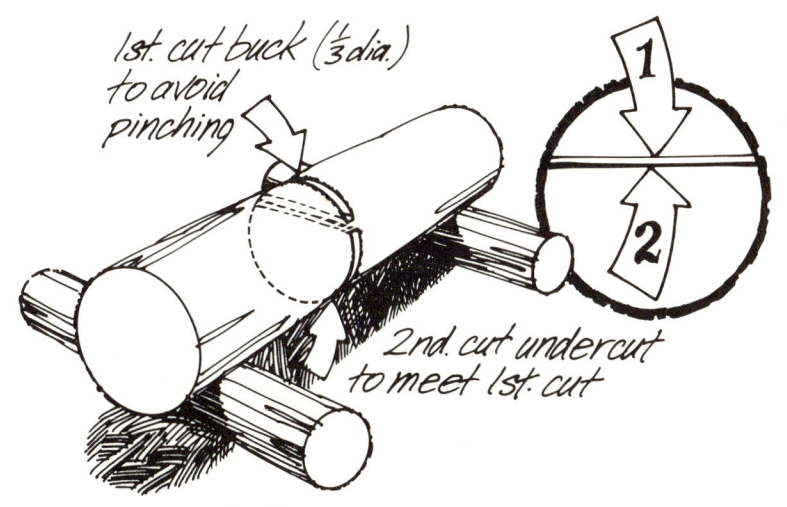

1st. cut buck (⅓ dia.) to avoid pinching

2nd. cut undercut to meet 1st. cut

SUPPORTED BOTH ENDS

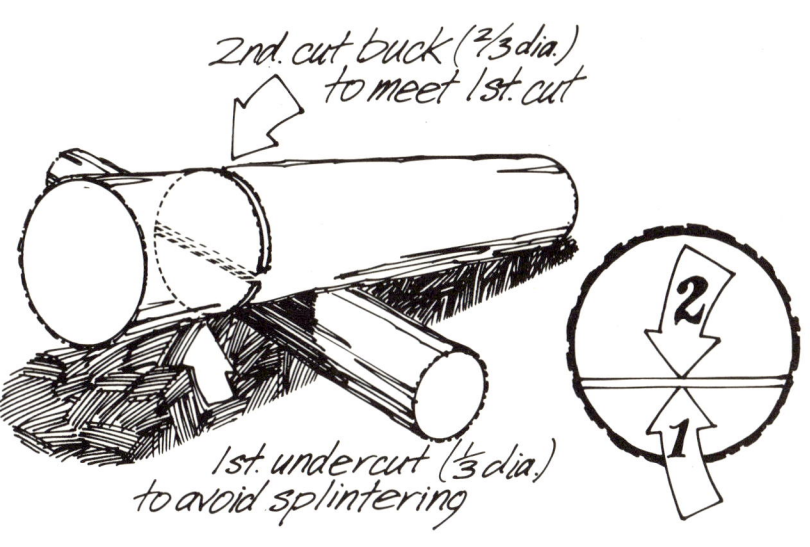

2nd. cut buck (⅔ dia.) to meet 1st. cut

1st. undercut (⅓ dia.) to avoid splintering

SUPPORTED ONE END

staples, or barbed wire. If the tree is covered with mud or has stones wedged in the fissures of the bark—as happens when a log is being skidded—use a wire brush to clean off all areas the chain will touch.

When bucking, try to keep the cuts straight. Your stove can be loaded more efficiently with blocks that have straight ends; it is easier to split blocks when they can stand up on their own.

SKIDDING WOOD

If the woodlot is near your home, consider skidding the logs out of the bush in long lengths. They can be placed in your yard and then cut, split, and stacked without having to make the journey into the forest. Whenever you plan to drag full-length trees, a logging skidder or team of heavy workhorses will be essential. A tractor can be employed if the trees are slender or if larger specimens are cut into twelve- or sixteen-foot portions.

When a log being skidded becomes jammed behind a rock or stump, try to free it manually with a peavey, not by revving up the tractor or having the horses pull harder. If this does not work, slacken the chain and move the machine or team so that it is pulling from a new direction.

One approach for those with a truck but no skidding equipment is to cut the logs into lengths that can be lifted by two or three people—a recommended size is four feet. This length is practical because most stoves take the twelve-, sixteen-, or twenty-four-inch-long pieces that can be sawed without waste from the four-foot log.

It is obviously necessary to know the length of your stove's firebox before any bucking can be done. Carry a tape measure or a stick marked in multiples of the length you need. After a short time, you should be able to estimate accurately how long the pieces need to be.

HAULING WOOD

As wood is piled in the truck or trailer, keep an eye on the springs to make sure you do not overload. Most modern trucks have leaf springs that are concave when the cargo area is empty. As the weight increases, they begin to flatten out; never allow them to become horizontal or convex, as a hard bump can snap the spring. Similar damage can be done to coil models, so always leave some play.

Overloading can also put severe strain on the brake system and cause the truck to become back-heavy, which will make steering difficult. Be cautious, especially during the first few trips. The terrain over which you will be hauling is also a consideration. If you live in mountainous country, less wood can be moved per load than on the plains.

If your truck can safely handle a load of fuel wood that rises substantially higher than the box's metal sides, wooden walls for the sides and rear should be constructed or borrowed. It is dangerous to move towering loads of wood without these in place, because of the possibility of dropping chunks onto the road. You might be charged if wood from your truck causes an accident. You can also run afoul of the law if you load a truck beyond its Gross Vehicle Weight (GVW). This figure is generally found on the truck's registration form. It is difficult to accurately estimate a truck's weight without experience so, when in doubt, load light.

SPLITTING

There are few outdoor chores more satisfying than splitting wood. When the day's work is done, the large pile is your tangible reward. Remember that newly felled wood splits easily and that bitter cold weather makes the process even simpler.

Most rounds of softwood slice apart without much effort, and the majority of hardwood logs can be split by a beginner. However, even the veteran will have occasional problems with an extremely gnarled and twisted chunk, or with elm, which is notorious for its tough fibers.

Beginners find it difficult to hit the same spot repeatedly with a lightweight axe. The heavier splitting maul, which has reappeared on the market in recent years, will split most chunks after two or three even scattered strokes. However, some people will not be strong enough to use a maul for an extended period of time. A delivery that makes aiming relatively easy is a modified baseball swing that begins over one shoulder; the neophyte usually has a tendency to bring the axe down from directly over his head.

With experience, you will learn where to hit the round. Split parallel to knots and as far from them as possible. If you cannot avoid one, strike on a line that goes through the center of the knot. As the wood seasons, cracks will appear in the ends; the heartwood, located in the middle of each round, will usually have one major fissure. Split as close as possible and parallel to it.

Knocking the wood in half is usually the hardest; once this is accomplished it is not difficult to create smaller pieces. Before beginning the splitting operation, measure your appliance's firebox door so that the chunks you turn out will fit through the opening. Whole rounds will ignite more quickly if a portion of the bark is sliced off and the exposed wood is then set down into the fire.

Wood is split most simply if the top of the chunk stands between the level of your knees and waist and is placed on a wide, stable piece of wood known as a chopping block. By striking the block instead of the ground, you will prolong the life of your axe or maul head.

To avoid mangled shins, bend your back and knees to keep your lower legs away from the action. Always wear long pants, safety boots, and shin protectors; tight-fitting gloves should prevent blisters.

If you prefer not to use a splitting maul, purchase one or preferably two six- or eight-pound steel wedges. When used with a bush axe and a sledgehammer, these wedges will force apart almost any kind of wood. It is easier to start the cut with an axe and then place the wedges. Once an indentation is made, the wedges can be driven in.

Many greenhorns snap a lot of axe handles, for three reasons. The first is that they often overaim, hitting the edge of the round with the handle instead of the blade. Until you become experienced, a piece of rubber, some wire, or friction tape wound around the handle directly under the axe head will help.

A second cause of broken axe handles is that they are sometimes left outside during winter. This causes the handle to freeze and, when put under stress, it often snaps. This happens especially during bitterly cold weather that can also lead to the axe head's becoming brittle and fragmenting when struck against wood. Store the axe where it will stay warm. However, do not leave it close to your wood stove—the handle will dry out and cause the head to come loose. The third reason why a handle will break is that it may have been cut across the grain of a block of wood, rather than parallel to it.

MECHANICAL SPLITTERS

There are two main types of mechanical splitters—screw and hydraulic. The former bores its way into the wood. As the thicker part of its shaft enters the wood, the fibers are torn apart, splitting the log. Some of these come with their own gasoline-powered engine, while others attach to the wheel of a stationary vehicle. The latter style takes quite a while to install, and, unless you have an old car or truck that can be pressed into service, your vehicle will be immobilized while this device is used.

The hydraulic version works on the ram principle, with the wood being slammed with great force against a wedge-shaped object, or vice versa. These units are usually larger and heavier than screw models. Some have their own trailer and others are fastened to the three-point hitch found on many tractors. Most operate on gasoline, but a few smaller models use electricity.

To be capable of splitting large chunks, a hydraulic splitter needs a minimum of ten tons of ram force. Extreme caution should be used when the machine is in operation, since it is powerful enough to crush a hand. A splitter will be needed only a few days each year, because it prepares a great quantity of wood at one time. Consider buying it with neighbors or renting one.

DRYING AND STORING WOOD

It is essential that dry wood be burned whenever possible. However, cutting the wood eight to twelve months before it will be employed is not enough to guarantee seasoning. It must also be properly stacked.

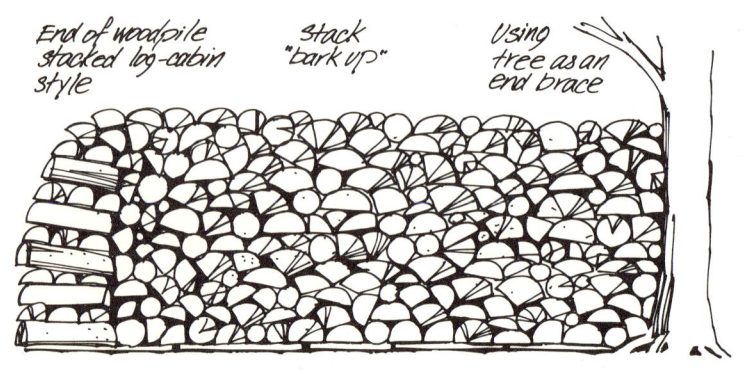

End of woodpile stacked log-cabin style *Stack "bark up"* *Using tree as an end brace*

PROPERLY STACKED WOODPILE

Rather than throwing the wood in a haphazard heap, use long neat rows that allow air to circulate between the pieces. These piles should be established on high, dry, sunny, exposed land and the wood should be piled rather loosely.

To keep the bottom course of the row dry, old boards or fuel wood should be laid on the ground before the row is started. The new wood is then placed, with its bark up, across the scraps.

The ends of the pile can be held in place by a number of different methods. The wood can be set between two trees, but this means it will be primarily in shade during the summer months, when the sun is most powerful. The log cabin method can be used, with the direction of each level of end wood being alternated. A third technique is to construct braces out of lumber or two pairs of hardwood poles driven into the ground at each end.

To keep snow and rain off the wood, shield the top with plastic or old plywood, held down by blocks of wood. Make sure that air circulation through the sides of the pile is not hindered. If the pile has not been covered, and the wood is to be put in a shed or basement, do so only after a few days of sunny weather, to allow surface water to evaporate.

Wood can also be stacked in a tall cylinder. According to Hans Klunder, who wrote about such "holzhaufens" several years ago for *Home Energy Digest*, they take up less space than a rectangular woodpile, dry the wood faster, and let the homeowner know when the wood is seasoned. Wood set in a holzhaufen must be split and between twelve and twenty-four inches in length. All pieces must be of uniform size and the terrain must be level.

To begin, a vertically level pole, the exact height of the planned pile, is erected. A four- to six-foot-diameter circle is drawn around it on the ground and a line of scrap wood is laid end to end around the circle's circumference. The first row of wood is then piled on these pieces—at a right angle to them with the thinner end toward the center. This wood must slant in— the outside end should be about one inch higher than the inside end—and it is vital that each layer be level. Some wedges may need to be inserted.

When wood has been piled to a height of two feet, the inner space is filled with wood set on end. Klunder notes that odd-shaped pieces can go in here; it is important that this wood not apply pressure on the outside row.

Up to a height of four feet, the holzhaufen can be constructed from the outside, but once this level is attained, the builder must work from the middle. Obviously, this is much more easily done if a helper hands the wood in.

A common height for the complete pile is ten feet. At seven feet, the pile should begin to taper in to the center. (This tapering should always begin a yard from the top, regardless of the height.) A top cover that will shed rain is provided by pieces of wood laid bark side up.

Since wood shrinks as it dries, the pile will settle. When approximately one-quarter of the center pole is visible, the wood is seasoned. It can be practical, and fun for children, to mark each foot on the pole before construction begins, so that progress toward seasoning can be followed. Klunder claims that a holzhaufen six feet in diameter and ten feet high can be erected in one hour. Although one properly built will be solid, children should not be allowed to climb on it.

Once the wood has dried, it is best stored inside a woodshed built close to where the fuel will be used. It is not essential for a woodshed to have solid walls, as long as it has a tight roof supported by stout poles; wood piled around the outside will act as a weather break. Always place the driest wood at the front of the shed, to allow the green chunks time to season.

Some people store wood in their basement. This practice can introduce insects into your home.

If you do not possess a shed and are not pleased about using your cellar, wood can be left outside. However, the moisture content will rise during the autumn; in winter, unless the wood is covered, snow will build up on the top chunks. And, although the pieces should be stacked closer together than in a seasoning pile, even those in the lower courses will likely freeze together. A good whack with a sledgehammer, the back of an axe head, or another block of wood should be enough to free the pieces you want. These are drawbacks, but thousands of people do leave their wood outdoors year round.

18
Chain Saws and Axes

THE CHAIN SAW

Thirty years ago, the chain saw was an expensive, snarling, inconsistent monster usable only by burly loggers. Now, however, it has been tamed and made available to the masses. With hundreds of thousands being sold annually, the chain saw is almost as common as the lawn mower.

Both the body, which contains the engine, and the length of the bar, which holds the chain, can vary considerably in size and weight because of the different tasks each model is designed to perform.

The Mini-Saw (about 25 cc)

Though it may appear to be a toy, do not be deceived as the mini-saw, weighing seven or eight pounds and possessing a ten-inch bar, can be every bit as dangerous as a much larger model. Mini-saws, made by most saw companies, are ideal for such light jobs as the trimming of branches. They are used by professionals such as tree surgeons and power company crews.

The mini-saw is relatively inexpensive, but its uses are limited. If you expect to need a saw of these dimensions only occasionally, you may be better off purchasing a manually operated bow saw for a few dollars.

The Lightweight Saw (25–40 cc)

A step up from the mini-saw, the lightweight saw can handle small- and medium-diameter trees. Weighing from nine to twelve pounds, it is ideal as an occasional-use home and garden tool, but for the person who will be cutting several cords of fuel wood each year, the lightweight is simply too small and underpowered.

The Middleweight or Farm Saw (45–60 cc)

The middleweight saw is the ideal tool for the fuel wood harvester. A middleweight saw weighs twelve to fifteen pounds, light enough to use all day without fatigue setting in, yet it has sufficient durability and power to be capable of cutting virtually any tree you will come across. A range of bar lengths is available. For the fuel wood preparer, the optimum length is usually fifteen or sixteen inches. It should be noted that these and the heavier lightweights can be tremendous labor savers for anyone involved in log or heavy timber construction. Notches can be made, beams smoothed and logs cut, safely and rapidly, even far above the ground.

The Heavyweight Saw (up to 80 cc)

With bars as lengthy as sixty inches, weighing fifteen to thirty-five pounds, and high prices, heavyweight saws are designed for the professional logger and are far beyond the requirements of the person who cuts a few cords of wood each year.

Special Features

After you visit a few showrooms, your head will be swimming with thoughts of roller-nose bars, chain brakes, kickback guards, antivibration devices, and automatic oilers. In some cases, one feature does the same chore as a different apparatus found on another brand of saw. Many of these devices are recent innovations designed to aid the comfort and safety of the operator.

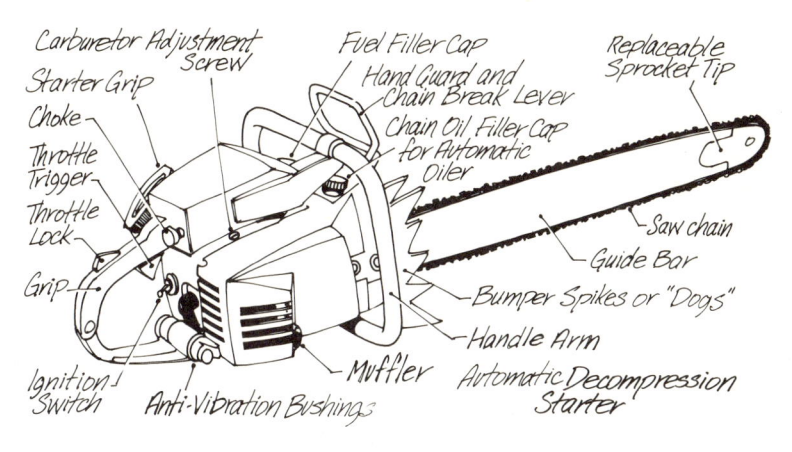

CHAIN SAW

ANTIVIBRATION EQUIPMENT

Many older loggers have become afflicted with what is popularly known as white hand disease, which attacks the nervous system and cuts down circulation of blood. It is caused by the constant vibration that can accompany the operation of a chain saw for long periods of time. To prevent this illness, and to generally lessen user fatigue, equipment has been designed that is claimed to remove 80 percent of the vibration. It is standard on most larger saws and available as an option on nearly every other unit manufactured.

The main improvements are handles that are padded and independent from the rest of the machine (shock absorbers are installed at the connecting points). Though they add weight and expense, antivibration systems are extremely worthwhile, especially if you expect to put in quite a few day-long cutting sessions annually.

KICKBACK GUARDS AND CHAIN BRAKES

If the top portion of the chain becomes pinched or hits an object on the far side of the wood being cut, the saw will be thrown back toward the operator. The kickback guard, a stationary piece of heavy plastic or coated metal mounted forward of the top, front handle, can prevent the operator's upper hand and face from being struck.

On some saws, a chain brake mechanism is built into the guard. When the saw is suddenly jolted, the reflex action of the operator's upper hand pushes the guard, disengaging the chain. The brake can also neutralize the chain when the saw is being started or carried to a cutting site.

THROTTLE SAFETY CATCH

The throttle safety catch performs a task similar to the latter function of the chain brake, but instead of disengaging the chain it holds the throttle closed. As these two features avoid the need to turn the saw off each time it is moved, they will substantially reduce wear on both the saw's starter assembly and the operator's pulling arm. Transporting a running saw without one of these devices is dangerous.

REAR OR RIGHT-HAND GUARD

The right-hand guard is designed to protect the operator's trigger hand from being hit by a swinging branch or a broken or derailed saw chain.

AUTOMATIC OILERS

When cutting hardwood, the saw's chain can get very hot, especially if it is dull. To keep the chain and bar from overheating, every saw is equipped with an oiler that injects fluid into the bar's groove, lubricating and cooling the assembly.

On all older models and some newer ones this is done manually, every few seconds, by pressing down a button with the thumb of your trigger hand. But on an increasing number of saws, this is handled automatically. Now becoming popular is a worthwhile combination approach—an automatic oiler with a manual override.

It has been proven that the automatic system, because of its regularity, is more efficient and induces longer bar and chain life. But if it breaks down while you are in the boondocks, the manual button can be used. For heavier than usual cutting, the manual button is also helpful.

ROLLER-NOSE AND SPROCKET-TIP BARS

Roller-nose and sprocket-tip bars are two names for the same feature—a bearing located in the tip of the saw's bar that reduces chain friction and wear plus allowing the saw to cut faster. Some are sealed, while others must be lubricated regularly.

MUFFLERS

A hot muffler can inflict a bad burn. Look for a design that covers the muffler with a guard or places it where it is not a menace. Also try to select a machine that directs the exhaust fumes and noise away from the operator or uses special noise-reducing devices. The front is becoming a favored location for mufflers, though fumes will occasionally bounce off the log and into the operator's face.

CHAIN TENSION ADJUSTMENT

When cutting hardwood, the tension of the chain must be adjusted regularly because heavy use stretches it. If the chain becomes too loose it can fly off, damaging the cutting teeth and injuring the operator of a saw not equipped with safety shields.

Opt for a model that makes this chore easier, requiring the operator only to loosen a pair of bolts, hold the bar up with one hand, and turn the tension screw with the other.

COMPRESSION RELEASE BUTTON

The compression release button makes starting easier by reducing the compression or pressure within the engine. Rarely found on lightweight or middleweight saws, which normally start with a solid one-hand tug, this is usually standard on the massive heavyweights.

EASE OF USAGE

Since gasoline and chain oil will be added to their respective tanks several times a day, check how easy the saw will be to fill. Also simulate the various operating procedures to determine whether the various controls are well situated.

Where to Buy

New saws can be bought in many types of retail outlets. According to one manufacturer's literature, the staggering sales figures of recent years make the chain saw "a must product for successful merchandisers." This may be true, but, as with the wood appliance, it is best to buy from a shop that sells only chain saws or stocks them as a major sideline.

If you patronize a department or hardware store, chances are that they will not service what they sell. They will either refer you to a repair shop—where you will likely find that your saw is fixed after regular customers are looked after—or tell you to send it to the manufacturer. If you have found two or three people to help you for a day, and the saw suddenly breaks down, you do not want to be informed that the unit will have to be taken two or three hundred miles to be fixed.

The specialty chain-saw store will usually fix the saw while you wait, or within a few hours (unless the damage is serious). The easiest way to locate the best outlets is to ask full-time bush workers where they deal; they cannot afford downtime, and neither can you. If a woodsman cannot be found, query another professional such as a tree surgeon, nursery operator, or surveyor. Quick, reliable service is so important that it is best to buy a brand of saw that can be repaired close to where you will be using it. Keeping this in mind, if you live in a city but expect to use the saw primarily at a retreat or cottage, purchase it nearby.

Most of the best known chain saws are about equal in quality. In each size class, features and weight may differ, but reliability and performance will be similar.

Renting Saws

Saws can often be rented by the day or week, offering an easy solution when only a small amount of cutting has to be done each year. Before you leave the rental outlet, check to see that the saw is performing properly and that you understand the function of each control.

Renting is also a good way to check out saws before you

buy. For a few dollars, you can examine and operate a saw, away from a salesperson's perfect patter.

Used Saws

Buying a used saw is chancy. Unless you know the former owner, the tool's history is a mystery. This is not to say that bargains cannot be found. Trustworthy dealers refurbish saws taken in on trade and have former demonstrators and rental units available. Some consumers acquire a saw and soon realize that it is not right for their needs, and once in a while saws in almost new condition come up at estate or farm auctions.

Examine a used saw carefully. Start it up several times, both when it is hot and cold. If it requires many tugs in either situation, pass on it unless the saw is sound otherwise and you are skilled in repairing small engines. Starting the saw should require a stout pull. If it does not, the compression may be low, which is the sign of a dying engine.

The saw should be responsive to the touch of the throttle. Ask to cut a few rounds of wood so that you can judge its cutting power. If you have never bought a saw before, try to take along a friend who knows chain saws and can appraise one in fast order.

Check the condition of the chain and bar. The bar is worn out when the chain can be moved freely from side to side in the slot and when small cracks appear, especially along the front edge of the bar.

As with new saws, buy a used model that can be easily serviced locally. Do not purchase an obscure brand. You may pick up such a saw cheaply, but unless you can find one or two more to scavenge for parts, repairing it will be difficult, if not impossible.

The Owner's Manual

When you buy a new saw, make sure that it is accompanied by an owner's manual that matches the model number of your unit. Read the guide thoroughly with the saw in front of you, so that you can familiarize yourself with the function and operation of each control. Refer to the owner's manual after a few months of using the saw to be sure you are taking care of all needed maintenance.

If you acquire a major brand secondhand saw without a manual, you may be able to order the manual through a dealer. If you do not get a manual with the saw, have the former owner show you how everything works, and take notes.

If you intend to maintain the saw yourself, consider purchasing the shop or mechanic's manual that corresponds to your saw. The local dealer can order it.

Basic Chain-Saw Safety

Always keep both hands on the saw, and your mind on what you are doing. Don't daydream; the work may get monotonous, but it requires full, constant concentration. Before every cut is made, assume a sawing position that gives safe, solid footing and proper balance—this will help to avoid the kickback problem. Since striking branches, rocks, and old logs can cause the saw to rebound, try to remove any such obstructions prior to starting the saw.

Never grab a chain while it is moving. Before you touch it, have the ignition switch at the off position and allow the chain to cool off.

When refueling a saw, be very conscious of the fire danger, especially during late spring and summer months when you are surrounded by dry vegetation in the woods. Don't smoke any time you are working around chain saws and wood, and after refueling move the saw at least ten feet away before starting it. Keep the saw's handles clean; gas and oil can make them very slippery.

Maintenance

With a chain saw, there are several cleaning and oiling chores that must be carried out at frequent intervals. One of the most important tasks is to fill the chain oil tank each time gasoline is needed. Proper chain oil can be purchased from any saw dealer. Ordinary motor oil is not as efficient because it does not adhere to the bar as well, but it can be used if there is no alternative.

It is essential to use the grade of oil that corresponds with the outside temperature. The warm days of late spring, summer, and early autumn require heavy 30-weight oil. From 32 to 0 degrees, 20-weight oil is needed, and for 0 degrees and downward, switch to 10 weight. If you are using too heavy a weight of oil in cold weather, the saw will let you know, as the oil will come out in globules and the chain will refuse to turn. In this situation, with a manually oiled saw, the oiler button will be hard to push down. If the bar begins to smoke, turn the saw off to prevent damage.

The tension of the chain must be adjusted frequently. The amount of play needed varies; saws equipped with a roller-nose or sprocket-tip bar can have the chain tighter than units without one. Consult the owner's manual for the proper setting. Once you have done this a few times, you will recognize the proper tension both by the amount of underside of each chain tooth visible when the chain is tugged on, and by how the saw performs after the adjustment is made; when the chain is too tight, it cannot turn. Experience will also tell you when adjustment is needed.

The groove in the bar that holds the chain should be cleaned once each day the saw is in use. This can be done while seeing to the chain's tension; loosen the chain by turning, in the opposite direction, the same screw that tightens it. Then take the tip of a slot screwdriver and run it along the groove, removing the oil and wood chips that have accumulated.

Each time the chain is tightened, remove the metal cowling that covers the base of the chain and clean around both it and the oiler mechanism. If this is not done regularly, this zone can become jammed with chips and stop the saw.

Roller-nose chain bars may need to be lubricated. Ask the dealer about this when the saw is purchased, or if you buy a replacement bar with this feature.

The air filter that protects the carburetor from the dirt, sawdust, and chips that fly around during cutting should be cleaned before the saw is operated, by hitting it gently with your bare hand or a glove or by using a small whisk broom. At the same time, also tighten all visible screws, as vibrations of the machine can cause them to loosen up.

Performance Adjustments

If the saw is hesitating or missing while idling, chances are the carburetor needs adjusting. Consult your manual or a mechanic on how to do this.

When the machine misses while being run hard, a few components should be checked. Examine one at a time and see whether performance improves. First, take out the spark plug and clean it. Then see if the gap between the bottom of the plug and the metal arm has to be modified. Additionally, the rubber plug cover should be blown clean, as dirt can accumulate and ruin the connection.

When the plug becomes badly pitted, replace it, and always carry an extra one with your tools. To remove it from the engine, use the large end of the chain-saw wrench. This multipurpose tool can be bought for a few dollars from any saw shop. Some dealers include one free of charge with each new saw.

The gas filter, which is located inside the gas tank, can also cause the saw to miss if it becomes clogged. With the gas cap removed and the level of fuel in the tank low, reach inside with a finger. You'll find a hose and, on the end of it, a bulb containing the filter screen. Without disconnecting the hose, carefully remove it and the bulb from the tank. Cover the mouth of the receptacle so that dust cannot get inside, but don't sever the hose. Blowing on the filter is usually enough to clean it.

For the same reason that a chimney sweep is brought in to inspect and clean the system annually, the saw should be overhauled yearly by a professional, just before fuel wood cutting is to begin.

Fuel for the Chain Saw

Saws have two-stroke engines, so, two-stroke engine oil must be added to regular gasoline before the gas is put into the saw. Never mix the two in the machine's tank, and use the proper oil. Some saw manufacturers require a specific brand if the warranty is to remain in force. Your manual or dealer will be able to tell you the proper oil-to-gas ratio—stick faithfully to what is recommended.

Even though there is a filter, be sure that dirt and wood particles do not find their way into the gas can or the saw's tank. Keep the top closed on the storage container except when filling the saw, and wipe the area around the saw's tank clean before adding fuel. Use a container or funnel with a mesh screen.

Sharpening the Chain

When a chain saw is first purchased, the consumer often runs it until he realizes it is no longer cutting and takes it to the dealer or a professional saw sharpener. Shelling out several dollars each time the saw becomes dull will get expensive, so it makes sense to purchase the needed tools and learn how to do it yourself.

There are several types of saw-sharpening equipment, ranging from simple file holders to elaborate jigs. Check your dealer's stock and choose one that suits your budget and is easy to operate even with gloves on. Follow the procedure outlined by its manufacturer. Remember that the rakers between the teeth have to be filed periodically so that they remain level with the teeth. When having the saw maintained professionally, have the chain inspected and either replaced or sharpened.

Ensure that the integral round file fits the teeth of the saw. Replace the file whenever it begins to wear out and keep two or three in reserve.

AXES

For the fuel wood cutter, the best axes are a mediumweight, general purpose model and a splitting maul. The general purpose or poll axe is used a great deal by bush workers. As well as being ideal for brushing and limbing, it is useful when doing heavy timber or log construction and is employed by many for fuel wood splitting.

When purchasing an axe, pick up a few and decide which one suits you best. Is the head too heavy? Could you wield this tool all day in comfort?

Avoid axe handles that are painted. It is difficult to tell how the grain runs, and the paint causes the handle to be slippery, especially when wet. Also stay away from axes that have the handle held tight to the head with plastic, as it makes removal of a broken handle complicated. Stick to a plain wooden handle held in place with traditional steel wedges. Sight along the handle from its bottom or heel to make sure it is straight; aiming an axe with a crooked handle is almost impossible.

The handle that will last the longest has a straight grain. Check the dark lines in the wood; they should run vertically down the length of the handle. Some stove and hardware stores stock fiberglass handles. They are much more expensive than wood models, but most have lifetime guarantees.

Replacing an Axe Handle

Panic is normal the first time a handle breaks. Removing the top part from inside the eye or hole of the axe head can take hours for the beginner.

A simple method is to place the head in a vise or on two blocks of wood. Using a wide piece of metal as a ram, drive the wood down and out of the hole. If it is difficult to remove, expand the head with a propane or acetylene torch; never throw it into a fire, as the temper or hardness of the head can be ruined. Be sure not to touch the hot metal with your bare hands.

It may be necessary to whittle some wood from the new handle to allow it to fit inside the head's eye. Once the handle does start to slip in, turn the axe upside down. By hitting the heel of the handle with a hammer, you will firmly seat the head. Once the top of the handle appears above the eye, saw it off level, if necessary, and pound in a couple of steel wedges to keep the head tight. With a general purpose head, you will notice that one end of the bit or cutting edge flares out more than the other. It is intended to be at the bottom.

Sharpening an Axe

How an axe is sharpened depends on what it will be used for. The bit of an axe used for limbing and brushing should be finely honed and razor sharp. A splitting model should be kept thicker near the bit, and duller, because a sharp axe is hard to pull out of a log, and many prefer having a splitting axe head wedge shaped. If you can afford only one axe and want a dual-purpose model, keep it at a medium taper.

An axe is most easily sharpened within a vise. When one is not available, use a block of wood. Set the axe down on its side or cheek with the bit out over the end of the block, and hold the head secure with your foot.

Using a flat steel file, sharpen from beyond the bit toward the back of the axe head. Work from the bottom of the bit toward the top, with steady continuous strokes. Repeat this process several times on each side. After nicks are removed with the file, use a combination medium-fine sharpening stone and plenty of oil to finish the job.

If you will use the head only for splitting, do not file much into the head past the bit, as you want the cheeks to stay fat; for bushwork, however, file the cheeks down. An old pedal-powered grindstone is excellent for axe sharpening, but never use a modern high-speed grinder, since the intense heat it creates will destroy the temper of the head. Having a veteran woodburner show you these basics in person will save time and virtually guarantee that your new axe will be kept in proper condition right from the beginning.

Bibliography

BOOKS

Adkins, Jan. **The Wood Book.** Boston: Little, Brown and Company, 1980.

Bartok, John W. **Heating with Coal.** Charlotte, Vt.: Garden Way Publishing Co., 1980.

Cohen, Maurice. **The Woodcutter's Companion: A Guide to Locating, Cutting, Transporting, and Storing Your Own Fuelwood.** Emmaus, Pa.: Rodale Press, Inc., 1981.

Cooper, Jane. **Woodstove Cookery—At Home on the Range.** Charlotte, Vt.: Garden Way Publishing Co., 1978.

Curtis, Christopher, and Post, Donald. **Be Your Own Chimney Sweep.** Charlotte, Vt.: Garden Way Publishing Co., 1979.

Eastman, Margaret and Wilbur F., Jr. **Planning and Building Your Own Fireplace.** Charlotte, Vt.: Garden Way Publishing Co., 1976.

Gay, Larry. **Central Heating with Wood and Coal.** Brattleboro, Vt.: The Stephen Greene Press, 1981.

———, ed. **The Complete Book of Insulating.** Brattleboro, Vt.: The Stephen Greene Press, 1980.

———. **Heating the Home Water Supply.** Charlotte, Vt.: Garden Way Publishing Co., 1982.

Hall, Walter. **Barnacle Parp's Chain Saw Guide.** Emmaus, Pa.: Rodale Press, Inc., 1977.

Hoadley, R. Bruce. **Understanding Wood—A Craftsman's Guide to Wood Technology.** Newtown, Conn.: The Taunton Press, 1980.

Hotton, Peter. **Coal Comfort: An Alternative Way to Heat Your House.** Boston: Little, Brown and Company, 1980.

Kern, Ken. **The Owner-Built Home.** New York: Charles Scribner's Sons, 1972.

———, and Magers, Steve. **Fireplaces.** New York: Charles Scribner's Sons, 1978.

Langdon, William K. **Movable Insulation.** Emmaus, Pa.: Rodale Press, Inc., 1980.

Mazria, Edward. **Passive Solar Energy Book.** Emmaus, Pa.: Rodale Press, Inc., 1979.

Michaelson, Michael. **Firewood—A Woodcutter's Fieldguide to Trees in Summer and Winter.** Mankato, Minn.: Gabriel Books/Minnesota Scholarly Press, Inc., 1979.

Osgood, William E. **Wintering in Snow Country.** Brattleboro, Vt.: The Stephen Greene Press, 1978.

Shelton, Jay. **The Woodburners Encyclopedia.** Waitsfield, Vt.: Vermont Crossroads Press, 1976. A thorough revision of this book is being issued in the fall of 1982 as **Jay Shelton's Encyclopedia of Solid Fuels** (Charlotte, Vt.: Garden Way Publishing Co.).

———. **Wood Heat Safety.** Charlotte, Vt.: Garden Way Publishing Co., 1979.

Sherman, Steve. **Home Heating with Coal.** Harrisburg, Pa.: Stackpole Books, 1980.

Sussman, Art, and Frazier, Richard. **Handmade Hot Water Systems.** Point Arena, Calif.: Garcia River Press, 1978.

Tresemer, David. **Splitting Firewood.** Brattleboro, Vt.: By Hand & Foot, Ltd., 1981.

Vivian, John. **Wood Heat.** Emmaus, Pa.: Rodale Press, Inc., 1976.

Wik, Ole. **Wood Stoves, How to Make and Use Them.** Anchorage, Alaska: Northwest Publishing Co., 1977.

REPORTS AND MANUALS

"Installation and Instruction Manual." For HS Tarm boilers. The Tekton Corporation, Conway, Mass. 01341.

Island Energy Associates. **Wood-Fired Residential Heating Demonstration: Final Report and Appendices.** Prince Edward Island, Canada: The Institute of Man and Resources, 1980.

Shelton, Jay. **Air Pollution from Residential Woodburning Appliances: An Annotated Bibliography,** 1980. The Western Sun, 715 Southwest Morrison, Portland, Ore. 97204.

———. **Measured Performance of Fireplaces and Fireplace Accessories,** 1978. Available from the author—Shelton Energy Research, Box 5235, Santa Fe, N. Mex. 87502.

———, and Barczys, Cathleen. **Research Report on Chemical Chimney Cleaners, 1980.** Available from Shelton Energy Research (see preceding entry for address).

Smith, Nigel. **Worldwatch Paper 42, Wood: An Ancient Fuel with a New Future.** Washington, D.C.: The Worldwatch Institute, 1981.

PERIODICALS*

Blair and Ketchum's Country Journal, Box 8600, Greenwich, Conn. 06830.

Canadian Consumer, Consumers Association of Canada, 200 First Avenue, Ottawa, Ontario, Canada K1S 5J3.

Consumer Reports, Box 1949, Marion, Ohio 43305.

Family Handyman, 52 Woodhaven Road, Marion, Ohio 43305.

Harrowsmith, Camden East, Ontario, Canada K0K 1J0.

Mother Earth News, Box 70, Hendersonville, N.C. 28739.

Maine Times, 41 Main Street, Topsham, Me. 04086.

New Hampshire Times, 20 Montgomery Street, Box 35, Concord, N.H. 03301.

New Shelter (Incorporating Home Energy Digest), 33 East Minor Street, Emmaus, Pa. 18049.

Popular Mechanics, Box 10064, Des Moines, Iowa 50340.

Popular Science, Box 2871, Boulder, Colo. 80302.

Rain Magazine, 2270 Northwest Irving, Portland, Ore. 97210.

Renewable Energy News, Box 4869, Station E, Ottawa, Ontario, Canada K1S 5B4.

WoodenBoat, Box 17, Brooklin, Me. 04616.

Wood 'n Energy, 13 Depot Street, Box 2008, Concord, N.H. 03301. (For professionals in related fields only.)

Woodstove, Fireplace and Equipment Directory, Box 4474, 106 Market Street, Manchester, N.H. 03108.

ORGANIZATIONS

Canadian Wood Energy Institute, 16 Lesmill Road, Don Mills, Ontario, Canada M3B 2T5.

National Building Code of Canada, National Research Council, Division of Building Codes, Montreal Road, Ottawa, Ontario, Canada K1A 0R6.

---

* *These are among the periodicals that regularly carry articles of interest to the woodburner. Many are available on most newsstands.*

234 Bibliography

National Fire Protection Association, Batterymarch Park, Quincy, Mass. 02269.

Underwriters' Laboratories, Inc., 33 Pfingsten Road, Northbrook, Ill. 60062.

Wood Heating Alliance, 1101 Connecticut Avenue N.W., Suite 700, Washington, D.C. 20036.

Index

add-on furnace, 43–46
air flow
   patterns of, 16–17
   preheating of, 15–16, 18
   regulation of, 9, 16
airtight stoves. *See* controlled-combustion appliances
Anthony, C. H., 49, 59–60, 84–88
antique appliances. *See specific type*
appliance efficiency, defined, 12
appliances. *See* wood appliances
asbestos gasket, 93
asbestos millboard, 141–42
ashes
   removal of, 97, 156, 172
   uses for, 172–73
axe(s)
   selection of, 227–28
   sharpening of, 228–29
axe handle
   broken, 212–13
   longest-lasting, 228
   painted, 227–28
   replacement of, 228

back cut, 203
baffles, 14–15
barrel stove, 62
Base-Burner coal appliance, 5
Be Your Own Chimney Sweep (Curtis and Post), 165, 168, 173–74
boilers, 7
   clearances for, 140t
      reduction of, 151
   with existing systems, 46–47
   features on, 47–51
   floor protectors for, 148
   with heat storage units, 53–55
   multi-fuel, 47
   standards for, 51
   wet- and dry-base units, 47
   See also central heat system

236 Index

box stoves, 56
  cast models, 57
  sheet steel, 58–59
  stepstoves, 57–58
brick shields, 147
British Thermal Units (BTUs), 8
  wood fuel output in, 193, 196
  stove sizing and, 84–89
Bryant, Bea, 4
Bryant Stove Museum, 3–4
bucking-up technique, 208–10

cap, chimney, 36, 116, 128–29, 169, 175
cast-iron appliances
  box stoves, 57
  cleaning and maintenance of, 76
  firebox liners in, 92–93
  reproductions of, 79
  vs steel, 89–91
catalytic combustor, 17–18, 43, 96–97
ceiling protection
  clearances for, 139–40
  shields for, 141–47
central heat system, 7
  installation of, 41–42
  during power failures, 41
  pros and cons of, 39–41
  recent advances in, 51–55
  sizing of, 88–89
  See also boilers; furnaces
ceramic liners, 119–21
ceramic tile heaters, 63–64
chain saw
  back cut with, 203
  bucking up with, 208
  face cut with, 203
  fuel for, 226–27
  maintenance of, 224–25
  owner's manual for, 223–24

  performance adjustments for, 226
  rental of, 222–23
  safety precautions with, 224
  sharpening of, 227
  sizes of, 217–18
  sources for, 222
  special features on, 218–21
  starting procedures for, 201
  trapped, 206–7
  undercut with, 202–3
  used, 223
chimney(s), 8
  cap, 36, 116, 128–29, 169, 175
  cleaning of, 165
    chemicals in, 171–72
    equipment for, 167–68, 170
    with fireplace insert, 34
    flue, 168–70
    frequency of, 170–71
    inspection for, 167
  cleanout door on, 122, 129, 170
  dimensions of, 107–8
  existing units, 127–30
    relining of, 130–32
  with fireplace insert, 35–36
  inspection of, 129
  installation of, 108–9
  liners, 119–21, 124, 130
  masonry. See masonry chimneys
  prefabricated. See prefabricated chimneys
chimney fires
  containment of, 176–77
  with controlled-combustion stoves, 107
  smokepipe in, 132, 133
  See also fire safety
chips, wood, 52–53, 55
circulating fireplaces, 28–30
circulating heaters, 60–62

Index 237

Clarion stoves, 5
Class A chimney. *See* prefabricated chimneys
clothing, for wood cutting, 196–98
coal appliances
  with Class A chimney, 110
  combination units, 59–60
  as primary heat source, 5
colonial period, wood heating in, 3
combi-fire units, 8, 36–38
combination furnace, 42–43
combination heaters, 59–60
combustion
  defined, 9
  design features for, 14–18
  efficiency measures of, 12
  problems with, 10
  stages of, 9–10
controlled-combustion appliances
  ash removal from, 97
  chimney for, 107, 108
  design features of, 14–18
  emissions from, 11
  introduction of, 5–6
  misrepresentation of, 23
  sealing of, 92
cookstoves, 7
  antique, 70–77
  clearances for, 140*t*
    reduction of, 144*t*
  European, 23, 24
  firing procedures for, 159–60
  heat distribution in, 160–61
  heating with, 23–24
  Scandinavian, 23
  traditional, 22–23
  types of, 21–22
  utility of, 21
  workmanship on, 24–25
cord measure, 8
Creelman, John, 23, 90

creosote deposits
  chemical cleaners on, 171–72
  and chimney fires, 107
  in cookstoves, 23
  with fireplace inserts, 32, 34
  formation of, 10–11, 156–57, 158, 170–71
  inspection for, 129
  liquid, 122
  in smoking problems, 175
Curtis, Christopher, 165, 168, 173–74

damper, 9
dealers
  appliance, 101–4
  wood fuel, 191–92
doors
  ease of use for, 97
  safety features on, 93
downdrafter design, 16
draft
  controls, 9
    on cookstoves, 159–60
  in firing process, 156, 157, 158–59
  in low setting, 10, 11
  safety features on, 94–95
  in smoking prevention, 175
  defined, 8–9
  intake, 9, 16
ductwork, clearances for, 149–51

efficiency
  appliance, 12
  overall, 12
emissions, 11, 54
European cookstoves, 23, 24

face cut, 203
firebox, 8
  door, 97

firebox *(continued)*
   insulated, 18
   liner, 92–93
fire extinguishers, 179
fireplace, 7
   chimney cleaning with, 166
   freestanding, 8, 30–31
   glass doors for, 27–28
   as heat source, 3, 26
   liner, 7, 29
   operating procedures for, 27
   popularity of, 26
   tubular grates for, 28
   zero-clearance, 7–8, 28–29
fireplace insert
   defined, 8
   design problems with, 32–34
   direct connections for, 34
   popularity of, 31
   safety of, 31–32
   selection of, 34–36
fireplace-stoves, 8, 36–38
fires. *See* chimney fires
fire safety
   equipment for, 179
   precautions for, 177–78
   with visitors, 178–79
fire starters, 156
firestop, 124–25
fireviewer, 8, 36–38
firing procedures, 10, 155–59
   for cookstoves, 159–60
Fisher, Robert, 57
flammable liquids, firing hazards with, 156
floor protection, shields in, 147–49
flue
   cleaning of, 168–69
   collar, 97–98, 134
   defined, 8
   screen cover for, 169
   sealing of, 119

Franklin stove, 36
Frazier, Roger, 67
freestanding fireplace, 30–31
fuel. *See* wood fuel
furnaces, 7
   add-on, 43–46
   antique, 77
   chip and pellet burners, 52–53, 55
   clearances for, 140*t*
   duct, 149–51
   floor protectors for, 148
   multi-fuel, 42–43
   wood, 42
   See also central heat system

gasket, asbestos, 93
Gay, Larry, 67
glasses, safety, 199
Glenwood stoves, 4
green wood, 10–11
Grubka model stove, 63
Gyproc shields, 144

Handmade Hot Water Systems (Sussman and Frazier), 67
hardwood, 183
   density and heat production from, 8, 184*t*
   moisture content of, 10
Hayden, Skip, 14, 16, 29
heater. *See* space heaters
heat exchanger, 8
Heatilator, 7, 29
Heating the Home Water Supply (Gay), 67
heat shields. *See* shields
heat-transfer efficiency, 12
Hendrick, Lewis T., 193
Hill, Richard, 52, 54
holding-a-side technique, 203–4
hollow trees, 200
holzhaufens, 214–15

humidifiers, 161–62
hydrocarbon emissions, 11

insert. *See* fireplace insert
Institute of Man and Resources,
    central heat experiment of,
    52–55
insurance premiums, wood-
    heating effects on, 151–52

Jagels, Richard, 67–68

kachelofen model stove, 63
Kern, Ken, 62
Klunder, Hans, 214–15

legs, bolt-on, 93
logging operators
    purchases from, 190
    woodland contracts to, 189
logs. *See* wood fuel
log splitting
    broken axe handle in, 212–13
    with mechanical splitters, 213
    method of, 211–12

masonry chimneys
    cleanout door in, 123
    clearances for, 124–25
    foundation of, 122
    horizontal connector in, 125
    materials for, 118–20
    older units, 129–30
    top cover, 127
masonry heaters, 63–64
mineral wool batts, 141
mobile home stoves, 68–69
multi-fuel
    boilers, 47
    furnace, 42–43

National Fire Protection Association (NFPA)

on chimney liners, 120, 121
    clearance guidelines of, 135,
        137*t*, 139, 140*t*
    reduction of, 141, 144*t*, 147,
        148, 151*t*
nickel plate, cleaning of, 76
Nott, Eliphalet, 5
Nutek 500, 173

Owner-Built Homestead, The
    (Kern), 62
oxygen flow. *See* air flow

Page, Charles, 94
Park, Brian, 40–41
pellets, wood, 52, 53, 55
plenums, 8
    clearance reduction for, 151*t*
polycyclic organic material (POM)
    emissions, 11
portable fence, 94
Portland Stove Foundry, 5
Post, Donald, 165, 168, 173–74
prefabricated chimneys
    cap for, 116
    construction and design of,
        109–10
    height of, 116–17
    high-range units, 117–18
    installation of, 110–11
    problems with, 110–11
    used, 128
Prince Edward Island, central heat
    experiment in, 51–55
pyrolysis, 141–42

refractory cement, 119
relining products, 131–32
replacement parts, for antique
    stoves, 72
Revere stoves, 6
rods, for chimney cleaning, 168,
    169

240 Index

safety boots, 197
safety gear, 198
Scandinavian appliances
   boiler, 53–54
   box stoves, 56
   cookstoves, 23
sheet metal shield, 141, 142, 145
Sheetrock shield, 144
sheet-steel stoves, 58–59
Shelton, Jay, 7, 9, 16, 124, 135, 185
   on chimney cleaners, 171
   on fireplace performance, 27, 29–30
   on floor shields, 147–49
shields
   brick, 147
   building materials for, 141, 144*t*
   construction of, 145–46
   floor, 147–49
   for furnace ducts, 151*t*
   operation of, 142
   UL-listed, 142–43
   uncertified, 144
   wall and ceiling, 141–47
ship stoves, 67–68
short cord, 8
sidedrafter design, 16–17
skidding procedures, 210
slabwood, 190
smoke detectors, 179
smokepipe
   in chimney fires, 132, 133
   clearance reduction for, 135, 137
   collar, 8
   defined, 8
   elbows in, 134–35
   for fireplace inserts, 34
   horizontal rise in, 135
   inspection and cleaning of, 167, 170

   interior accessories of, 137–38
   joints of, 133–34
   length of, 34
   life expectancy of, 135
   materials for, 132–33
   smoking, causes of, 175–76
soapstone heater, 63–64
softwood, 183
   density and heat production from, 8, 184*t*–185*t*
solar homes, 40
space heaters
   antique, 77–78
   box stoves, 56–59
   circulators, 60–62
   clearances for, 140*t*
      reduction of, 144*t*
   defined, 7
   with humidifier tray, 161–62
   kits and homemade, 62–63
   masonry, 63–64
   for mobile homes, 68–69
   ship stoves, 67–68
   sizing of, 84–88
   vertical units, 59–60
   water, 64–67, 173–74
spark arrester, 116
   cleaning of, 169
stack. *See* chimney
stacking techniques, wood, 213–15
Stanley stoves, 6
steel appliances
   vs cast iron, 89–91
   firebox liner in, 92–93
   quality of, 91–92
steel brushes, in chimney cleaning, 167, 168, 169
stepstoves, 57–58
stoves. *See* cookstoves; wood appliances
Sussman, Art, 67

sweeps
  equipment of, 167–68
  selection of, 165

thermometer, cookstove, 160–61
thermostat, 93–94
thimble, 125
trees
  felling methods for, 201–5
  hollow and rotten, 200
  hung-up, 206
  placement of, 200–201, 203–4, 205
  under pressure, 207
  See also wood fuel
truck, for wood hauling, 210–11

undercut, 202–3
Underwriters' Laboratories (UL) standards, 96
  for chimneys, 109, 113, 117–18
  for fireplace inserts, 34
  for shields, 142–43, 148

vertical heaters, 59–60

wall protection, clearances for, 139–40
warranties, 98
water heaters, 64–67, 140*t*, 144*t*, 173–74
wedges
  in log splitting, 212
  in tree felling, 204–5
Weir Stove Foundry, 4
white hand disease, 219
winter cutting, 195
Wood and Bishop Foundry, 4–5
wood appliances
  aesthetics of, 100
  air flow in, 9, 15–16
  antique, 3–5, 70–78

baffles on, 14–15
cast iron *vs* steel, 89–92
catalytic combustors on, 17–18, 96–97
clearance for, 139–41
  reduction of, 141–47
controlled combustion, 5–6, 14–18, 23, 92, 97, 107, 108
dealer selection for, 101–4
defined, 7
ease of use in, 97–98
efficiency measures for, 12–13
firing of, 155–59
inspection and cleaning of, 164–66
insulated, 18
manufacturer selection for, 98–99
nonairtights, 92
owner's manual for, 99
safety hazards for, 93–95
secondhand, 78–79
shield installation for, 141–49
sizing technique for, 83–88
smoking of, 175–76
warranties for, 98
See also specific parts and types
Woodburners Encyclopedia (Shelton), 7, 9, 185
wood fuel
  cutting of, 194–95
    amounts in, 196
    axes in, 227–29
    bucking-up technique in, 208–10
    chain saw in, 217–27
    clothing for, 196–98
    equipment for, 199–200
    method of, 201–5
    problems in, 205–7
    safety gear for, 198–99
    season for, 195–96

wood fuel *(continued)*
   tree placement in, 200–201, 203–204, 205
   chips and pellets, 52–53, 55
   conventional fuel cost comparison, 193
   cord measure of, 8
   drying of, 10
   hardwood *vs* softwood, 8, 183–84, 184–85*t*
   hauling of, 210–11
   heat output from, 8, 196
   skidding procedures for, 210
   sources of, 185–86
      from dealers, 191–92
      government programs, 189–90
      from loggers, 190–91
      scrounging, 191
      woodlot ownership, 186–89
   splitting of, 211–13
   stacking of, 213–15
   storage of, 215–16
wood furnace, 42

wood heating
   air circulation in, 162–63
   combustion process in, 9–11
   emissions from, 11
   history of, 3–5
   home humidifier with, 161–62
   home insurance and, 151–52
   terminology of, 7–9
Wood Heating Alliance, 109
Wood Heat Safety (Shelton), 124, 147, 149
woodlot ownership
   initial clearing in, 188
   inventory taking in, 187–88
   logging contracts in, 189
   log skidding in, 210
   pros and cons of, 186, 189
   selection criteria for, 186–87
Wood 'n Energy magazine, 26
woodrange. *See* cookstove
woodsheds, 215–16

zero-clearance fireplace, 7–8, 28–29